Case Based Teaching and Learning for the 21st Century

Nigel Courtney,
Christian Poulsen and
Chrysostomos Stylios

Case Based Teaching and Learning for the 21st Century

Nigel Courtney,
Christian Poulsen and
Chrysostomos Stylios

Foreword by
Richard McCracken

Published in 2015 by Libri Publishing

ISBN 978 1 909818 56 9

Copyright © Libri Publishing

Authors retain copyright of individual chapters.

The right of Nigel Courtney, Christian Poulsen and Chrysostomos Stylios to be identified as the editors of this work has been asserted in accordance with the Copyright, Designs and Patents Act, 1988.

All rights reserved. No part of this publication may be reproduced, stored in any retrieval system or transmitted in any form or by any means, electronic, mechanical, photocopying, recording or otherwise, without the prior written permission of the copyright holder for which application should be addressed in the first instance to the publishers. No liability shall be attached to the author, the copyright holder or the publishers for loss or damage of any nature suffered as a result of reliance on the reproduction of any of the contents of this publication or any errors or omissions in its contents.

A CIP catalogue record for this book is available from The British Library

Cover design by Helen Taylor

Design by Carnegie Publishing

Libri Publishing
Brunel House
Volunteer Way
Faringdon
Oxfordshire
SN7 7YR

Tel: +44 (0)845 873 3837

www.libripublishing.co.uk

Contents

Foreword by Richard McCracken, Director of The Case Centre
(formerly The European Case Clearing House)   iii

Part 1

1 "Case Based Teaching and Learning for the 21st Century: an Introduction by the Editors"   1
By Nigel Courtney, Christian Poulsen and Chrysostomos Stylios

2 "Exploring Cases Using Emotion, Open Space and Creativity" 19
By Grier Palmer and Ioanna Iordanou

3 "Structured Controversy Cases in Theory and Practice"   39
By Eva Dobozy

4 "Strategies to Enhance Students' Capabilities of Abstract Thinking – the Use of Cases in Different Learning Situations" 59
By Ola Mattisson and Ulf Ramberg

5 "Case Study as – and within – Simulation: a Mobius Loop for Analysis and Learning"   81
By Elyssebeth Leigh and Kate Collier

6 "Case Based Learning Approaches Used in Business Schools in Western Greece: the Experiences, the Values, the Good Practices"   101
By Ioanna Ath. Giannoukou and Chrysostomos Stylios

7 "Towards New Genres for 21st Century Business School Case Studies"   121
By Clive Holtham

Part 2

8 "Didactic Categories for Organising Dimensions of Case Based Teaching 137
By Thomas Muschal

Part 3

9 "Students as Collaborators, Contributors and Co-creators" 153
By Margrethe Mondahl, Lisbet Pals Svendsen and Daniel Horn

10 "Representation: Objectivity and Artistry for Trainee Lawyers" 171
By Nigel Duncan

11 "Real World Cases in Virtual Environments: Blending Environments, Bringing Teacher Training to Life" 199
By Graham Lowe, Dario Faniglione, Mark Hetherington and Luke Millard

12 "Benefits of the Use of Video in Case Based Teaching" 221
By Christian Poulsen and Steffen Löfvall

13 "ICT Tools and Approaches to Support and Enhance Case Based Learning" 237
By Stefanos Petsios, Petros Karvelis and Chrysostomos Stylios

14 "The Use of Fuzzy Cognitive Maps for Learning and Development of Medical Case Learning Scenarios" 257
By Voula Georgopoulos and Chrysostomos Stylios

Collected Bibliography 277

Appendix 315

The Casemaker Platform User Manual A1
By members of the Casemaker R&D team

Foreword

I am comfortable with doubt. My instinct is to take the opposite view, to question orthodoxy.

Yet I have absolutely no doubts about the power of the case method and its ability to fundamentally transform learning in business schools. So what happened to my natural scepticism? Particularly as I came to the case method relatively late in life and, as the saying goes, it can be difficult to teach an old dog new tricks.

I became Director of The Case Centre (formerly The European Case Clearing House) just over six years ago. I had a paralegal background specialising in intellectual property rights and I understood cases in the context of the UK legal system: lawyers refer to particular legal 'cases' to understand how written laws have been interpreted by the courts.

In business cases, I found something that seemed both familiar and yet very alien. I set out to read as many cases as I could and observed a number of The Case Centre's case writing and teaching workshops. Not unexpectedly, given my predisposition, doubts began to enter my mind. I found the writing style of some of the cases I read to be somewhat bland; surely business students would find nothing stimulating or inspiring here? I questioned whether the cases were too hermetic, too self-contained and anecdotal to produce universally applicable learning outcomes. Can there ever be an answer to any given management conundrum? And I began to wonder if the case method might, in fact, be a negative influence, offering students the illusion that life can be neatly packaged and solved like a crossword puzzle. My scepticism grew.

Then came my first experience of a classroom case discussion: it was a revelation.

I was immediately transfixed and totally engaged in the process, as were the students; I came to understand how the written case can be transformed in the course of a discussion, and that the case itself is just one part of the case method package. When combined with a skilled tutor (plus, very often, a well-written teaching note) the case method takes on a life of its own in the classroom, an almost alchemic reaction that creates more than the sum of its parts.

How does this happen? Humans are storytellers by instinct. Since the dawn of recorded history, and probably before, we have told stories to each other. It's our way of passing on experiences, wisdom and learning, of creating a sense of community and fostering cohesion and shared values. And it's an enjoyable pastime, too, of course! At their most succinct, stories can be reduced to aphorisms and proverbs, sometimes delivering important lessons in a fast and memorable format or, conversely, perpetuating socially conservative or outmoded thinking. Contradictions creep in, too: do too many cooks spoil the broth or do many hands make light work? Which stories do we believe?

Combining the Power of Storytelling with Critical Discussion

The case method combines the power of storytelling with critical discussion, shared experiences, and rigorous academic practice and theory. I realised during my first experience of a class case discussion that the essence of the case method is not finding a single 'right' answer but of arriving at a number of preferred answers. The best outcome is the best one possible in the circumstances – but it will rarely be a perfect solution. The case method enables the application and testing of theory, it encourages questioning of accepted practice, and it incubates essential dialogue between business practitioners and academics.

Before looking forward and embracing what the future holds for the case method it is instructive to look back and remind ourselves of its beginnings in ancient culture. We can trace its roots in Socratic dialogue, or 'questioning' used to prove the falsity of an assumption, as well as in Aristotelian logic and the method of argument and counter-argument. This long history over more than two thousand years is indisputable evidence of the case method's staying power and its enduring value and irreplaceability. It was far more recently that the case method was codified by Harvard Business School in the early twentieth century, as well as by other leading business schools. We should remember we are standing on the shoulders of giants!

The Case Method's Rich Diversity

So where are we now in the twenty-first century?

It is a small foible of mine sometimes to refer not to 'the case method', but 'the case methods'. I believe we can get bogged down in dogmatic efforts to define the case method once and for all, as if it is a static and inflexible entity. I like to compare the case method with another great art form (for I believe that the case method is an art): that of jazz. Jazz – like the case method – has many variants, each of which may differ enormously while still being recognisably jazz. And jazz, in common with the case method, provokes arcane and internecine arguments between its most committed devotees about whether jazz fused with folk traditions, hip-hop, rap, or rock can ever really be called jazz.

I say categorically that it can, and I believe the same is true in relation to the rich diversity of the case method. It must be part of our brief continually to reinvigorate the case method and take a pioneering approach to its development and use. We must find new ways to, for example, meet the needs of different cultures and geographic regions, to fully exploit emerging technologies, and to address the fundamental social and economic challenges that present themselves as society evolves. We must respect the foundations from which the case method grew, while at the same time building anew. And we mustn't be afraid to experiment.

The Case Method Community's Energy, Commitment and Vitality

It is part of The Case Centre's role to champion creativity, innovation and original thinking in case teaching and writing. We're enormously privileged to be part of that process and to work with so many dedicated case method practitioners. I would like to take this opportunity to share just some of the exciting developments I have witnessed over the past few years; I never fail to be impressed by the forward-thinking energy, commitment and vitality of the case method community.

A number of case writers and teachers are making the most of technological advances to ensure their cases remain relevant and appealing to students while maintaining rigorous learning objectives. A perfect example is one of The Case Centre's recent prizewinners, *Teaching the Virtually Real Case Study*. This is an innovative approach to case teaching developed by Sabine Emad, University of Applied Sciences (UAS) Western Switzerland - Geneva School of Business Administration, and Wade Halvorson, SP Jain School of Global Management, Singapore & University of Western Australia. They transformed the format of a written case by introducing on-line gaming techniques and virtual simulation, providing a truly engaging experience for a new generation of students who are always on-line and comfortable in virtual environments.

Case method practitioners who resist the opportunities presented by technological innovation may be interested in some recent research conducted by Stuart Read, Professor of Marketing at IMD Business School, in collaboration with The Case Centre. He found that of all the independent variables, the inclusion of video material had the biggest impact on case sales, selling on average 413 more copies than a case without an accompanying video. A more detailed analysis of this topic can be found in chapter 12 of this volume which explores the benefits of video as part of case based teaching.

I believe that we ignore at our peril rapid technological advances and the resulting transformation of students' expectations and demands. Case writers should at the very least consider multi-media options when researching and writing a new case if they are to be sure of meeting the needs and preferences of their technically sophisticated students – many of whom arrive in the classroom with a correspondingly short attention span. They challenge us to make the case method relevant to their generation; I'm confident that it can adapt and change to meet that challenge head on.

Another sea change that many business schools are currently grappling with is the phenomenon of MOOCs – massive open on-line courses. To some, this presents an exciting opportunity to engage with previously unreachable students across the globe, while others perceive MOOCs as a possible threat, potentially undermining a school's reputation or devaluing its offering by allowing free access to previously elite educational opportunities. I can't claim to have definitive answers to these complex conundrums, but I do believe that the current debate surrounding MOOCs, and whether or not it is possible to replicate traditional case teaching in an online environment, is further evidence of the case method's resilience and flexibility in the face of previously unimagined change and upheaval.

Responding to Change: the Endlessly Inventive Case Method

In addition to technological change, the case method is currently struggling to reflect some huge cultural shifts that have taken place in many regions of the world over the past fifty years or so. A prime example of this has been highlighted in an important piece of research carried out by leadership coach and mentor Lesley Symons as part of her 2014 INSEAD MA thesis (as yet unpublished). She found that of 53 of The Case Centre's award-winning and bestselling cases, just seven featured female protagonists. She also notes in her thesis that gender balance at middle and senior levels in organisations is currently a hot topic. The 2011 European Business School and European Commission Call to Action Report states that business schools have a vital role to play in shattering the glass ceiling. The report recommended that business schools could help to increase men's awareness of gender issues by revising teaching materials and using more cases about women leaders.

And in an unprecedented move earlier this year, Harvard Business School Dean, Nitin Nohria, apologised for how the school had treated women in the past. He pledged to double the number of business case studies that feature a woman as the protagonist to 20% over the next five years.

Again, this gives me cause for optimism: the case method is endlessly inventive, able to recreate itself and emerge strengthened and renewed in the face of fundamental change.

Far-reaching and Positive Outcomes for Institutions and Individuals

The benefits of adopting the case method are numerous for both institutions and individuals. As a relatively recent convert, I am still astonished by the depth and breadth of its positive effect and influence. Students can gain so much from the case method; within the context of real-life decision-making, they can learn business and management theory while at the same time developing a wide range of vital skills. These include negotiation, analysis, defending and challenging viewpoints, team and lone working, and guarding against making decisions based on too little information. The beauty of the case method is that it both harnesses and challenges the wisdom of the collective.

Faculty find that it changes the dynamic of the classroom, creating powerful relationships between teacher and students resulting in far more meaningful engagement on the part of students, and an exponential increase in job satisfaction for the teacher. A successful case method session can be an intoxicating and hugely uplifting experience for students and teachers alike.

In addition, writing a case can provide faculty with unique behind-the-scenes access to a company, often offering opportunities to develop or deepen research into an individual business, sector or industry. This encourages an invigorating synergy between teaching and research, with case teaching sessions providing the perfect setting for disseminating research findings and benefiting from in-depth feedback.

Business schools, too, can only benefit from encouraging and supporting their faculty to adopt the case method as a key teaching tool. It provides hard-wired links between the school and industry, highly beneficial to students and also helping to eliminate accusations of being out of touch or of operating within a remote 'ivory tower'. Publishing good quality cases will enhance a school's brand, help to raise its profile on an international basis, and improve its accreditation performance.

Finally, it is our experience at The Case Centre that more and more companies are keen to be featured in cases written by leading academics or specialist faculty. It can be a huge learning experience for them during which they gain invaluable insights and advice from some of the best business brains in the world. Many are proud to be the subject of a case and use the final product to support their brand.

Conclusion

I welcome this volume; it offers a fascinating snapshot of the current state of play in relation to the case method, covering a diverse range of ideas, innovatory techniques and fresh thinking. It forms a fitting tribute to the invaluable contribution made by the EU-funded Casemaker project and will, I hope, serve to disseminate the project's achievements more widely.

Finally, I would like to say how proud and honoured I am to be the Director of The Case Centre, a unique and invaluable international institution. I welcome open and ongoing dialogue and discussion with the world's case method practitioners and champions – and also with its detractors, for there are still some (and as explained here, I was almost one myself). As a not-for-profit organisation, our mission is to advance the case method worldwide, sharing knowledge, wisdom and experience to transform business education across the globe. I consider this work to be among the most valuable and important of my career so far.

Richard McCracken
June 2014

About the Author

Richard McCracken is Director of The Case Centre (www.thecasecentre.org). The Case Centre's collection includes more than 50,000 cases covering an extensive and diverse range of management disciplines and international contexts. Most are available electronically for preview and delivery. He can be contacted at this email: richard@thecasecentre.org

Chapter one

Case Based Teaching and Learning for the 21st Century: an Introduction by the Editors

Nigel Courtney, Christian Poulsen and Chrysostomos Stylios

This anthology has been created to foster contemporary ideas and practices in case based teaching and learning (CBT), to present how new information and communications technologies (ICT) are increasing the scope and reach of CBT, to introduce and discuss innovative design approaches of CBT, and to support and help disseminate the achievements and results of the EU-funded Casemaker project.

The Theory and Practice of Case Based Teaching and Learning

What Is Case Based Teaching?

Characteristically, the traditional approach to teaching would start with the premise that the teacher has a superior knowledge in the subject area compared to the students. Following the traditional approach, the goal of the teaching would therefore be to transmit the teacher's knowledge to the students in the lecture hall. The student would continue to attend their educational institution until this transmission of knowledge has been successful. The typical student will leave academia after a number of years, will wander out in the world and start to test out the theories that he or she has learned. Often this meeting with the empirical world will prove to be a shock for the ex-student. Although the process of transmission might have been successful, the transformation from theoretical knowledge to practical ability is a challenge that is left to the ex-student and the businesses she or he is working with.

It has fallen to such businesses, and the Professions, to press academia constantly to introduce practical knowledge into education. This has resulted in the emergence of a growing range of pedagogical approaches which aim to embed practice-based knowledge acquisition into university teaching. Pedagogical methodologies that have addressed this issue successfully include Problem-based Learning, Inquiry-based Learning, Project-based Learning and Case-based Teaching and Learning (CBT).

CBT has a long history and is increasingly applied in teaching and learning situations. The advent of Information and Communications Technologies (ICT) which are low-cost and easier to use has accelerated the accessibility and effectiveness of CBT and greatly widened the range of techniques available to teachers. Today we live in a connected world where new media are central for both education and entertainment and access to the Internet is widely available via numerous devices including laptop, tablet, and smart phone. So, in this anthology we set out to describe this evolution and to promulgate both traditional and innovative forms of CBT.

We will start with a broad definition of CBT which can accommodate all the different ways of applying practical examples to teaching. There is no one best way of applying CBT. Cases can be used with beneficial learning effects in a multitude of settings and arrangements.

In order to provide a standard of comparison we offer for CBT the following Weberian 'ideal type' (that is, an idea construct that characterises a complex social phenomenon).

A teacher is planning to use a case with a Masters-level group of service management students. He knows the students quite well because he had them for a class on bachelor level. The students have little work-life experience but have some training in CBT. The teacher decides on a four page case which describes a real problem occurring at a hotel. The case has three exhibits: a photograph of the backstage of the restaurant, a photo of the hall connecting the kitchen with the reception, and a one minute long sound file where one can hear an argument between the chef and one of the receptionists.

Before the students discuss the case in plenum they are instructed to discuss the case in small groups of five students. The instruction includes questions about the case and a list of relevant literature. Once the students are gathered together in plenum one of the groups is asked to present their answers to the case questions. Their presentation serves as a starting point for a plenary discussion of the case. The teacher facilitates this discussion in order to cover the themes he had thought would be relevant to the case and the interesting new angles that the students provide.

When the class ends each student has worked for one hour on reading the case text and studying the exhibits, a further hour on small-group preparation, a quarter of an hour listening to the case presentation and three quarters of an hour participating in the plenum discussion. A total of three hours.

After class the students go to the cafeteria for a coffee and evaluate their group's performance. The teacher looks for a quiet place to evaluate the teaching, the case and the exhibits.

In this anthology, you will see numerous variations to our ideal type of CBT. The only common factor is that in each instance a group of students is provided with some kind of case material, they study it and it is followed by a case discussion.

CBT and the Harvard-style approach

In the ideal type the teacher's role is to pose questions to the students both before and during class. These questions would be of a reflective nature in order to encourage students to formulate answers and new questions. In a Harvard-style setting they would, in addition, discuss and analyse the *"solution of relevant and practical problems"* (Erskine *et al.*, 1981).

For many educators the relevance of a case problem is an important attraction of the CBT approach. The Case Centre (2014) reports its survey findings that researchers are calling for cases with a recognisably local setting. Thomson & Baden-Fuller (2010) assert that the introduction of such problems should be relevant to the students in their life off campus and in terms of their future career; and these authors 'practice what they preach' by featuring non-USA cases. CBT provides safe circumstances in which the student can take on the roles of specific people in specific organisations that are faced with real problems (Leenders *et al.*, 1973). The case has the role of bringing actual practice into the class room (Leenders & Erskine, 1989).

If, in our ideal type case, we add a crescendo at the end of the written case material when our main character, the chef, is about to make an important choice we would allow the student to step figuratively into the position of the decision maker (Maufette-Leenders *et al.*, 1997). The focus on decision making is a strong feature to the Harvard case-based tradition. The questions, and particularly the small-group discussions, also help the students to *"learn (...) by doing and teaching others"* (Erskine *et al.*, 1981; Leenders *et al.*, 1973).

In contrast to the traditional 'transmission model' of teaching we have described, the CBT-approach also lets students *"apply theory to practice, instead of learning by memory"* (Erskine *et al.*, 1981). Cases effectively serve as the basis on which student can explore whether theories are needed and can apply theories to simulated practice (Leenders *et al.*, 1973). In this way cases serve as an example of active learning (McShane & Von Glinow, 2009).

Ideally the CBT approach should provide the student with a series of skills which supplement the learning goals of a particular lesson. In addition to the sorts of skills already mentioned, Maufette-Leenders *et al.* (1997) in their canonical 'Learning with Cases', highlight analytical skills, oral communication skills, time management skills, interpersonal skills and creativity.

Origins and Influences of the Case Method

Case examples have helped people to cope with the unpredictability of life for a very long time. Originally this was through storytelling, sometimes with the support of painted images. About five thousand years ago tablets bearing cuneiform writing began to record harvests. Exhibits which are not so far different from the images, videos and spreadsheets that typically accompany contemporary case studies.

Accounts of the experiences of real or fictitious others – for example, in Biblical parables and medieval plays – have prepared and educated many generations. More formally, a case study by Galileo enabled him to correct Aristotle's law of gravity (Flyvbjerg, 2006).

Since the mid-19th Century case based learning has been an integral part of education in medicine, legal process and social science. Operating theatres were set up to enable would-be doctors to witness and learn from operations being performed on patients (eg: The Garrett built in the church at St Thomas's Hospital in London (http://www.thegarret.org.uk/oot.htm). And since 1860, statute law in the UK has been supplemented by 'case law' whereby law is established by judicial decisions in particular cases, instead of by legislative action (http://dictionary.reference.com/browse/case+law).

In 1829 Frederic Le Play's studies of family budgets introduced the case-study method into social science (Healy, 1947). Harvard Law School followed suit and since the 1910s Harvard Business School the case method has underpinned its reputation so that today with Christensen (nd) claiming that *"more than 80% of HBS classes are built on the case method"*.

The Evolution of Modern Case Based Teaching

Although the era of personal computing began in the 1980s, the use of information and communications technologies (ICT) to animate case based learning really took off after Berner-Lee's invention of the world wide web in 1989 (http://webfoundation.org/about/sir-tim-berners-lee/). By the end of that millenium Kozma and Anderson (2002) were able to report that 28 countries were using ICT to innovate pedagogical practices.

The continuation of these trends has greatly increased the range of possible applications of case based teaching. Initially, the case method was applied mainly in the diciplines of management, business, law and medicine. A further trend is that teachers today are applying it in many more discplines. Indeed, authors in this anthology seek to foster this trend by describing for the reader their experiences of using case based teaching in engineering, computer science, artificial intelligence and the social sciences more generally.

The traditional approach pioneered at business and medical schools is characterised by face-to-face interactions between student and tutor. It continues to be highly effective in higher education – notably at Harvard and Ivey – and is widely used in vocational education and executive development. This popularity has fostered the development of innovative methods that also rely of face-to-face interaction. These include simulation, role-play and case debates.

At the same time the availability of simple and inexpensive desktop publishing software and website design and video editing tools – combined with ubiquitous and free searching and hyperlinking capabilities – has allowed tutors and students to expand case based teaching into new realms.

About Casemaker

Casemaker is a 3-year transversal research and development initiative co-funded by the EU (Project # 531169-LLP-1-2012-1-DK-KA3-KA3MP for the EU Lifelong Learning Programme, Key Action 3 (ICT), Multilateral Projects).

Casemaker aims to promote new learning and teaching practices in higher education and secondary vocational education and to create an innovative open source web-based ICT-platform specifically designed to enhance case-based teaching and learning. The overall rationale for initiating the Casemaker project is to further integrate academia and practice in order to enhance student learning, help students develop transferable skills and improve students' employability, and at the same time provide advanced sophisticated tools to teachers and professors.

The Project Partners, who are co-funding the project, are Copenhagen Business School Denmark, Lund University Sweden, Birmingham City University UK, Cass Business School UK, Lűbeck Fachhockschule Germany, Technological Educational Institute of Epirus Greece, and the Danish software house Phases. The Case Centre (formerly the European Case Clearing House) is an Associate Partner.

Casemaker enables three communities – case writers, teachers and students – to develop and work with case studies, to review progress of study (of individuals or groups), and to give feedback. In short, to foster and gauge the learning taking place.

The software development is supported by this anthology on the theory and practice of case based teaching – particularly that which takes advantage of advances in ICT and multimedia. Accordingly we include in this anthology a User Manual to help people to take full advantage of the freely available Casemaker software.

A Road Map for Navigating this Anthology

This anthology has been created by international scholars and practitioners who share a desire to foster and enhance case based teaching and learning. These authors, some of whom are collaborators in the Casemaker project, have designed a mapping space (Figure 1) that illustrates and accommodates the evolution and expansion of CBT.

The horizontal axis focuses on the design approach for the creation of a case. It offers a spectrum ranging from traditional types of case based teaching to innovative forms that are being developed by pioneering teachers and case authors. The vertical axis concentrates on the delivery mechanism used to deploy cases. It ranges from person-to-person interaction to ICT-enabled delivery.

In this mapping space the sort of CBT traditionally used on the

Harvard Business School MBA programme is likely to be located in the bottom left quadrant. On the other hand, CBT that makes use of scenarios acted out in video clips and deployed via a virtual environment would appear in the top right quadrant.

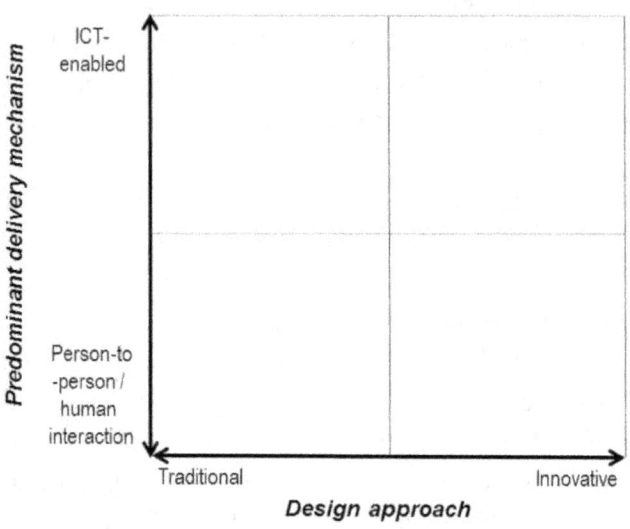

Figure 1. *A mapping space for case based teaching approaches*

Getting Started

Our aim is to make it easier for you, the reader, to navigate directly to information that addresses case based teaching issues that are currently of particular relevance to you. Accordingly each author has captured 'in a nutshell' exactly what their chapter is about. See Table 2.

Chapter #	The key message of the author(s)
Part 1: Focusing on Face-to-Face Interaction	
2	"Exploring Cases Using Emotion, Open Space and Creativity" by Grier Palmer and Ioanna Iordanou. We describe an innovative case teaching method ('creative criticality') to engage students by means of imaginative case materials and their enacted interpretations. We contrast this with the successful but overly analytical Harvard case method. Student feedback and practitioner advice is provided.
3	"Structured Controversy Cases in Theory and Practice" by Eva Dobozy For learning to have a transformative effect, academic disagreement needs to be embraced as a valuable pedagogical strategy. The dual purpose of structured controversy case pedagogy is the teaching and learning of particular subject matter and the development of positive personal attitudes.
4	"Strategies to Enhance Students' Capabilities of Abstract Thinking – the Use of Cases in Different Learning Situations" by Ola Mattisson and Ulf Ramberg Teachers need strategies when teaching undergraduate students with cases. This chapter equips teachers to select appropriate cases and teach in a manner that will enhance students' learning outcomes. A comparative study of six different course settings is presented.
5	"Case Study as – and within – Simulation: a Mobius Loop for Analysis and Learning" by Elyssebeth Leigh and Kate Collier Case study and simulation are similar in form and use but are rarely connected. We explore why this is so and demonstrate how to integrate them in practice using concepts of Stopped Time and Living Time in a hybrid example. The Mobius Strip is offered as a metaphor for the process.

6	"Case Based Learning Approaches Used in Business Schools in Western Greece: the Experiences, the Values, the Good Practices" by Ioanna Ath. Giannoukou and Chrysostomos Stylios Following a review of the pedagogy of case based learning we report on the application of teaching case studies in business schools in Western Greece. We analyse the different methods employed and highlight how case debates have emerged as a popular and effective approach.
7	"Towards New Genres for 21st Century Business School Case Studies" by Clive Holtham The traditional Harvard case study is increasingly challenged by novel case study methods which are founded on fundamentally different pedagogic assumptions. Such methods include games, simulations, emulations, role play, 'student as co-author', and may depend on ICT enablement.

Part 2: A New Pedagogical Theory	
8	"Didactic Categories for Organising Dimensions of Case Based Teaching" by Thomas Muschal The literature on case based teaching presents very different dimensions and perspectives. To summarise the pluralism a model of seven didactic categories by Baumgartner (2011) is used to structure relevant didactic decisions to facilitate discussion of this teaching method.

Part 3: ICT-enablement of Case Based Teaching	
9	"Students as Collaborators, Contributors and Co-creators" by Margrethe Mondahl, Lisbet Pals Svendsen and Daniel Horn We identify which ICT tools support students' intrinsic motivation and deep learning. But students are also motivated particularly by one extrinsic factor: exams. So how can the education system balance the two motivation types via ICT for better learning outcomes?

10	"Representation: Objectivity and Artistry for Trainee Lawyers" by Nigel Duncan
	Lawyers must develop artistry in a reflective practice enabling them to represent their client's interests using objectivity, analysis, and oral and written communication skills. This chapter presents and evaluates a longitudinal case study method designed to achieve this.
11	"Real World Cases in Virtual Environments: Blending Environments, Bringing Teacher Training to Life" by Graham Lowe, Dario Faniglione, Mark Hetherington and Luke Millard
	Our chapter describes a pioneering example in which online simulation has been developed for Initial Teacher Education in England and the impact this new type of encounter has had upon the students' perceptions of their self-confidence.
12	"Benefits of the Use of Video in Case Based Teaching" by Christian Poulsen and Steffen Löfvall
	Our chapter reviews articles on the use of video in case based teaching. It divides the articles into a typology of closed and open case based teaching and practical and theoretical-lensed cases and then analyses each type. The chapter then proposes the optimal use of video at different stages of the teaching process.
13	"ICT Tools and Approaches to Support and Enhance Case Based Learning" by Stefanos Petsios, Petros Karvelis and Chrysostomos Stylios
	Information and Communication Technology (ICT) tools handle information and provide access to knowledge but also have great potential in any educational procedure. This chapter compares and contrasts ICT tools available to support and promote case based learning and offers recommendations.

12   CASE BASED TEACHING AND LEARNING FOR THE 21ST CENTURY

14	"The Use of Fuzzy Cognitive Maps for Learning and Development of Medical Case Learning Scenarios" by Voula Georgopoulos and Chrysostomos Stylios
	Fuzzy cognitive mapping (FCM), a soft computing approach, is introduced as a methodology for case based learning in situations characterised by uncertainty and vagueness. We explain the application of FCM as an interactive learning procedure and present its implementation for medical decision case scenarios.

Table 2. Each chapter author's(') key message

Using the mapping space, our authors and their peers have collaborated to position the 'centre of gravity' of each chapter and create the road map depicted in Figure 2.

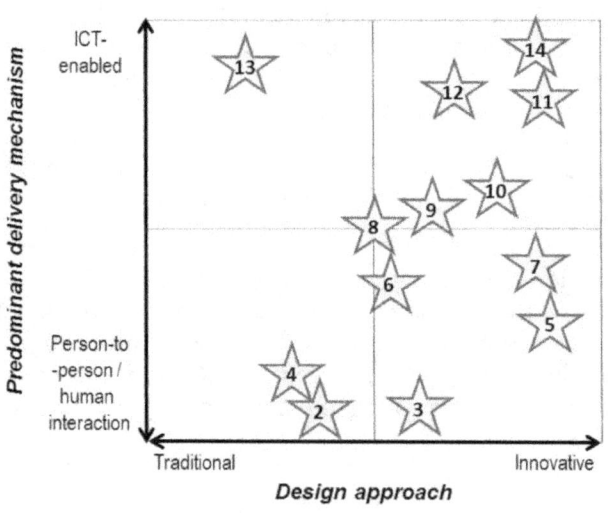

Figure 2. The road map for the chapters

As can be seen from Figure 2 the chapters' foci are well dispersed across the mapping space.

Chapters 2 to 7 address both traditional and innovative design approaches that promote learning through person-to-person interactions. These comprise Part 1 of the book.

Chapter 8 is a standalone chapter that offers a pedagogical theory that will greatly assist the design of learning materials and settings.

Part 3 of the book contains chapters 9 to 14. These look at how ICT is enabling new forms of both traditional and innovative approaches to case based teaching.

These sections are followed by a collected bibliography which offers in A-Z order all the references cited in each chapter.

The book is completed with the Casemaker User Manual.

The Future of CBT is Electronic

In this introduction we have paid due tribute to the important contribution that Erskine and colleagues (Maufette-Leenders & Erskine, 1973; Erskine, Leenders & Maufette-Leenders, 1981; Leenders & Erskine, 1989; Leenders, Maufette-Leenders, Erskine & Leenders, 1997) have made to case based teaching. However, those authors pay little attention to the role of ICT in the advancement of CBT – not least because their contributions were made quite early in the emergence and evolution of ubiquitous ICT. The realm of CBT is now much broader than the traditional Harvard- and Ivey-style approach and our ideal type must now accommodate several adjustments and new layers in the way CBT is used throughout the world.

There are several reasons for the opening up of CBT. This broadening is partly due to the greatly increased capabilities of ICT (including, for examples, cheaper and easier access, miniaturisation, fast broadband, video streaming and YouTube). At the same time it is also because of the increased take-up in Higher Education of learning approaches based on interpersonal learning activities requiring little or no ICT (for examples: simulations, role play, and case debates).

One of the key contributions of CBT to higher education today is its ability to bring the outside world into the classroom and at the same time to transfer the classroom, through new media, onto the screens of students' pads, laptops, smartphones and other connected devices. In this way, ICT accentuates the realism of CBT that is often reported by users and teachers. For example, Shareville is a 'virtual learning room' that includes simulations, role plays and cases (Lowe et al., this volume). Students report that Shareville's use of video-filmed, realistic situations *"made it feel more true-to-life and less like a video game"* (Hollyhead, 2010). Users of Shareville also report that the use of video triggers students' engagement in the education (ibid), a finding that is also reported in other studies (Brundvand, 2010; Hakkarainen & Saarelainen, 2005; Hakkarainen et al., 2007)

So why does the introduction of ICT tend to result in students being more engaged with case- and other activity-based teaching approaches? In some cases there might be a novelty effect (Poulsen & Löfvall, 2014) but an alternative explanation might also be the change of students' expectations of Higher Education Institutions (HEIs). Dobozy (2011) reports that a rising trend in the development of HEIs is that students now see themselves as consumers. HEIs that take full advantage of modern ICT make it possible for their teachers to meet this expectation.

The availability of online case catalogues – managed, for example, by the Harvard Business School in the US, the Ivey Business School in Canada and the UK's The Case Centre – has made it possible for today's enhanced capabilities of CBT to be taken up and exploited in many parts of the world. This volume presents developments in seven nation states – a small but representative sample which highlights the European context.

The feedback from non-North American or British educators has led these case centres to seek to publish cases which have been developed in other parts of the world and this, in turn, has spread the usage of CBT to yet more countries. In addition, the advent of Learning Management Systems (LMS) such as Moodle has provided an effective and low cost way to store locally produced case materials.

Erskine and colleagues at Ivey School in Ontario (ibid), and Christensen (1987) at Harvard, are among the many acknowledged experts who have reported evidence that the traditional, face-to-face case method can be highly effective. After all, it has kept Harvard among the top 5 business schools worldwide for many decades. But a widening range of ICT-enabled variants of the case method is now available to teachers.

Because of the relative newness of ICT-enabled CBT, published work showing that it is effective is less plentiful but no less powerful. In comparison with traditional lecturing, ICT-enabled case based teaching is building up a proven record for enhancing student learning outcomes.

This is notable in the context of acquiring decision-making skills (Harrington, 1995; Kolodner *et al.*, 2003) while the use of video to promote case based reasoning is promoted by Perry and Talley (2001) and Schrader *et al.* (2003). More recently Han *et al.* (2013) have set up an experimental design that shows that multi-media cases strongly assist students to achieve learning goals because they enrich the learning context; in their study, they found that students using multi-media cases benefitted from better knowledge acquisition and integration than the control group. The CBT approach has also been found to be particularly effective as a practice-based approach when it comes to teaching teachers (Çevik & Andre, 2014) and tackling societal issues (Wright & Heeran, 2002).

Although more research on the learning effects of ICT-enabled case teaching will be welcome there are already compelling indications that teachers in Higher Education Institutions can enhance students' learning outcomes by introducing CBT and ICT-enabled CBT approaches. Indeed, the chapters in this anthology provide a comprehensive examination of current issues in the field; over 350 sources of relevant work are cited and many of the chapter authors offer first-hand qualitative and quantitative evidence of benefits obtained in practice. They also highlight how to avoid potential pitfalls. We cordially invite you, the reader, to take full advantage of their experiences and recommendations.

About the Editors

Nigel Courtney took the BSc at University of Manchester Institute of Science and Technology and then gained the MBA, with distinction, at Cass Business School, City University London, UK where he was awarded his PhD. He is an Honorary Senior Visiting Fellow at Cass, a visiting fellow at the University of Technology, Sydney and formerly a Visiting Fellow at the Australian Graduate School of Management, Sydney.

Nigel is a Chartered Engineer, a Certified Management Consultant, a fellow of the Chartered Institute of Management, a Certified IT Professional and a Freeman of the City of London. He has extensive experience in project and general management and clients of his firm Courtney Consulting, which specialises in information systems strategy, include the European Commission, Deloitte & Touche, Metropolitan Police, Transport for London, The Post Office and the UK National Endowment for Science Technology and the Arts. Nigel co-authored the British Standards Institute's PD7502 on Knowledge Management and is co-originator of the Skills Framework for the Information Age (SFIA.org.uk).

Nigel's teaching practice includes MBA programmes on Business Information Management and the Management of Technology, and MSc courses in Economics and on Information Leadership. He has taught/lectured in Australia, China, many parts of Europe, the Middle East, South Africa, and the USA. His research interests include innovation in education, business innovation, the extraction of business value from ICT investments, and the use of communications technologies for social change. He can be contacted at this email: nigel@courtneynet.com

Christian Poulsen studied sociology, political sciences, economics and welfare studies for the Masters diploma at the University of Lund, Sweden, where he was awarded his PhD in Sociology. The PhD programme was completed at the Complutense University of Madrid and the University of Lund.

Christian's teaching practice includes bachelor and master-level courses in Organisational behaviour, Quantitative methodology, Service management and Theory of the project. His research interests include sociology in the contexts of education, feminism, and knowledge and learning in the tertiary sector. His current focus is on learning analytics and ICT-enabled teaching. He can be contacted at this email: cp.ioa@cbs.dk

Chrysostomos Stylios is an Associate Professor at the Department of Computer Engineering in the Technological Educational Institute of Epirus, Greece. He is also a research collaborator at the Computer Technology Institute & Press "Diophantus", Patras, Greece and was a visiting assistant professor at the Computer Science Department of the University of Ioannina. He received his PhD from the Department of Electrical & Computer Engineering of the University of Patras (1999) and the diploma in Electrical & Computer Engineering from the Aristotle University of Thessaloniki (1992). He has published over 135 journal and conference papers and book chapters. His main scientific interests include: Fuzzy Cognitive Maps, Soft Computing &, Computational Intelligence Techniques, Signal Processing methods, Decision Support Systems, Modeling and Simulation. He is member of the IEEE and a member of the TC 8.2 and TC 5.4 of IFAC.

Chapter two

Exploring Cases Using Emotion, Open Space and Creativity

Grier Palmer and Ioanna Iordanou

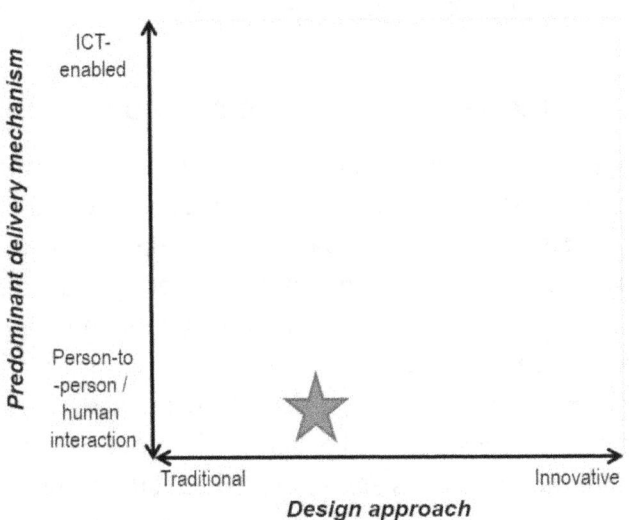

Introduction

Business education has tended to emphasise rational and analytical processes as a way to dissect and manage situations requiring executive decisions. Understanding how to manage has principally been taught via the case method. The educational aim, typically framed by the Harvard Business School (HBS) case format and class review, is to develop executive analytical skills in the student, the latter working as the protagonist in real business examples.

In this chapter, we describe and discuss the practices in the classic and pre-eminent HBS case method. In particular, we review its pragmatic pedagogy and highlight that theory is, therefore, light in the method. Then a different approach is presented through an innovative case in which we illustrate key alternatives for the design of the learning experience. These innovations are principally the inclusion of emotion and an heightened presence of the affective domain, the use of non-traditional space and classroom set up, and, above all else, the emphasis on creativity processes. Creativity infuses a case in format and content. The teacher introduces processes of creative ensembles and the students are challenged to use their senses and imagination to develop and apply 'creative criticality' to complex case material. The challenges of this approach for practitioners are discussed by a case teacher, and a package of suggestions is presented.

The Harvard Business School Case Method

HBS cases today dominate the international academic market (HBS claim an 80% share), 90 years after the case method became *"the dominant mode of instruction"* at HBS (Garvin, 2003:60). The HBS case teaching culture, method, and materials are especially related to its student audience of primarily future consultants and financial executives. This audience's future employment explains the large number of cases studied (over 500 on the MBA two-year course), because the material provides, in the classroom, vicarious experiences of a wide range of industry sectors and management situations. These real life cases also help early career MBA students understand the management protagonist through their classroom practice of executive decision making in 'participant-centred learning'.

HBS cases are developed within the School's format and style, generally heavy on detail and aiming to challenge analytical skills. The learning approach places a large emphasis on individual preparation of issues in the case, before a class discussion, in which contributions can account for 50% of an MBA student's grades. The approach of the HBS case class teacher is to 'choreograph' or guide the 90 students' dialogues and debate by, for instance, the opening 'cold call' questions. The higher aim for HBS teachers, however –

above analysis and persuasive communication – is to help students develop leadership character and courage in the face of uncertainty or complexity (Garvin, 2003:62).

The sustained success of HBS (1st in FT Global MBA rankings 2013) is linked to its case method but this does not preclude a critical review of it. Indeed HBS itself has been reviewing possible weaknesses. For instance, Datar *et al.* (2010) identified inter alia a lack of cultural awareness and global outlook, as well as little sense of the business as an integrated whole. Especially critical as an outsider has been Mintzberg (2004), who argues for more students in the classroom with more business experience and, therefore, more sharing of those managers' knowledge. He proposes that managers need more learning that facilitates self-awareness, reflection, and the ability to relate to others. These softer characteristics, he believes, balance business schools' emphasis on analysis (techniques) and action driven leadership (fast decisions).

Despite the longevity and global success of the Harvard method, we observe several potential weaknesses and risks in the current practices in case-based education. These are:

- a convergent (Kolb, 1984) emphasis, searching for the one right answer.
- a leadership style biased to decisions and action, and light on explicit reflection.
- an emphasis on defining the solution, not the people involved in it.
- a rational and analytically bounded approach, versus imaginative and creative interpretation.
- a disciplinary/functional separation, versus the integrated and overlapping nature of business.
- a focus on how to do it, not why – i.e. short on values and ethics.

The Pedagogy of Case Teaching and Learning – Theory and in Practice

The central HBS cultural features of 'real world' situations and 'business relevance' have influenced the managerial focus of business school education across the world, particularly through the case method. Appropriately, in 2001 a major literature review and research of case teaching practice in relation to learning was completed by Burgoyne and Mumford. In their review, they positioned case teaching as a diametrically opposed alternative to the lecture, and also inherently a-theoretical in its pragmatic pedagogy of management practices for decisions and action. Significantly, their conclusion was that the case method is neither grounded in any particular learning theory nor does it itself stimulate theory building. As one interviewed practitioner said: *"You don't need a theory – you do it because Harvard does it"* (Burgoyne & Mumford, 2001:49).

From a pedagogical perspective, one of the most worrying conclusions of their review is that *"there is a great tendency for the Case Method to homogenise the learner"* with limited design or response to individual differences in styles and learning strategies (Burgoyne & Mumford, 2001:6). It seems obvious from this comprehensive review that 'classic' HBS pedagogy can be best described as pragmatic and craft-based, as seen in the sub-title of a key Harvard text – 'artistry of discussion leadership' (Christensen *et al.*, 1991). It is also not surprising that the HBS pedagogy is developed mainly through observation of practice, complemented by academic group discussions sharing class experiences, methods, etc.

In published HBS writings the pedagogic authority principally cited is Dewey but we can also recognise Kolb's (1984) Experiential Learning, especially the *convergent* style. We see Rogers also present, in terms of HBS valuing the student as the independent learner (Christensen, 1991) in partnership with the class and teacher. Despite these underpinnings, the HBS case method does not come without challenges to university teachers. They will possibly have personal concerns about the skills needed for successful leadership of discussions; they may not be confident in depending on students as the core learning element in the class, versus their own PowerPoint-based lectures; they may be worried about covering curriculum content sufficiently; finally, they may have concerns about a potential conflict between the student expectations of the professor and a 'participant centred' class.

Cases can be used at the lowest end of Bloom's (1956) Taxonomy of educational objectives to build and check knowledge and understanding, both especially relevant for undergraduates or students early in their postgraduate course. From the detail of the case, their learning can be demonstrated by identifying and describing key features in the narrative and material. Students will need to show they can recognise key elements in the mass of details or from a narrative.

More frequently, case teaching tends to focus on Bloom's more difficult cognitive levels of application, with students using models and analysis, breaking down the detail, problems and issues in the case. These lower/middle level activities can be useful for earlier stages of a course, or be relevant to less experienced students, thereby supporting a more student-centred approach to teaching. For example, 'knowing' can help memorisation and 'understanding' can help by explaining in one's own words. The applied use of models can provide a feedback loop on the student's understanding of and skill in applying, say, Porter's Value Chain or the analytical challenge of deconstructing a case.

A teacher can, by selecting the appropriate cognitive activity, use a single case at different stages in a course, or to different student levels from Undergraduate through Masters/MBA to Executive Education. A more challenging and significant goal for case teachers is to incorporate two other parts of Bloom's Taxonomy – the affective domain that includes emotions, feelings and values in learning, and creativity, highlighted in the later taxonomy revisions (e.g. Krathwohl, 2002, although Creativity is somewhat narrowly scoped).

Affective development is recommended by Barnett (2004:247) as essential in a *"pedagogy for human beings"* to help develop qualities like *"thoughtfulness... receptiveness, courage"*. Reviewing affect (or lack of it) in legal education, Maharg and Maughan (2011:1) propose that a barrier is *"the view that affect is irrational and antithetical to core Western ideals of rationality"*. Cownie's (2011) study concludes that, for lawyers, *"clear boundaries are drawn between law and morality. The law student is taught to 'think like a lawyer', learning how to separate 'legal' issues from social, political, moral and other kinds of issue."* Burgoyne and Mumford (2001:64) also regret *"the absence of emotional content"*.

Creativity pedagogy assumes that creativity is 'learnable' in terms of facilitating natural talent, curiosity and imagination (Robinson, 2001). In arguing for more emphasis on emotion and the use of the senses in the classroom, Palmer and Leonard (2012:4) suggest that *"creativity in critical thinking rather than 'dry' rational analysis of information"* may help students *"ask more sceptical questions, such as why is the information structured and presented in this way, how is it manipulating me and why am I reacting in this way?"* Adriansen (2010) also concluded that there can be complementarity between studying creativity and criticality. Similarly, Bailey and Ford (1996:11; see also Darso, 2004) argued that management should be taught as a craft, which allows for active exploration of and experimentation in *"ambiguous, contextually-bound problems faced by practitioners"*.

How Practitioners Teach Cases

In a survey of a UK business school's case teaching, its academics* defined what they understood as a case (Palmer, 2005; Paroutis & Palmer, 2007). The main descriptions were of a situation-based case, with Professors tending to add 'a story' to their definition. For instance, a case was defined as a good story about a real situation with an important dilemma. Cases were seen as an opportunity for students to demonstrate and practice analysis and decision making. There was also a preference for a real company as the case's base and for a significant amount of detail. (*Similar practice by Strategy professors was found in a number of leading European Business Schools, indicating the HBS case format is widespread in use but not its class discussion.)

The need for detail linked to a preference for a case of 10-15 pages, although, in fact, most cases exceeded the 15 pages. A lecture was normally linked to the case and generally delivered before the case session (i.e. presenting a model to be applied). In line with this, questions were given to the students for their preparation of the case before class. Student participation was primarily through group presentations.

Significantly, Greiner *et al.* (2003) found, in top US schools, theory and lectures tending to replace the case method. Similarly other research suggests that university teachers, even in professional domains like Business, tend to be more knowledge centred, with an epistemological emphasis in their teaching rather than the development of their students' imagination and leadership behaviours. Also, the previous pedagogic discussion of lack of affect may indicate a reluctance to integrate emotion and feelings into a case class. Additionally, in the UK (Paroutis & Palmer, 2007), MBA alumni were seen – as corporate executives – to be in need of different capabilities from the Strategy techniques taught them. Especially weak were their meta skills, emotional sensitivity to organisational politics, and imagination for sense-making and visioning. These and other findings prompted pilots of innovative case teaching.

Innovative Case Teaching: Cases, the Student Experience, and Practical Advice for Teachers

The case of 'Critical Issues in Law and Management'

The authors of this chapter – a senior veteran educator in academia and an early career academic committed to developing innovative teaching expertise – collaborated in an ongoing institutional initiative to enhance the student learning experience in ways that transcend the traditional lecture-led teaching methods. The module 'Critical Issues in Law and Management' (CILM) was created by the former and handed over to the latter in 2013. CILM is a compulsory module for third year undergraduate students who study Law and Business at the University of Warwick in the UK. This module is run jointly by Warwick Business School and Warwick School of Law. It aims to enhance the students' critical thinking abilities by means of *creative criticality* (Palmer, 2013), which in CILM means the critical interpretation of issues dramatised in case studies. Specifically, in groups, students are tasked with exploring real-life multi-dimensional case studies through the medium of dramatisation and performance. They are invited to engage emotionally with case studies (Palmer & Leonard, 2012) and then embody these in open space (Monk *et al.*, 2011). In the process they utilise props, space, emotion, and each other. The students enact the roles and their perspectives of the issues set in three cases (Neelands, 2009; Palmer, 2006), including one that is assessed.

Palmer and Leonard (2012:11-12) explain that *"three innovative cases were designed in Autumn 2011"* – the first of which concerned policing London's Notting Hill Carnival. The first set of case material was designed to prompt exploration – *"a list of sources: legal, government, media and academic"* – and the second was intended to stimulate critical interpretation through the format of *"a 'factional' case, which contained elements that could be true, but delivered through a portfolio of dramatised narratives in emails, media reports and official documents."* To help frame the case, a fictional Commission was proposed. The students were split into syndicate groups and asked *"to dramatise their perspectives, issues, and arguments depending on the stakeholder role assigned"*. One syndicate group, for instance, played the London Mayor, plus the London Metropolitan Police Authority. The case included objective legal references but, overall, *"emotions were prominent, for example, in the crafted correspondence between a local councillor and the Carnival organisers"*.

The emphasis of CILM is placed on the critical analysis and interpretation of contemporary legal and corporate phenomena through the students' sensory engagement with a case. This process is followed by the embodied enactment of the students' ideas, rather than simply reporting and commenting on the case. The module therefore aims to provide an environment conducive to creative risk-taking (Amabile, 1998; Beghetto, 2010).

In order to underpin the learning that is fermenting through their creative criticality, students are subsequently asked to reflect on their experience of the presentations through post-session group reflection and a reflective essay – both also helping to monitor critical development. The students' reflective essays offer valuable insights into their experience of this innovative way of learning. In order to assist the reader to gauge the challenges and benefits of this mode of teaching some of the 2013 students' comments follow below, supplemented by material from the 2011 class. The analysis of the material was based on a review of the reflective essays. The process of data analysis was informed by the principles of grounded theory with simultaneous data collection and analysis (Strauss & Corbin, 1998; Suddaby, 2006). All essays were analysed iteratively and coded by hand. Analytical themes were generated during the stages of data analysis as suggested by Miles and Huberman (1994).

On Creativity and Criticality: the Student Voice

In their reflective essays nearly all students commented on the novelty and subsequent challenges that this new method of delivery engendered. When asked to present their critical analysis of the cases through dramatisation this initially caused all sorts of uncomfortable emotions from anxiety to frustration. As two students graphically observed:

"I was lost in abstraction!"

"I felt like the mundane educational context had been shaken!"

Our introductory meeting with the students focused deliberately on the drama-linked elements, namely ensemble building, the engagement of feelings, physical 'performance' and communication. The classroom was more like a rehearsal studio, with a flat floor, no tables and stackable chairs on wheels. Using open space, the drama-trained tutor engaged students in several creative exercises in order to build trust and help them to start appreciating the notion of presenting critical thinking through actions, rather than only words. The initial effect was not the one we had hoped for, with one student observing:

> "After the first two sessions, I nicknamed the course 'The Shakespeare Class'."

The creative character of the module broke the boundaries and pushed the students out of their comfort zones and their expected environment. High grades are generally their top priority in the current educational context, so they prefer clearly signposted ways and specific instructions for success. A prescriptive and familiar way of delivery – preferably through lectures and set texts – is, therefore, the preferred pedagogic approach. As a result, it is perhaps understandable that, overall, the initial reaction to CILM methods was frustration.

> "Being accustomed to operating with facts, figures and theories, I was quite exasperated."

> "I had my reservations of how useful this module was and I immediately thought it was going to be a struggle to get to grips with. I was further apprehensive, as I have never been hugely keen on acting which made me think of myself: 'I do Law and Business, not Drama!'"

Generally, the novelty and apparent idiosyncrasy of the CILM pedagogic methodology was too overwhelming for the students to see initially that they still had to deliver the mainstream academic thinking – specifically here, criticality – by demonstrating and communicating this in more creative ways. Thankfully, there was a minority of students whose first reaction to the dramatisation of the cases and the unconventional space was less one of shock and nervousness, but rather of excitement and relief. As one student put it:

> "The module provided a breath of fresh air and an escape from the monotony of learning case after case and theory after theory."

Also, the module's creative challenge to authority (Mingers, 2000) helped some elicit a positive critical transformation as the term progressed.

> "This is perhaps one of the things I have begun to learn – there is often no right or wrong answer."

> *"I have just been accepting ideas and believing that information was 100% acceptable."*

For us, the pedagogic challenge of teaching cases creatively was amplified by the principal objective of coaching and encouraging criticality. Teaching students how to engage in critical thinking is, as one of them put it, an *"ambitious intention"*.

> *"I was brought up by what is known as 'spoon-feeding education' –that teachers feed information and knowledge to students that we need not question."*

Indeed, communicating the essence of criticality is one thing; getting the students to actively question four sensitive elements – rhetoric, objectivity, authority, and tradition (Mingers, 2000) – is a challenge of a higher level, especially when this criticality is packaged in creativity. The inherent difficulties of genuine critical analysis is one issue, especially at an undergraduate level where mastery of professional knowledge has been emphasised. A further challenge involves facilitating the learning of students who come from cultural and educational backgrounds where the norm is to absorb and remember information, not question it. This underlying controlling layer produces worry and hesitation if the conventional teacher-student-knowledge matrix is disrupted. We must then, as educators, help students to transcend their cultural upbringing and begin to gain confidence in learning in different ways. This is a precondition for their effective engagement with criticality and their development of higher thinking skills. Students reflected very candidly on this issue:

> *"I was disciplined for nearly twenty years at home, at school and even on the society level, not to challenge the authority and obey traditions orderly."*

It was in this context that the practical application of criticality had to be conveyed to the students, in the session following the opening performance and bonding class. After a lecture on 'What is it to be critical?' students were asked to watch a short televised interview with the CEO of a global corporation. They were then invited to discuss critically the CEO's credibility, focusing on his rhetoric and objectivity. This mini exercise seemed to work. Moving on to question tradition and authority, the students saw two photos of the first moon landing and were asked to discuss the credibility of the event based on what they saw in the photos. Some of the hoax theories behind Neil Armstrong and his team's accomplishment generated critical questioning and debate. The effects were astonishing!

> "I was shocked when I discovered that the photo of Armstrong [on the moon] might be false. I felt like a kid [who] discovered that Santa Claus never existed. Thinking back, I think that what shocked me was to realise how strongly accustomed we are to listen to our teachers' words. Honestly, it has never bothered me before."

It was these exercises that provided an early catalyst for students to understand, in practice, the several possible viewpoints of reality and, in consequence, the need to explore these. As one of them remarked:

> "It takes courage to argue an alternative point of view. Such courage is essential for our development since, without people questioning established views, we could still leave in belief that the earth is flat."

From that point on, during the successive five weeks of classes, students worked on the three different case studies, critically analysing and interpreting them by means of performance-based group presentations. With the guidance of the performance specialist, they were gradually immersed in the creative process through practice and group cohesion, whilst constantly being reminded of the need to be critical. As one student put it, they were using their developing ability to:

> "...think, not only inside and outside the metaphorical box, but under, over, around and whilst taking a backwards step."

Overall, due to their novelty, the activities were not easy for the students. Especially challenging was the process of effectively combining the approaches of creativity and criticality. Over time and through practice, however, students started to show an appreciation of this new mode of activity, learning, and delivery. Indeed, attitudes and behaviours started to shift. One student elaborated on this:

"I had no idea how you would unite these two disciplines, but after one session, I began to realise that there is far more to critical thinking than I'd ever anticipated."

Ironically, like Koestler's 'bisociation' (1964:27), it was the amalgamation with creative processes that enhanced the students' understanding of criticality (Adriansen, 2010). Some students described their understanding thus:

"Critical thinking is not assessing what we find natural to question, but rather, quite uncomfortably, to question things that are obvious."

The freedom of thought and action in this creative approach helped students discover a new landscape of possibilities. Firstly, this included autonomy in the way they worked and dealt with the material. In the opinion of one of the students:

"The module gave me the chance to decide the pace and scope of my learning."

This also had an impact on group-work:

"Having a less structured atmosphere allowed our group to bond on a personal level."

Secondly, the dramatisation of the case studies offered students the possibility to expand their viewpoint of various phenomena and see things differently through practising divergent thinking (Kolb, 1984):

"The process of de-compartmentalising and subverting knowledge allowed me to see how there is a spectrum of truth dependent on whose perspective is put forward."

This is because students were asked to present the point of view of stakeholders with whom, at times, they held opposing views and values – e.g. capitalists or activists. The startling outcome of this requirement was increased empathy that amplified the students' emotional engagement with the material. Engagement with case studies in a creative way, embodying and enacting the case's subject matter, allowed for a more pluralistic overview of the case and richer sense-making of the issues. One participant explained that,

> *"Seeing how someone's background influenced their views really helped. The criticality through empathy allowed us to get into the shoes of those involved and see the conflict of interests, how the issues affect people's lives, and their perceptions of the issues."*

By the end of the first term, many students acknowledged insightful moments of knowledge generation. In a deeply introspective letter to herself, one of the students rationalised that she never considered critical thinking as creative discourse, mainly because she chose to position herself as non-creative. She had been surprised to discover that:

> *"Creativity isn't reserved for the arts alone, being a broader notion of exploration and thinking beyond the limits imposed by convention. It is a notion that questions the efficacy of those limits. So, why should we be confined in certain ways of thinking and certain ways of presenting?"*

In a similar vein, another learner became conscious of her initial misconception that:

> *"Theory-based learning methods are the only effective means of imparting knowledge."*

Overall, the creative embodiment of the case studies opened up an impressive number of different avenues of thinking on a specific case.

The Teachers' Conclusions

CILM was originally created to mirror a similar module in Warwick Business School based on a mix of principles (Mingers, 2000) – particularly complexity – in response to the creators' intention to bring the study experience as close to complex real-world situations as possible. However, the design of CILM was to innovate by employing a delivery approach of creativity and drama in order to facilitate students' imagination and willingness to explore ambiguous and pluralistic cases. The intention was to *"provide different ways of both describing and relating to that complexity, thereby offering novel ways of responding"* (Ladkin & Taylor, 2010:235). CILM's creative engagement, taking place after two years of textbook and lecture-based learning, aims to accelerate the emergence of the independent thinker, focusing on the ability to move beyond formal knowledge. Some students reported a change:

> *"CILM has triggered a significant personal transformation: becoming an autonomous thinker."*
>
> *"In a world with increasing illusions of choice, this creative module has encouraged me to trust my own choices, whilst staying open to different ways of seeing."*

We understand that this mode of case delivery is not applicable to every academic context: constraints of time and resources, combined with institutional pedagogic strategies and priorities, can pose barriers. In a similar educational frame, not all students will welcome this novel, holistic, and more demanding approach to learning. Moreover, it takes time for the coaching and practising to 'stick'. CILM uses two terms to develop the new practices of learning. In the second term the creative criticality switches focus to reviewing texts and writing essays, with more individual study. This change challenges the sustainability of the new approach.

Palmer and Leonard (2012:17) report that *"aspects of 'story' performance encourage Emotion and a deeper engagement"*, whereas *"trying to get the students to read emotionally, to feel and talk"* in CILM's second term is a much more difficult outcome. This is a weakness we acknowledge. In consequence, we are exploring ways to sustain the learning experience when transferring this innovative approach to non case-based (and non group-based) material.

Overall, we hope to have demonstrated that creativity and criticality can coalesce effectively into *creative criticality* when teaching with cases. This is because engaging with cases creatively encourages a pluralistic mode of exploration. As a result, study practices can become more independent and imaginative. In conclusion we offer three takeaways that we hope will encourage teachers to develop or adopt this approach. These are concerned with the production of new cases, the practice reflections of a teacher new to this approach, and 10 Habits (*pace* Covey!).

Three Takeaways
The Case for Creative Case Writing

Partly as a result of the creative emphasis in teaching cases at WBS a bespoke Case Writing Programme has been set up. The programme trains doctoral and early career researchers to write cases in a customised way, using research data generated by themselves or WBS academics. Built on a pedagogic agenda that places great emphasis on interdisciplinarity, the programme draws on the input and expertise of specialists from a variety of disciplines. Great weight is placed on training writers to produce cases that a) are different from an academic thesis or paper, yet just as rigorous and thought provoking, and b) have the potential to ignite the students' curiosity to engage actively with the material. Cases are designed in a variety of creative formats, for instance film, picture/photographs, and acted cases.

Ioanna's Reflections and Suggestions from Practice

"When I was asked to take on CILM and teach cases through dramatisation in open space, I was excited and daunted at the same time. The prospect was as novel to me as to the students and, in this respect, our initial reaction of numbed surprise was mutual. As a fervent exponent of experiential pedagogic methodologies who was armed with the guidance and collaboration of colleagues, I welcomed the opportunity.

"The challenges:
- how do I convince the students to overlook the assessment and immerse themselves in this challenging process?

- how do I get them to understand that the dramatised case is as content-rich as an actual lecture?

"I tackled these challenges by:
- enthusiastically conveying to the students my faith in the process.
- trusting my module colleague's skillful ability to lead the dramatization.
- allowing for reflection time at the end of every class.

"Constituents for success:
- genuine commitment to the pedagogic methodology.
- communication of this through enthusiasm, patience, and empathy.
- constant encouragement of the students to see past the surface of the performance and begin to generate creatively critical knowledge.

"As a final note, I would encourage you not to be disheartened by any initial reluctance of students. As is often the case for anything innovative and unknown, time for adjustment and acceptance are significant constituents of the process. Our experience has shown that, once the students bypass the initial 'shock' phase, they end up enjoying the process. The energy and passion they put into it is testament to the fun they are having while learning. Constant encouragement, enthusiasm, and faith in the process will be key. Ultimately, the potential 'bumpy ride' provides an excellent opportunity to reflect critically on one's own pedagogic approach."

Recommendations

We end by offering to the interested practitioner the following '10 Habits for Highly Innovative Case Teachers':

- Design in and facilitate group collaboration on the case and promote the concept that creativity and new ideas are not exclusive to a few but can emerge from group-work.
- Set up physical movement and stand-up activities in open space in order to release energy and involvement in the group work – plus fun and active use of the senses.
- Show that emotions, empathy and feelings are OK; give permission that insights from the senses can help with case interpretation.
- Coach that Habit 3's heightened Emotional Intelligence can help with seeing, and working on, how to persuade and involve people in implementation.
- Promote the positioning that a creatively critical approach can help one stand out to employers, and gives a wider portfolio of thinking and interpretative approaches.
- Encourage students to develop and practise a variety of 'lenses' for their diagnosis, and 'voices' using different media in communicating a case. Lenses could be functional, disciplinary, or critical (e.g. feminist).
- Help students to be aware of and open to the tensions, complexities, ambiguities of a case – reflecting the 'real world'.
- Set questions or tasks which allow for multiple thoughts or tentative reflections – not just 'the one right answer' or the definitive recommendation.
- Develop a portfolio of cases in different formats – paper, online, film, live. Design cases with multiple function angles,

e.g. Accounting and Human Resources Management. Have some cases set in real time or in emerging situations.

- Help students transfer their learning from case work to other studies and to their post-education roles as reflective life-long learners and adult citizens.

About the Authors

Grier Palmer is a Creativity Director and previously Assistant Dean of Creativity, Teaching and Learning at Warwick Business School, UK. He can be contacted at this email: gcap@talktalk.net

Ioanna Iordanou is a Teaching Fellow, responsible of developing the Case Writing Programme at Warwick Business School, UK. She can be contacted at this email: Ioanna.Iordanou@wbs.ac.uk

Chapter three

Structured Controversy Cases in Theory and Practice

Eva Dobozy

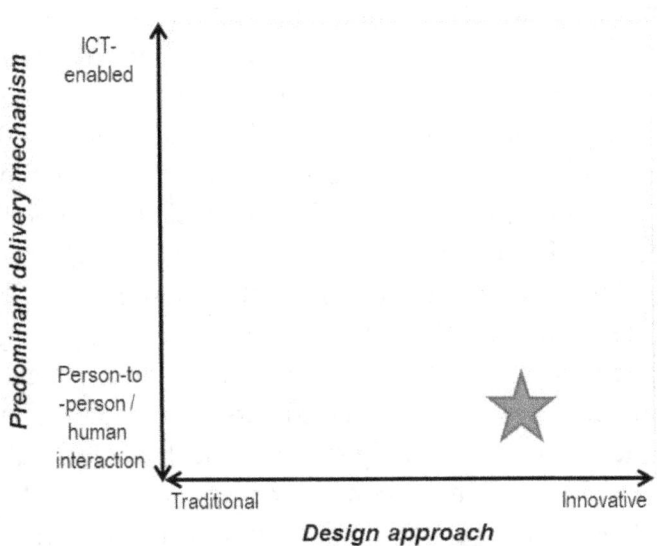

Introduction

Demands for highly trained individuals are increasing. No longer is it sufficient for 21st Century adult learners to acquire narrow technical knowledge and skills. To be employable in an increasingly competitive global economy, graduates at all levels of the education system will need increasingly to demonstrate competencies such as creative and critical thinking, team-based problem solving and effective communication, tenacity, goal orientation, open-mindedness, and intrinsic motivation. This list of highly sought-after competencies of present and future 21st Century workers and learners makes clear that a competency is *"more than just knowledge and skills. It involves the ability to meet complex demands, by drawing on and mobilizing psychosocial resources"* (OECD, 2005:4). These resources have been acknowledged as intangible assets, which do not lend themselves to direct translation into discrete and measurable learning outcomes. Nevertheless, they are clearly valued and increasingly important in today's business world.

Millennial Branding (2012) conducted a recent survey of US employers. Their results show that instead of narrow technical knowledge and skills, which are commonly tested in end-of-semester examinations at university, high on the list of important competencies of prospective employees were: communication (98%), positive attitude (97%), adaptability to change (92%), teamwork (92%), and goal orientation (88%). It is not surprising then that contemporary educators have a mandate to cater for these changed conditions and demanded learning outcomes. What is needed, therefore, is the successful implementation of learning-centric and future focused pedagogies (Reynolds, 2006), such as case-based teaching and learning (Branch et al., 2014) The learning-centric pedagogical models of contemporary education are diverse and include, but are not limited to, learning and teaching strategies such as classical case-based teaching (CBT), structured controversy case pedagogy (SCCP), problem-based learning (PBL), inquiry-based learning (IBL), and project-based teaching (PBT). What these approaches to teaching and learning have in common is a focus on learning-centric design aspects as a basis for student action, be this self-directed or guided.

The aim of this chapter is to explore the nature, purpose and practice of structured controversy case pedagogy (SCCP) in theory and practice. It is deliberately descriptive in nature, providing two practical examples from teacher education to illustrate the translation of SCCP theory into practice. It is hoped that this chapter will inspire others to engage in professional dialogue about their experiences and their views about the value and challenges of modernising teaching and learning practices in general and the benefits and/or disadvantages of technology-mediated SCCP in particular.

The chapter is structured as follows: First, SCCP is defined and contrasted with the classical Harvard-style case-based teaching approach. Second, the philosophical underpinnings of SCCP are explored and its relationship with transformational learning is explained. Third, a four-step SCCP model is introduced, which will illustrate the transformational power of SCCP in theory. Fourth, two case examples from teacher education will demonstrate contemporary, technology-mediated applications of this pedagogical model. Finally, some conclusions will be drawn concerning the practicalities of implementing SCCP in higher education.

Differentiating Structured Controversy Case Pedagogy from Classical Case-Based Teaching

Teaching and learning with cases is well established and was pioneered at Harvard University as early as the 1870s (Merseth, 1991). This approach is defined here as the use of real or fictitious narratives to provide the context for a team-based exploration of messy and complex problems in an authentic situation, allowing learners to make connections among systems and ideas as they present a 'best-fit' solution to a given problem based on text-book theory (Dobozy, 2014; Merseth, 1991; Yadav *et al.*, 2007).

Equally established are pedagogical approaches that are purposefully designed to incorporate controversy. Introducing learners to real world situations that are saturated with academic conflict, problems and dilemmas of practice is a pedagogy that extends the classical case-based teaching approach (CBT) introduced at the Harvard Law School so many years ago. This approach to teaching and learning is defined as a pedagogy that uses real or fictitious narratives to provide an anchor and practical examples of ethical dilemmas in practice and the application of theory-based decision making, enticing students (as professional novices) to learn to think and act like an expert in a given situation that demands the making of professional judgments based on theory, personal ethics and practical experience (Bennett *et al.*,

2002; Davies & Wilcock, 2003; Dobozy, 2014; Johnson & Johnson, 1988; Yilmaz & Seiffert, 2011). In other words, structured controversy case pedagogy (SCCP) values autonomous and reflective thinking and promises not simply subject-specific knowledge and skills development. More importantly, its intentions are the enhancement of identity or personality development (Johnson & Johnson, 1988) and the expansion of the 21st Century competencies outlined above (Yilmaz & Seiffert, 2011).

Similarly to the classic Harvard CBT approach, SCCP is underpinned by real world situations and is a method of teaching and learning that presents opposing views on a given topic, inviting students to take a particular position. Their personal opinions and values positions are first unearthed and articulated in a supportive team environment before being tested by fellow learners, who adopt different views. Students are required to confront peers who challenge their current belief systems and argue from different viewpoints. Through the strength of argument, personal values and ideologically coloured (and often taken-for-granted) views are exposed.

I argue that this process helps learners to develop and exercise their cognitive flexibility. Hence, there is a distinct difference between the classical Harvard-style CBT and SCCP. The former entices students, through design, to engage in problem framing and to arrive at a possible way forward for working through the given ill-defined problem. This is followed by a 'text-book solution' (Tang, et al., 1997). In contrast, SCCP guides learners through a specific set of learning activities that enables them to team up with like-minded peers to explore their current thinking. This helps them to formulate arguments cooperatively which based on evidence in the support of a community of learners that share similar beliefs. Finally they are guided through activities that allow them to test their thinking and, if necessary, change their minds.

Therefore, the multi-step learning activities are predefined and are naturally saturated with academic conflict, problems and dilemmas of practice to help students uncover hidden and taken-for-granted beliefs.

In other words, SCCP extends the classical Harvard style case-based teaching approach (CBT) in three distinct ways:

- SCCP is pedagogically structured, allowing students not familiar with self-directed learning practice or uncomfortable with exposing their personal views to delve deep into various value positions in a risk-free environment;
- SCCP demands that students engage with and argue for particular value positions and test their views with disagreeing peers, providing cognitive flexibility practice;
- SCCP helps students uncover hidden and taken-for-granted values. This demands that they acknowledge ethical dilemmas in professional practice for which decontextualised 'text-book solutions' are not available.

Despite the value attributed to SCCP, Johnson and Johnson (1988:58) explain that *"teachers often suppress students' academic disagreements and consequently miss out on valuable opportunities to capture their own audience and enhance learning"*. Hence, a central aim of this pedagogy is to get learners cognitively and emotionally involved in the learning activity through the expression and defence of their ideas and actions. Students are encouraged to take a stand on an issue, to deconstruct it, argue for or against it and, through the act of deliberation and debate, to enhance critical capacities and learn more about themselves and the subject at hand.

Philosophical Underpinnings

The use of explicit, systematic and comprehensive descriptors of properties of any event or phenomenon in a scientific manner is important in theory development. Distinguishing various characteristics of learning and teaching activities *"begs the question of whether we conceive of learning as a process or product"* (Bell, 2011:528) and this alludes to the important epistemological position from which learning theories originate.

The philosophical underpinnings of SCCP lay within an interpretive paradigm. It assumes that social reality is the result of subjective interpretation and personal meaning-making. *"To be locked in a particular paradigm is to view the world in a particular way"*, explain Burrell & Morgan, 1974:24). Or as Pansiri (2005:196) notes:

> *"Paradigms have been defined as 'world-views' that signal distinctive ontological (view of reality), epistemological (view of knowledge and relationships between knower and to-be known), methodological (view of mode of inquiry), and axiological (view of what is valuable) positions"*

Consequently, SCCP's theoretical framework can be characterised by a set of common principles and processes. According to Smith, Flowers and Larkin (2012:79-89) these are: committing to personal meaning-making in particular contexts and moving through deliberate reflexive engagement from a particular, individualistic view to a new and possibly shared understanding. In other words, the requirements of design are that the phenomena being investigated are clearly visible within the case's construction. Students require opportunities to apply their ideas systematically. At the same time they want sufficient flexibility to be imaginative and playful in order that they can develop a combination of reflective, critical, creative and conceptual thinking.

SCCP has the potential to provide a means for students to become more proficient critical thinkers who are actively engaged with each other in an ethical and respectful way. Furthermore it *"helps to minimize the suspicion of possible indoctrination and partisan influences"* (Leung & Yuen, 2009:19) when engaging with controversial topics and issues. This process may help learners understand the multiplicity of realities and experiences. Hence SCCP may contribute to the transformation of thought and being because, even when a learner indicates that something is 'right/wrong' or 'true/untrue', the perceived reality *"remains open to a reinscription because it is always haunted or bothered by its own impossibility"* (Vintimilla, 2012:94). As Stone (2011) explains:

> *"Meanings overlap, sometimes to the point that, when we feel our meaning is understood by others, there is an evanescent sense of spiritual communion. ... [t]he idea that meaning is both (i) personal*

and social and (ii) neither personal nor social is best understood as the idea that meaning is relational, or, more precisely, dialogical. The idea is encapsulated in the concept of dialogical thinking." (Stone, 2011:32)

The intention of SCCP is not only to develop professional knowledge and skills in the sense of 'vocational training'; in addition its aim is to be transformational in the sense of 'education' based on the German notion of 'Bildung'. Transformational learning combines professional, ethical and cultural development (Dobozy, 2011).

Transformational Learning with Technology-mediated SCCP

In the manner of David and Robert Johnson (1988), Henry Giroux (1994) and Paulo Freire (1970) are two of the more prominent education scholars who have pointed to the need of education at all levels to create opportunities for transformative experiences. For example, Giroux (2010:203) notes: *"Education cannot be neutral. It is always directive in its attempt to teach students to inhabit a particular mode of agency, enabling them to understand the larger world and one's role in it in a specific way."*

Moreover, following in the footsteps of Johnson and Johnson (1988) two decades ago, Dobozy (2007) and Todd and Säfström (2008) explain that education should take conflict seriously. They point out that contemporary pedagogical models of how to promote respectful learning in an active classroom often center on *"creating a conflict-free atmosphere ... [i]ndeed, conflict is often perceived as not simply being counter-productive to dialogue and conversation, but as being indicative of communicative breakdown itself"* (Todd & Säfström, 2008:1). Hence, the general reluctance to move out of one's comfort zone of like-mindedness and to confront opposition to personal views and values acts as a barrier to deep learning and this requires learners to develop *"strategic skills in mess management ... [and] a tolerance for ambiguity in the name of new knowledge, goods and identity production"* (Dobozy, 2011:20)

Accordingly I argue that academic disagreement should not be avoided. Rather, it should be embraced and used for the dual purpose of teaching learners about a particular subject matter and, equally importantly, to develop their 21st Century knowledge and skills and psychosocial capabilities.

The act of deconstruction and critical thinking unearths previously unquestioned assumptions, values positions and possible internal contradictions (Biesta, 2009). The guiding concept for the advocacy of this form of active and transformative education through the utilisation of SCCP is exposure. Focusing on a range of 21st Century skills, in particular higher order thinking skills, Hannam and Echeverria (2009) make the point that learning-centric pedagogies set the stage for interaction between four key elements, namely; critical thinking, creative thinking, collaborative thinking and caring thinking, and four categories of skills, listed as good reasoning skills, investigatory skills, conceptual skills and translation skills. The SCCP model that I have developed incorporates these elements into a clearly identifiable, logical structure (see Figure 1).

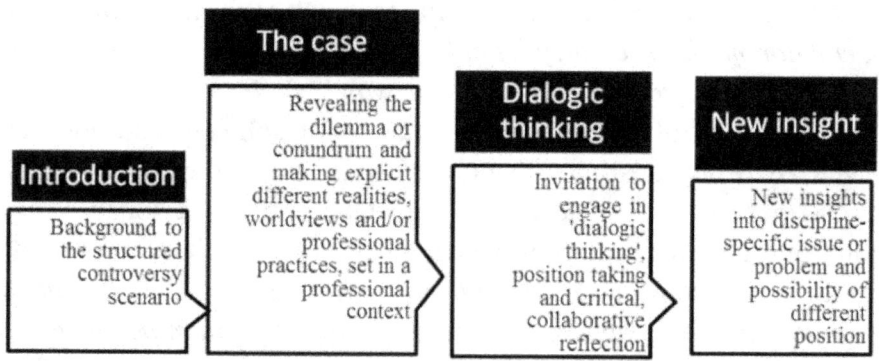

Figure 1: Four step Structured Controversy Case Pedagogy model

Moreover, to assist learners in the exploration of their personal values positions in a risk-free environment, step three of the four step model is the most critical and demanding for students. Because of this, the pedagogical design must guide them carefully through both the discussion and the debate phases in a way that makes them feel supported and ready to embrace the challenge to face people who hold opposing views. Therefore, a colour-coded diagram is introduced to learners to help them understand the pedagogical procedure (see Table 1).

Phase	Action	Diagram
1	Person A or B posts her/his views on the forum and meets up with a likeminded peer to form a small group, exchange views and construct initial argument	A+A and B+B
2	Likeminded groups join up to strengthen their arguments to pool their thinking	AA+AA and BB+BB
3	Phase 2 is repeated	AAAA+AAAA and BBBB+BBBB
	Two opposing parties are created and a spokesperson is elected to explain via video or audio link (or asynchronous forum post) the particular values position taken by the group	AAAAAAAAAAAA and BBBBBBB
4	Individual views and arguments are tested as students move out of groups of likeminded people to confront peers who hold opposing views. Hence, they progress from discussion to debate, testing the strength of beliefs and arguments	A+B and A+B
5	Some students may change position or request time to verify arguments presented by the opposition so they can update their arguments. Testing of arguments continues in small often uneven groups.	A+BB and AA+B
6	Testing continues as larger and more uneven groups are formed until students are certain they have sufficiently developed arguments to defend their values position and can resist 'groupthink' or assumed consensus.	AAAAA+BB and BBBBB+AA

Table 1: SCCP Dialogic thinking – moving from discussion to debate

After the scenario or dilemma is introduced, students are requested to take a position for or against a particular idea or action. In the discussion phase, students meet up with like-minded peers to exchange opinions and construct their arguments as to why this is the 'right' view to have. They are aware that their ideas will be tested. Therefore there is a requirement for their arguments to be theory and evidence based.

There is a clear difference between 'groupthink' and agreement among people on a particular idea or action based on deep seated beliefs. In groupthink situations conflict avoidance is the goal and 'not rocking the boat' is the major objective. In contrast, the genuine pooling of ideas to arrive at a values position shared by many requires debate and rigorous testing of ideas and arguments. SCCP enables and even requires students to move from a clear cut 'yes/no' position to a more realistic and questioning 'yes/no/maybe/yes' position. Hence, the 'changing of sides' and moving between A and B positions is encouraged as it reflects the cognitive struggle of the thinker. Moving through the six phases of the dialogic thinking stage of SCCP helps students to acknowledge the multiplicity of perspectives, enables them to question, challenge and argue for or against certain ideas or actions and act as sounding boards for their peers.

The conceptual model illustrated in Figure 1 was taken as the starting point for the development of an online learning module which involves the organisation and sequencing of learning material and learning activities according to pedagogical principles in preparation for delivery via the World Wide Web using an open source platform. This learning module's pedagogy is underpinned by Vygotskyian social learning theory (Woolfolk & Margetts, 2013) and fits seamlessly with the SCCP philosophy outlined above.

The Learning Activity Management System (LAMS) developed by Macquarie University in Sydney Australia was chosen because it is a user-friendly platform for learning designers and for students (Dobozy, Dalziel & Dalziel, 2013). As Dalziel (2011) notes:

> *"LAMS is used by thousands of educators in over 80 countries, is translated in 30 languages [and] provides an integrated Learning*

Design system, incorporating an authoring environment, a runtime implementation environment for students (including a suite of activity tools – 10 in the initial V1 release, 24 in the V2.3.4 release) and a monitoring environment for teachers to track real-time student progress." (Dalziel, 2011:19-20)

LAMS is as an ideal vehicle for learning-centric design because of its visual appeal for the designer and the user-friendly 'swim lane' structure for learners, providing logical design flows and time structure. The technology-mediated SCCP design allows for the seamless integration of external, digital, text-based and visual/audio material. This provides an effective and efficient way of providing contextual and foundational information to students in conjunction with procedural information necessary for authentic, technology-mediated SCCP.

Technology-mediated SCCP - Case Examples

Two technology-mediated SCCP case examples were developed for an Australian teacher education programme; one for a first year technology in education course and one for an introductory educational psychology (child development for educators) course. The programme is aligned with the new teaching standards and accreditation requirements for Australian teachers (Australian Institute for Teaching and School Leadership [AITSL], 2014). The purpose of the technology in education course was to enable students to appreciate the personal and professional implications of living and working in a technology-rich society. The design of the unit offered learning opportunities for the adoption of safe and ethical personal and professional practices. The introductory educational psychology course aimed to provide an overview of typical and atypical human development across physical, cognitive, social and emotional domains and to offer opportunities for effective engagement and interaction with various stakeholders and for the creation and maintenance of safe learning environments for children.

SCCP Step 1: Introduction

The introduction page constructed on the LAMS noticeboard provides background information about SCCP and procedural instructions (see Table 2).

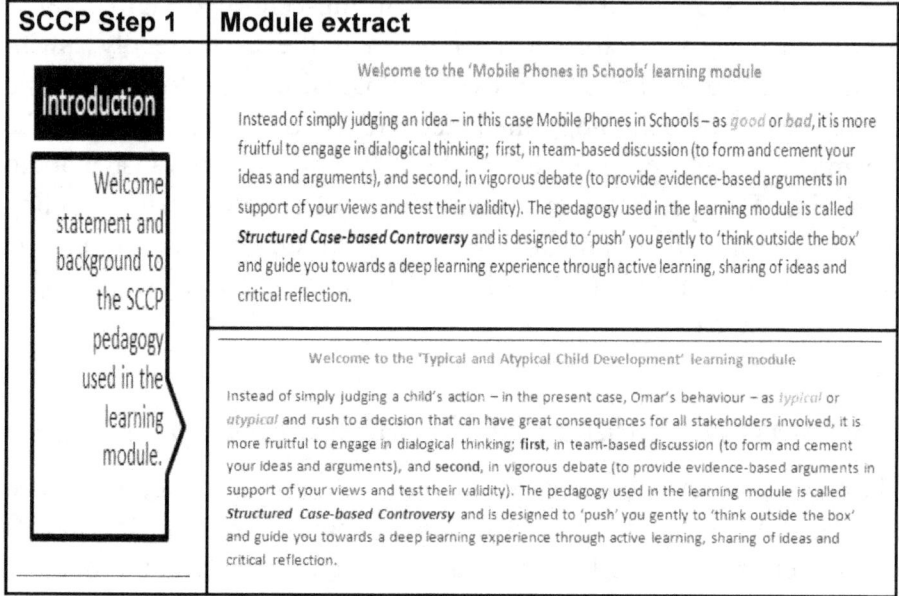

Table 2: Step 1 - Introduction

This introduction page alerts the reader to the need for deep, dialogic thinking, making explicit that there is an expectation of personal engagement. Moreover, it is made clear that students cannot stay neutral, but will need to commit to a values position and to explore, with like-minded people, why they believe in a certain idea or action. This discussion phase is followed by a debate phase, as outlined in Table 1, which stipulates that students should expect their ideas to be challenged and vigorously tested – even to the point where they are unsure if their arguments, based on deeply held beliefs, hold up to scrutiny. Finally, students are invited to change positions actively and thereby show cognitive flexibility.

SCCP Step 2: the Case

After setting the stage for the context-specific scenario, the case is introduced with the help of multi-media resources and hyperlinked academic texts providing convincing arguments and evidence for or against the adoption of a particular position (see Table 3).

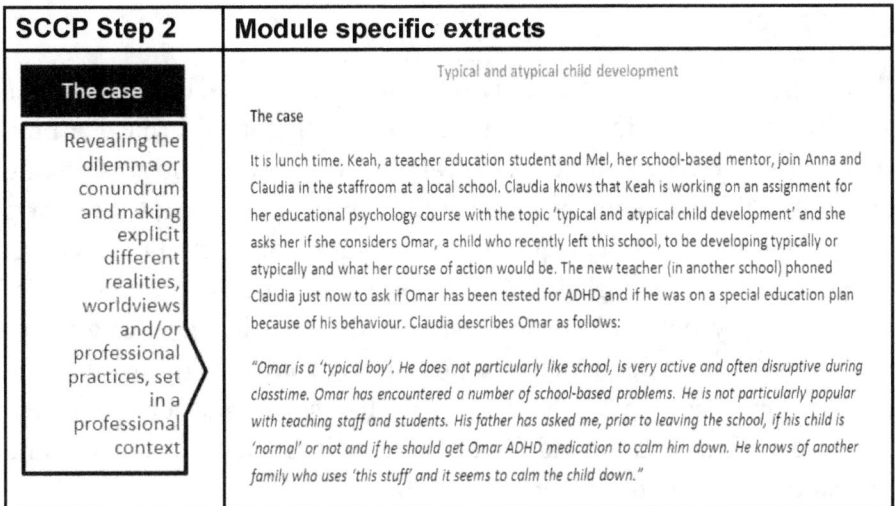

SCCP Step 2	Module specific extracts
The case Revealing the dilemma or conundrum and making explicit different realities, worldviews and/or professional practices, set in a professional context	Typical and atypical child development The case It is lunch time. Keah, a teacher education student and Mel, her school-based mentor, join Anna and Claudia in the staffroom at a local school. Claudia knows that Keah is working on an assignment for her educational psychology course with the topic 'typical and atypical child development' and she asks her if she considers Omar, a child who recently left this school, to be developing typically or atypically and what her course of action would be. The new teacher (in another school) phoned Claudia just now to ask if Omar has been tested for ADHD and if he was on a special education plan because of his behaviour. Claudia describes Omar as follows: "Omar is a 'typical boy'. He does not particularly like school, is very active and often disruptive during classtime. Omar has encountered a number of school-based problems. He is not particularly popular with teaching staff and students. His father has asked me, prior to leaving the school, if his child is 'normal' or not and if he should get Omar ADHD medication to calm him down. He knows of another family who uses 'this stuff' and it seems to calm the child down."

Table 3: Step 2 – the Case

In the case for the educational technology module the dilemma or conundrum presented to students is that although technology-enhanced learning in school education is more and more a reality in Australia and elsewhere, there is great opposition to the use of mobile phones in school, due to reports of frequent misuse and concerns about children's emotional wellbeing.

The case for the child development module aims to alert teacher education students to the conundrum of distinguishing between typical and atypical child development and to the difficulty of diagnosing learning disabilities, such as ADHD. In both modules, students are introduced to pro and con arguments through the use of external multimedia resources. At the conclusion of the online learning sequence in the educational technology module, students will need to articulate whether or not they would permit the use of mobile phones if they were the school principal or center director. In the child development module students must prepare effective responses to queries by the teacher at an imaginary practice school in relation to teacher's expectations concerning atypical and typical child development of children who are classified as 'active', 'often inattentive' and 'boisterous'.

SCCP Step 3: Dialogic Thinking

As in the Harvard-style case-based teaching approach, SCCP cases serve as an immersion tool for deep engagement with the learning material. However, as outlined in Table 1 above, the dialogic thinking step will guide students through the Discussion phase when they form their opinion and produce quality arguments in support of their views. Then, in the Debate phase, they must move out of the comfort of their currently-held beliefs and test their thinking in rigorous ways in what can often be perceived as a hostile environment. In this way the students are taken on a guided tour of self-discovery where they need to make choices and defend their decisions in the light of choices and decisions made by their peers (see Table 4).

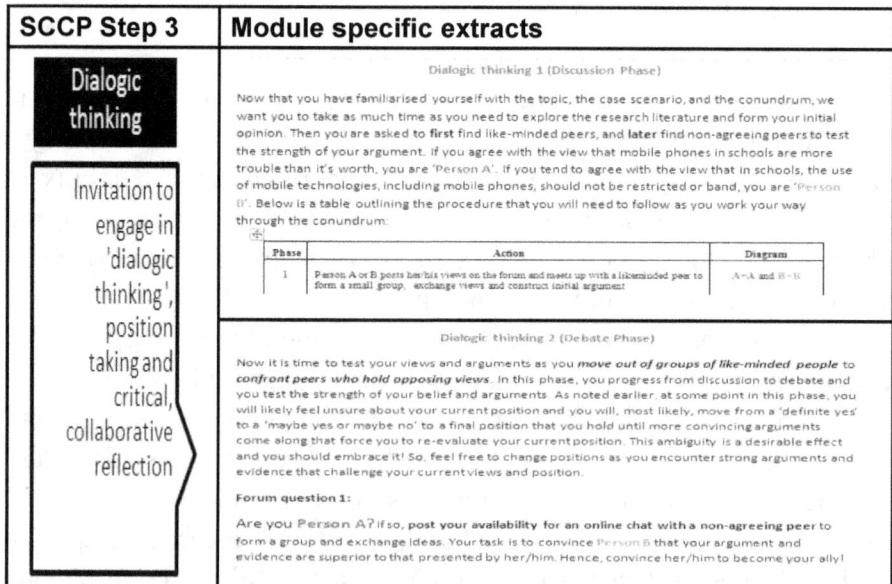

Table 4: Step 3 – Dialogic thinking

Because of the interactive nature of the modules learners are encouraged to provide personal viewpoints and elaborate on their decisions, understanding that there is no right/wrong answer. The underlying purpose of these forum tasks is the sharing of ideas and making explicit how meaning is constructed and applied to specific problems. The student teachers immerse themselves into the learning activities, constructing their arguments in support of their beliefs first in like-minded teams and later in situations that test the strength of their evidence and arguments. They do not simply engage with the learning material, they experience the meaning of transformational learning. The learning experience is deemed transformational because the student has to grapple with their personal ideas and deep-seated values as they use their knowledge and skills to build new mental models and learn the value of "*getting stuck*" (Whitehouse, 2011:58).

After students are carefully guided to explore and express their views in a risk-free and supportive learning environment (the discussion phase) they are prompted to move out of their comfort zone and test their ideas, evidence and arguments in a 'hostile environment'. This means that their debate partners will adopt different views and seek to find holes in the evidence and/or argument they are hearing to persuade them to join 'the other party'. In this debate phase of the dialogic thinking step, students should realise the tentativeness of values positions and the significance of scientific, evidence-based argument construction and testing.

SCCP Step 4: New Insight

The fourth and final step in the SCCP model is the generation and sharing of 'new insights' gained through engagement with the module, the embedded curriculum material and each other (see Table 5).

SCCP Step 4	Module specific extracts
New insight New insight into discipline-specific issue or problem and the possibility of producing high-quality ideas and evidence-based decision making	**New insights** Now that you have had the opportunity to broaden your perspective and arrive at a decision about an issue of great importance to teachers, first through engaging in discussion with like-minded peers (dialogic thinking 1), and later through the testing of the strength of your conviction, argument and evidence with non-agreeing peers (dialogic thinking 2), it is time to reflect on your learning. **Reflect on your subject matter knowledge:** What are possible symptoms of ADHD in the classroom and what can teachers do to help children with learning difficulties? **Reflect on your emotions:** During the dialogic thinking phase, did you feel supported by your like-minded peers? How did your emotions change when you were confronted with non-agreeing peers? **Reflect on pedagogy:** What is the value of structured controversy pedagogy? Why should school teachers consider using this social constructivist pedagogy in the classroom? What adaptations could/should be made?

Table 5: Step 4 – New Insights

Reflection is an important aspect of learning and knowledge maturation. It allows learners to document and analyse their knowledge and skills development from early, often unexamined and taken-for-granted beliefs and judgments about a given issue or problem in order to arrive at a more considerate, analytically sound, evidence-based and defensible values position.

Discussion

Benefits of SCCP

SCCP avoids providing the student with discrete facts using classical transmission education methods. Instead it seeks to entice the student to engage in problem-solving and to draw out their current knowledge and understanding of a problem or issue and engage in the sharing of personal reactions and evidence to enhance meaning-making. Classical CBT methods require students to engage largely in unstructured team-based problem solving. In contrast, SCCP is a teaching and learning approach that is highly structured, able to carefully guide students through various steps of dialogic thinking. This pedagogical approach is designed to take care of students' psychosocial needs and emotional wellbeing. In this way it is, in theory, able to move students out of passive learning modes Dobozy's 2011 discussion of 'consumer students' versus 'producer students') to become more active and engaged in their learning process. In particular it should help novices of learning-centric pedagogies to adjust their learning habits in a unique way.

This pedagogical approach has been tested in 2013 in four units as part of a larger study (Dobozy, 2014) showing that students are appreciative of the possibility of engaging with non-traditional pedagogies during their studies. However, it also makes clear that consumer students are not ready to switch modes and contribute to discussion and debate. The interactive process was designed to get students to articulate clearly a values position which is well-developed, consolidated and evidence-based (discussion phase of dialogic thinking). However, consumer students are classical 'lurkers' and want to remain invisible (Soroka & Rafaeli, 2006). SCCP is a learning-centric approach that provides an environment which assists learners to move out of their comfort zone and confront opposing views and values in a safe, supportive and pedagogically designed environment. This point is particularly important, because it is vital to help students become more cognitively agile and less risk-averse (Dobozy, 2011). However, the presented design is used differently by different student groups. Some students are motivated to engage with the learning material and each other, others are interested in having access to student interaction without being active contributors and others still do not seem to have the willpower and/or capacity to engage with anything that does not contribute to assessment points. They are simply absent from the learning experience.

During the discussion phase of stage 2 (dialogic thinking) students are encouraged to engage in divergent thinking in like-minded groups so that they can pool their ideas in an environment that is non-threatening. This design feature is particularly appreciated by teachers, because it provides opportunities for students temporarily to suspend criticism and critical judgment of the ideas and values of others while compiling their evidence and constructing their arguments in support of their position.

Teachers report (Dobozy, forthcoming) that students tend to be reluctant to engage with additional, non-assessed learning materials. Similarly, students are said to be simply 'too busy' to volunteer as study participants and test the online SCCP learning environment. Nevertheless, the teaching staff engaging with the SCCP design have noted that it is user-friendly and is assisting them in helping students move away from behaving like consumers. These teaching staff observe that a particular strength of the SCCP design is that it causes students to engage and then use divergent and convergent thinking sequentially. Hence, the SCCP model can be a powerful tool for providing students with a safe learning environment in which to examine their taken-for-granted beliefs, to construct supportive arguments, and then test their viability (Mannix *et al.*, 2009).

Limitations of SCCP

Despite its pedagogical value, SCCP is complex and time consuming. It requires dedication and practice from teachers and students, and additional resource allocations from education institutions. As noted above, students typically will endeavour to avoid conflict at all costs. Therefore explicitly designing conflict and controversy into the learning activity requires an understanding of its value-adding nature; it also requires strong pedagogical leadership. Despite the empirical evidence of SCCP's ability to increase students' preparedness for work in 21st Century global knowledge economies, more 'buy-in' from educational leaders and students is needed to foster a mindset that is open to challenge and various forms of learning centric pedagogies (Dobozy, 2014). The empirical findings provide additional evidence that the problem of consumer students, invisible participants and lurkers is a deep-seated problem that demands better understanding. Most importantly, as expectations of students change, the behavioural change will need to be made explicit and tackled at the systems level.

Conclusion

All pedagogies are underpinned by educational values, aims, purposes, and principles which align to a particular educational paradigm. The LAMS-based SCCP model introduced in this chapter is a learning-centric pedagogical strategy that has been designed to move beyond traditional transmission education pedagogies. Traditional transmission education methods rightly attribute importance to the expression and defence of deeply-held beliefs and the need to act upon those ideas and ideals using ethical and professional decision-making and judgment. SCCP goes further by provoking the testing and possible revision of those ideas and ideals and this makes it transformational in nature.

Through individual and collective engagement with the carefully crafted SCCP scenario and real-world professional dilemmas, learners are given an opportunity to engage in deep learning by reflecting about previously unquestioned assumptions, articulating and testing their views in a supportive and relatively risk-free educational environment. This process makes possible the detection of possible internal contradictions and misconceptions (Biesta, 2009).

In this chapter I have argued that, rather than subduing students' academic conflicts, introducing students to technology-mediated SCCP not only has the potential to enhance students' learning engagement and outcomes but also engages student in transformation learning. SCCP provides a means for students to become critical thinkers and to engage actively with each other in an ethical and respectful way. Students should appreciate the existence of different realities and priorities; working their way through the SCCP guided process helps them to understand the complexity of ethical and evidence-based professional decision making.

About the Author

Eva Dobozy, is a Senior Lecturer in the School of Education at Curtin University, Perth, Western Australia. She can be contacted at this email: Eva.Dobozy@curtin.edu.au

Chapter four

Strategies to Enhance Students' Capabilities of Abstract Thinking – the Use of Case in Different Learning Situations

Ola Mattisson and Ulf Ramberg

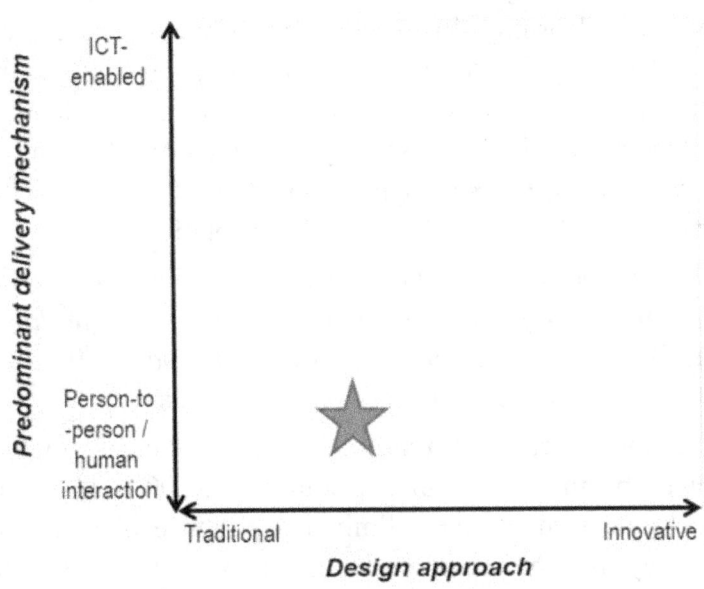

Teaching with Cases for Undergraduate Students

The pedagogical idea underpinning the Case Method originated from concepts such as empirical and authentic. A case will present a realistic situation that will be meaningful to those involved in the learning activity (Mattisson & Ramberg, 2013). This element of reality is an important reason why the method is used extensively in many areas of professional education. The case method is also an active learning technique in which students read, write, discuss, evaluate and reflect – that is, they do more than just listen (Auster & Wylie, 2006).

This approach allows active professionals to discuss perceived, relevant problems and solutions inspired by a piece of reality. It has proved very successful; not at least in MBA programs all over the world (Liang & Wang, 2004; Lee *et al.*, 2009). At its best it brings many voices, ideas, perspectives, experiences from life and work, and arguments into a discussion. When students who have accumulated life and work experience get involved in such a discussion they become engaged in a very powerful and formative learning process. Hattie's (2008) meta-analysis clearly points in that direction: the student's input into a learning situation (i.e. experiences, expectations and knowledge) is very important for the learning process. In line with Hattie, but put in a slightly different way by the Nobel laureate Aron Klug, *"One doesn't see with one's eyes, one sees with the whole fruit of one's previous experience."* (In Marton & Booth 1997/2009:83 from Marton *et al.*, 1994). Or as Ausubel (1968) put it:

> *"If I had to reduce all of educational psychology to just one principle, I would say this: the most important single factor influencing learning is what the learner already knows. Ascertain this and teach him accordingly."* (Ausubel, 1968:vi)

Recent decades have seen an increase in the use of the case method in undergraduate business programs (Booth *et al.*, 2000). However, most undergraduate students have limited experience of work and practical everyday life. In fact, it can be the opposite; they are likely to be more familiar with theory and critical thinking than with work practices and experience. Against this background the use of cases to enhance students learning settings can be problematic and potentially counterproductive. What kind of 'meaning shaping' process occurs in the students' mindset if their knowledge and experiences can't relate to a situation being presented to them?

This chapter elaborates on how case teaching strategies can be adopted in order to effect the learning outcome when teaching with cases in undergraduate classes, especially those for first year students. The chapter is based on development of conclusions in Mattisson and Ramberg (2013) and aims to equip teachers to select appropriate cases and teach in a manner that will enhance first year undergraduate students' learning outcomes. We will raise and discuss different strategies for case teaching in relation to student's capabilities of abstract thinking and their amount of empirical knowledge.

Perspectives on Learning

Our point of departure is that a business case is a piece of reality presented in an interesting way to reach different kinds of intended learning outcomes in a given learning situation. The case describes something problematic with a distinctive connection to reality which students discuss and solve interactively (Bengtsson, 1999). The intention is that students will understand the 'problematic something' a little bit better after the case discussion than before they started it.

The SOLO taxonomy (Structure of Observed Learning Outcomes) enables us to describe how this intended learning can evolve from quite simplistic understanding to more and more complex. According to Biggs and Tang (2007) the student's understanding can change in two ways – quantitative and qualitative – where the quantitative learning always occurs first. Understanding is concerned with both the amount of detail that can be handled in the discussion, and about how these details are structured in a more and more complex and relational way in the mind-set of the student.

According to this taxonomy, case discussion where a student reproduces one or two facts from the case will render low grades. To obtain a higher grade the student needs to do more. For example, to discuss many different details from the case, to relate those details to each other, to integrate those details into a new structure by means of theory or through others' experiences and, finally, to make reflections and generate new ideas. Put differently; to demonstrate the capability of higher order thinking skills (HOTS).

The capacity for HOTS is tightly connected to the idea of meaningful learning (Hattie, 2012). According to Ausubel and Robinson (1969) a learning situation must fulfil all the following conditions in order for the student to experience meaningful learning.

1) The student needs to be able to relate to the case content to a certain extent

2) The student must be able to pinpoint 'what is new' in the case relative to already assimilated experiences and

3) actually relate new experiences to existing knowledge.

Marton and Booth (1997/2009) summarise this perspective on learning as follows:

"Our point is that you can only learn something new about something, and by learning something new about something, that something will change, more or less, which implies that the whole must precede the parts. Moreover, the whole is, according to this line of reasoning, a part of wholes established earlier. One cannot learn mere details without having an idea of what they are details of. Learning is mostly a matter of reconstituting the already constituted world." (Marton & Booth, 1997/2009:139)

This reasoning emphasises the importance for case teachers of being aware that students will have different viewpoints on what constitutes the whole. This will always be the situation. Wahlgren and Ahlberg (2013) use case discussions to study progression in engineering programmes. In an experiment they found that first year students discuss and act differently in comparison with the way final year students discuss and solve cases. Final year students are more shaped by the content of their study programs than first year students. They identify the problems, connect the problem to a broader empirical and theoretical knowledge base, make the analyses and present solutions in a more straight-forward way than the first year students do. In other words, they have a more integrated and overall view to relate to than the first year students.

Using conceptual models in case teaching for first year students is demanding because the models represent and organise a reality they have little or no experience of. According to Hattie (2012) it is essential to be aware of what kind of learning and experience each student brings into the class. Allowing first year students to work empirically with detailed case studies enables them to gain business and organisational experience relatively quickly. The Case Difficulty Cube of Maufette-Leenders *et al.* (1997) can preferably be used both to design new cases and to choose cases for a case discussion in this respect. This Case Cube divides the complexity of a case task into three dimensions, namely; analytical, conceptual and presentational. Following this reasoning, the presentation dimension is of special importance when it focuses on the empirical content and on how it is organised.

Encouraging students to relate new knowledge to their previous knowledge can be troublesome. Maufette-Leenders *et al.* (1997) offer a three stage learning process for case teaching which can be one way to organise and encourage students to engage in this important kind of learning activity. Their process always starts with individual case preparations. These are followed by a student-led, small group discussion where each student needs to argue and defend their interpretation of the case. Finally there is a case seminar in full class.

This three stage learning process also puts the student in the position of being a learning partner and not merely a recipient of knowledge. This recognition of being a learning partner is an important factor for achieving effective teaching for first year undergraduate students (Allan *et al.*, 2009). It is also possible to elaborate on the case content in order to make the case more interesting to read for the students. According to Lynn (1999), the case features that students appreciate often differ from those that teachers prize – and this can be a problem. However, in the early semesters it can be wise to use cases that the students will like and appreciate. This means that cases should be well written and have interesting characters and stories that are filled with action, drama and heightened feelings. Useful teaching notes of intellectual quality are of subordinate importance (Lynn, 1999:114-118).

We argue that the learning curve and knowledge of students depend on the background knowledge of the individual. Furthermore, the amount of empirical knowledge is a crucial requisite for analytical ability. Another relevant dimension is the student's capability for abstract thinking and his/her ability to apply and use analytical tools. These two dimensions are illustrated in Figure 1 below, where arrow A represents 'learning concretisation' and arrow B represents 'learning acceleration'. We will return to these types later in this chapter.

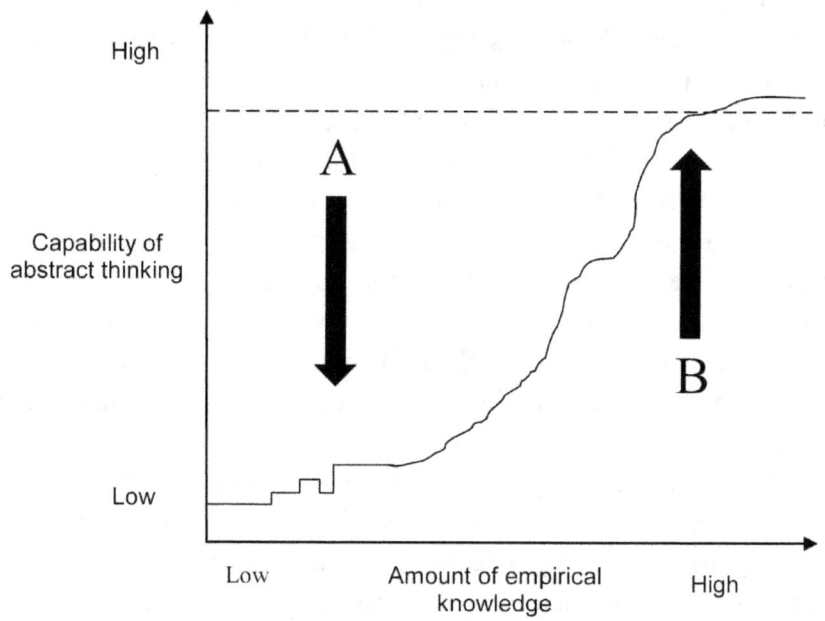

Figure 1: The typical student learning curve and how a case can infuse knowledge and learning in different directions. From Mattisson & Ramberg, 2013:98

In Mattisson and Ramberg (2013) we argued that the case method is very effective for integrating abstract thinking with empirically-oriented thinking. As Kolb (1984) asserts, as long as cases allow students to make associations with previous experiences they can be used for reflection, conceptualisation and experimentation.

Stimuli to arouse those sorts of experiences can be of different kinds, including texts, pictures, movies, paintings, and music. Therefore a broader palette of stimuli is to be recommended because most of the stimuli that students bring in to class normally come from concrete phenomena which are outside the world of books and readings (Palmer & Iordanou, this volume).

An orientation towards multimedia cases is also in line with the need to focus on the Case Cube's presentational dimension. Such materials give students the opportunity to explore different kinds of qualitative and quantitative presentations of data and this can stimulate them to take an active role as a partner in learning. As Liu (2012) shows, this can also affect when students' knowledge-seeking shifts from a focus on single aspects of a task towards getting a more comprehensive view of the task. In return this may also give more time for teachers to initiate and stimulate conceptual understanding and development. We will illustrate below the interaction between teachers and students, and between abstract and concrete knowledge, and how this can differ in case discussions.

Empirical Findings

The empirical data we will use stem from courses at two different departments at Lund University where we have been involved as teachers. We have collected data from two programs - Service Management and Business Administration – during two periods; namely, 1) between 2005 and 2010 and 2) during 2012 and 2013 when the teamwork case has been used. We have examined two perspectives. The first is concerned with the students' perceptions and opinions as gathered by course evaluation forms and formal discussions with students; the second perspective is that of the teachers. After every course, there is a staff meeting where the impressions from giving the course are gathered and summarised. We will show representative extracts derived from documents, notes and protocols from these sources.

The empirical evidence we give in this chapter stems from three different settings where cases have been used in our teaching. For each setting there is one example of case based teaching on an introductory course (first semester of a program) and one example from a degree level course (Bachelors or Masters). The empirical analysis is based on comparisons of case teaching between introductory courses and degree courses.

The examples featuring case based teaching (CBT) that we draw on in this study, and their contexts, are as follows:

1. Cases in service management from a four-year Masters program. The program includes different specialisations such as hotel management, tourism management and retail management. Here, examples of CBT come from two different situations. The first is an introductory course which forms the start of the whole program, while the second is the final theory course before the students sit their Bachelor exam.

2. Cases in organisation and strategy. At the School of Economics and Management of Lund University there are two courses on the bachelor program in business administration that are explicitly based on case pedagogy. The first is the introductory course in organisation theory (second half of the first semester). The second is a course in strategy and management control that students take as a final course before completing their Bachelor degree program.

3. Cases about efficiency in team work. The same case and assignment has been used in two different situations at the master program in Business Administration. The first situation was the introductory course starting the entire program (after less than a month) and the second was when the same exercise was used at the final semester for students immediately before their Masters thesis.

Table 1 offers information about the three case settings included in this study. It is important to note that every sample is drawn from the same cohort of students (dropouts excluded).

	Service management master program	Business administration bachelor program	Team efficiency case in business administration
Introductory level How the case work is structured and organised	Introductory course about service management in different service industries 200 students	Introductory course in organisation 200 students	Introductory course about business models 200 students
	Open general questions for discussion between students, and a follow up in class No detailed grading	Specified questions for discussion between students, and a class room discussion Detailed grading	Virtual group exercise (Harvard Business Publishing case about climbing Mount Everest) No detailed grading
Degree level How the case work is structured and organised	Bachelor degree course in strategy and management control 180 students	Bachelor degree course in strategy and management control 80 students	Elective course about 'Management' at the master level 40 students
	Open (problem seeking) questions for discussion between students and a formal class room discussion Detailed grading	Open (problem seeking) questions for discussion between students and a formal class room discussion Detailed grading	Virtual group exercise (HBR case about climbing Mount Everest) No detailed grading

Table 1: Characteristics of the three case settings in this study

From each of these settings we will present feedback and impressions of both students and teachers as they have been expressed in course evaluations and teachers' follow-up meetings.

Experiences with CBT on the Service Management Program

The comments from the students differ between the courses. Table 2 shows representative comments characterising the students' view of the courses.

Service management master program	Introductory level	Degree level
Feed-back and statements from students	Happy to get to know more about service industries Useful readings about service Good to discuss with others in the group Difficult with a vague task, where to focus? Difficult to learn "everything about a company in one day"	Interesting to use theories (not describe them) Focus on analysis Understanding crucial (not knowing by heart) Use other students as learning partner, the case is an arena to discuss Demanding situation to be graded on oral exam
Observations from teachers	Works good to introduce the topics Stimulates reading of the book Creates motivation to study and learn more Students needs help to go outside the story (case)	Case motivates to efforts Gradually less descriptions of theory and more applications, more synthesis No attention to choice of industries (empirical focus)

Table 2: The service management master program

To summarise the detailed findings: students on the introductory course do appreciate the case as a way to learn more about the service sector. The examples given of useful learnings relate mainly to empirical knowledge about companies, organisations and service concepts. Few comments relate to models or theoretical concepts for describing or analysing the case situations. It is also mentioned that it is difficult to work with an open assignment, i.e. without clear questions expecting well defined answers. Starting the case work with defining the problem/issue was not a familiar procedure. Instead they focused on finding and discussing facts about the case organisation. The teachers were available for students needing help in their discussions. Teachers' reflections were that the case method created a high level of involvement but that it focused mainly on what is considered familiar, i.e. facts and figures (and to some extent suggestions for improvements). To obtain a more formal analysis a higher level of teacher involvement and guidance would be required.

The same cohort subsequently reached bachelor level and then took a course in strategy and management control. In Table 2 it can be seen that the students now express more thoughts about issues arising from the course literature. It is considered important and relevant to be able to use the theories to sort out data in the case and synthesise it on a more abstract level. Discussions with other students are considered to be an important part of the preparations because these can bring multiple perspectives and raise more issues for analysis. Several students also mention understanding as important in contrast to learning by heart. Students found it necessary to genuinely understand a case in order to be able to solve it. A common theme is that students perceive the models and concept as 'useful'. Teachers noted that students pay little attention to the choice of a case and do not even discuss to what extent it is a service management case. Gradually the focus shifts from describing theories (and using theories to describe) towards synthesis and higher order thinking.

Experiences with CBT on the Business Administration Program

On the bachelor program in business administration the first course in organisation theory is based on cases. Reflections and statements representing the different views are summarised in Table 3.

Business admin. courses Bachelor program	Introductory level	Degree level
Feed-back and statements from students	Interesting to learn about the companies Much (too much) facts to learn Difficult situation discussing the case Difficult to choose what to focus on in the course book	Suddenly you saw something you hadn't seen before Defining the problem is crucial Finally, I learnt to do analysis first, then solve the problem You improve your skill to bring experience from one case to the next (even though they are about different companies and industries) Demanding situation to be graded on oral exam
Observations from teachers	Theories used to describe the case (low degree of analysis) Students use the case as an illustration of the theories Requires active teacher involvement to generalise outside the case	Case motivates to efforts Initially difficult to analyse before solving Theories more explicitly used for analysis Analytical focus improves case after case

Table 3: The business administration program

As in the previous example, students on the introductory course in Business administration are eager to learn about companies and industries. A large proportion of the case assignments on this course are designed to train students to problematise and define organisational problems. The course is based on thematic lectures and on five case discussions. Defining organisational problems is considered very difficult and students find it hard to choose models and concepts from the literature: *"There are so many concepts"*. Students say it is problematic to choose different approaches during the discussion. The teachers' view, to a high degree, is that student attention is oriented to facts. The students prepare individually before the case. During the classroom discussion the theories are used mainly to explain and iluminate practical concepts. A high level of teacher involvement and participation is needed to achieve this.

At the Bachelor level the students may choose to continue with a course in strategy and management control. It is a very popular course and, because it uses many graded cases and an extensive literature, it is perceived to be very demanding. There is a clear analytical focus in the case instructions and the students are encouraged to analyse the situation and define the problem before suggesting actions. One common comment in the course evaluations is that this is the first time students have used theories to both widen and deepen the analysis themselves. The use of concepts from the literature helps students to organise the data and make a structured analysis of the situation. Another comment is about integration; earlier in their studies the students will have taken specific courses in different specialities, one at a time. At this course there is an explicit intention to stimulate integration of concepts and dealing with a comprehensive picture. In this case context it is now possible, and necessary, to combine all tools. Initially it is believed to be a problem but after the course many students mentioned this aspect. From the teachers' point of view there has been a consensus to put analysis in the foreground as a basis for suggesting actions. This is believed to have worked well. During the course the students appear increasingly to apply higher order thinking skills to apply theoretical concepts in order to make a formal and structured analysis.

Experiences with CBT on Team Efficiency

The third setting of case use on the Business administration course is a team efficiency case from Harvard Business Publishing. It is a computer-based, interactive simulation of an expedition climbing to the summit of Mount Everest. The same case was used on both the introductory course and the final semester course. Representative reflections and opinions of students and teachers are summarised in Table 4.

Team efficiency case	Introductory level	Degree level
Feed-back and statements from students	Fun. We learnt how to organise group work Got an idea of what it means to be a leader Difficult to deal with the software. No feeling for the Everest challenge – could have been any challenge It was fun and interesting, but what did I learn?	Good to think about your actions in a team Forced you to act, and to reflect afterwards Difficult to deal with the software – stole focus Good to act and be practical, AND also use theory and analyse "Demanding, but rewarding to bring out general learnings from the case"
Observations from teachers	Difficult to make the students reflect on issues and on their own actions. A lot of energy but theory has low impact on the actions (and reflections afterwards)	Follow-up reflection crucial for learning. Great variety in use of theories for reflection (students use option to choose freely) Individual reflection appreciated Personal reflections to a high extent related to literature

Table 4: The team efficiency case

On the introductory course the student expectations of this case were very high. Afterwards many students were disappointed because it gave no flavour of how such an expedition takes place. Some students believed it were just about *"pushing buttons."* As every group had an assigned leader, this role came into focus. Students with other roles believed they had less fun and less impact on the process. Students, took one of two standpoints in the reflections afterwards, irrespective of what role they had been assigned to. A minority claimed it was a great learning experience because it required them to reflect upon their own actions independently of which role had been assigned to them). However, the majority claimed they were uncertain about their learning because they had no experience of the setting (climbing Mt Everest). Furthermore, several students felt it was not much use because *"they were never to do such an expedition."* From the teachers' perspective there was agreement that the students found it difficult to reflect upon their own actions, even when aided by theory. Many students merely described their day.

Half a year later we used the same case assignment on a Masters course in management. The design of the event was similar to the one for the introductory course. In the evaluations afterwards a majority of the students claimed this to have been the highlight of the course which, overall, got good marks (4 out of 5). The students' view starts with the importance of trying something in practice. It was considered very important to have the case as a setting for practising team work. The course provided a structured process for reading course literature and preparing for the case and afterwards reflecting upon what happened; this earned high merits. The reflections were considered difficult but, as the students were highly motivated and made good use of teacher attention, it was considered to be a highlight. From the teacher perspective the high level of student motivation was noted; the impression was that students were mature enough to drive this process themselves. The final discussion and reflection was to a large extent driven by students with little teacher involvement. It is worth noting that for their individual work students used many different sources from the literature (there was a long list to choose from). When used in classroom discussion the teachers noted a wide variety of perspectives in the analysis, i.e. using higher order thinking skills. However, it appears to be necessary for teacher involvement to structure and set the activities.

Taking the Student View

Our starting point was to look at theories about learning – especially meaningful learning – and some examples of CBT at different levels. We will now elaborate on how case teaching strategies can be adopted in order to affect the learning outcome when teaching with cases in undergraduate classes.

We believe the empirical findings and theoretical perspectives convey three key messages. To be successful in enhancing the students learning by case teaching, it is important to:

- ensure students really sense that a case displays an authentic reality
- ensure students understand what a problem can be/is within an organisation
- appreciate how problem-solving is a useful way to understand different kinds of organisational contexts.

Ensuring students' recognition of reality is a key issue. If the students don't have any previous knowledge, it is difficult (impossible?) to appreciate and internalise new knowledge that arises in a discussion. In that instance the learning progression will be zero. Therefore, the teacher needs to find ways to ascertain what kind of relevant knowledge each student brings to the case discussion. The relevant knowledge is mainly connected to the course content and intended learning outcomes. It is very demanding to ascertain what each student brings to the class. One way of getting this information is to interview each student before class or have them fill in a form.

Depending on class size and the frequency of case use this approach is resource demanding but it does give the teacher good quality data. The data can be used both in selecting cases and in the interaction with students in class. This kind of documentation can be transferred between teachers, courses and programs. If the cost of doing so is too high it is possible to treat a group of first year students as resembling the average of the student population. As a part of such a population they probably have some experiences of 'everyday' organisations, such as public transport and restaurants, which they can relate to in a given learning situation.

Understanding a problem is strongly connected to how the teacher involves the students in a learning activity. The teacher has to encourage students to make investments in individual case preparations, but also to discuss case material in smaller groups. Through questions and other remarks during class the teacher needs to ensure that the students assimilate the kind of problem that the given case illustrates. Similar teaching procedures are also necessary to secure students' understanding about the process of problem-solving and how closely this is related to understanding the context of the problem.

Relating a problem to a specific context and generating different kind of solutions is a distinct step towards the use of 'higher order thinking skills' (HOTS). But is it possible to steer students' thinking even more towards HOTS? Is it possible to talk about case teaching strategies to achieve this goal?

Strategies to Enhance Learning Outcomes

According to theories about meaningful learning, the content of cases used in the initial semesters, and how the teacher chooses to apply them, need to be adapted to the experiences that students bring when they first come to the course. To understand business situations you must be able to describe them (Mattisson & Ramberg, 2013). By increasing the students' acquaintance and empirical knowledge a case can promote learning concretisation (as denoted by arrow A in Figure 1). However, the aim is to foster HOTS and the *teacher role* is gradually to introduce abstract thinking by conceptual models and theories. Starting with the empirical knowledge obtained, a learning acceleration (arrow B in Figure 1) takes place when abstract models are applied. When students apply conceptual thinking to their empirical knowledge more things can be seen and conclusions can be developed in more depth.

We set out to elaborate and discuss strategies for applying the case method to its full potential. Our research has shown that there are at least four dimensions to such a strategy:

- The case characteristics/content
- The preparation and direction of the case discussion in class
- The teacher's role and the development of students as learning partners
- The grading of learning development

The Case Characteristics/Content

The experiences presented in this chapter highlight some characteristics that enable CBT to be effective on introductory courses. Firstly, it is a good opportunity to amplify the students' interest in the factual conditions in organisations and industries. One way is to choose case settings (products and services) that students can to some degree understand and relate to (eg: restaurant, clothing store, library). It has also proved to be a good idea to keep down the amount and complexity of data in the case. A lower level of complexity makes it easier to grasp and follow the overall aim and conclusions from the case, otherwise the good learning points in the case might be lost. Shorter cases (some might say incomplete) that are well structured may also stimulate students to look up and find out for themselves things about the case (which is good habit for future activities in academia and working life). In terms of priorities, it is probably better to have more short cases and fewer long cases. Since students at this point usually lack experience of work and organisations it is better to provide them with more empirical settings to broaden their base of knowledge and frame of reference. It is only once they have 'seen' many different examples themselves that they can start to look for similarities and general patterns – that is, theories about how things are.

At the degree level the situation is different. These students have now been trained in using academic models and have a broader experience base. Therefore they can be asked to deal with bigger and more complex data sets (i.e. cases). As both their empirical knowledge and conceptual ability is more developed, it is easier for them to deal with case settings and products they are unfamiliar with.

The Preparation for and Direction of the Case Discussion in Class

When handing out a case to students it is important to guide students in their preparations. One important way to do this is through the design of the assignment questions. Unless the teacher is aiming for something very specific these should be of an open nature. Our experience is that questions should not be too specific or too analytically demanding. It is better to recognise the students' empirical interests and encourage them to find facts and describe situations or problems. If the circumstances allow they can also be asked to search for other examples to use for comparison. It can be of help to highlight particular literature but leave clear directions about what concepts and models to use. Giving too many choices tends to result in a shallow tour around all of them, leading to cursory results or arbitrary conclusions. The experiences also show that giving an assignment that is too complex or complicated to structure can force the students to 'make a decision' (because that is often required) without really being able to explain or justify it. If the case is too difficult their attention will be directed toward the decision itself and not to an analysis and argumentation for it.

At the degree level it is possible to give more complex situations and deeper assignment questions including more components for analysis. This will allow more student initiative as to what theories and concepts could be used. It is also possible to require more benchmarking and referral to facts outside the case in order to put it into perspective.

The Teacher's Role and the Development of Students as Learning Partners

The teacher's role varies somewhat depending on the course. At the introductory level the teacher is required to be active and formative in actions. Even though the aim is to be a partner for discussion there is a need to structure the situation and guide discussion. By doing this the teacher illustrates how theories and concepts help in describing and analysing. It is also possible to use the case to illustrate theoretical concepts and to point out how different things link together within processes. Our experience shows that one should not expect the students to do make such illustrations and connections by themselves. By giving them an empirical focus in their preparations the case discussions can then be used to show the role and importance of theoretical concepts and their potential to organise the analysis of a case. The teacher must expect to take a leading role in these discussions, and also be prepared to summarise and conclude step by step.

On the other hand, degree students are better equipped to do this themselves and their initiatives are more likely to lead the discussion forward in a constructive way. This means the teacher can adopt the role of a discussant and provider of expert comments and other perspectives.

Grading the Development

The question whether or not to use differentiated grades when having case discussions, especially in the initial courses in a program, is open to debate. In one sense it is a part of the course curriculum and its intended learning outcomes. However, first year students can find it uncomfortable to discuss and articulate their own opinion in open plenary. Based on our examination of the literature and our own empirical findings, we can recommend using a system with pass and fail only. Even though this system may appear blunt it affirms participation and reduces stress in class.

Creating a learning climate of confidence, and ensuring that students really dare to participate in class discussion, is key to enhancing their higher order thinking skills (HOTS).

Final Comments

The discussion in this chapter has concentrated on the case discussion in class. Our purpose has been to help and inspire teachers and students interested in and/or actively employing CBT and case solving.

To ensure that a high student's involvement pays off it is important to design the learning activities in such a way that it fits well with the experiences and abilities of the students. Trying too much and being too focused on conceptual thinking might impair the learning outcomes if students are not equipped for it – so it is important to carefully choose the case setting and amount of data. By gradually increasing the complexity of facts it is possible to develop abstract thinking at the same gradual pace.

In higher education, the fostering and enhancement of abstract thinking by different pedagogical methods and instruments is such an important and broad subject that it cannot just be limited to what can result from a case discussion. It is a strategic issue for the leadership teams in most of the higher educational systems around the world. Hopefully, the thoughts presented in this chapter will give these teams some inspiration for further efforts in this direction, and for the higher educational system as a whole.

About the Authors

Ola Mattisson is associate professor in Business Administration at the School of Economics and Management, Lund University. He can be contacted at this email: Ola.Mattisson@fek.lu.se

Ulf Ramberg is associate professor in Business Administration at the School of Economics and Management, Lund University. He can be contacted at this email: Ulf.Ramberg@fek.lu.se

Chapter five

Case Study as – and within – Simulation: a Mobius Loop for Analysis and Learning

Elyssebeth Leigh and Kate Collier

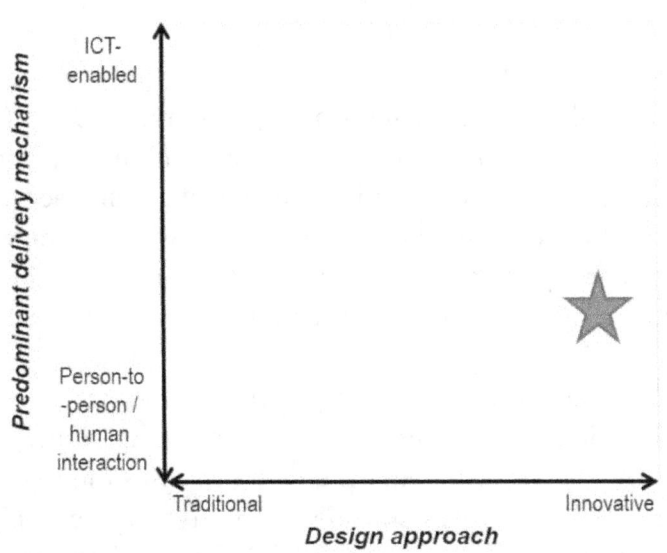

Introduction

As a form of active learning, case studies are most appropriately located as a sub-set of simulation and games-based learning strategies. All such strategies use condensed versions of real time events to generate initial conditions for learning (Ellington, 1999) and draw on formalised *"abstractions of reality used for a purpose"* (McGarrity, 2011). Locating case studies in this wider context allows them to be used in more diverse ways. Those working in the field of simulation and games-based learning regularly identify this relationship, while educators focusing solely on case study strategies appear not to have made the same connection. For example, Teena Clerke (2013) in an extended literature review on case study revealed no cross-referencing to simulation games or related literature. This chapter therefore argues for recognition of the connections between case study and simulation, and asserts that locating case study within this broader domain of learning increases the educational benefits. The work of practitioner researchers (e.g. Duke, 1970; Ellington *et al.*, 1987; Ellington, 2000; Leigh, 2012) illustrates how sets of common structural characteristics inextricably link case studies to games and simulations. We make this argument explicit through an analysis of an extended activity entitled "Yuppies Go Home" (Collier, 2000).

The chapter begins by reviewing how case study is defined more generally within the teaching/learning literature. Use of two categorisation models position case study as – and within – the broader spectrum of simulation-based activities to demonstrate the theoretical and practical connections among case study, games and simulation. In addition the concept of active learning, often used to distinguish case study from more conventional teaching modes, is shown to be problematic.

While the term active learning is regularly used to describe case study-based learning, the nature of such activity is largely disembodied, in comparison with that generated through simulation and games. While case study users consider themselves to be applying active learning principles, there is a clear difference between how they perceive action and how users of simulation and games perceive it. We argue that this disconnect is a major factor preventing these strategies from being seem as educationally contiguous.

The final task of this chapter is use of an analysis of Yuppies Go Home to draw out ways in which case study belongs as a sub-set of simulation-based learning strategies and can extend the learning possibilities for all these strategies. The metaphor of the Mobius Strip is offered as a new way of thinking about how to integrate the embodied action of games and simulation with the objective analytical focus of the case study method. This approach engages the learner creatively, physically and intellectually in an active and immersive learning environment.

What is a Case Study?

There is no single, universally applicable definition of 'case study', 'simulation' or 'game' (see for example Oren, 2012). Nor is there likely to be. There are, however, apparently limitless ways of enacting processes described by these terms. As Wittgenstein (2014) argues, the meaning of words is constituted by the function they perform within any given 'language-game' so that concepts do not need to be over-defined to be meaningful. His concept of language-games was intended *"to bring into prominence the fact that the speaking of language is part of an activity, or a form of life."* (Wittgenstein, 1953:23). Thus he asserts that no word has only one meaning, and meaning is shaped by the way words are said and the context of use.

Given this, we chose three propositions to illustrate characteristics of case study pertinent to this analysis. The first of these asserts that *"The purpose of a case study is to identify the relations between causes and behaviours in a bounded instance"* (Love, 2014) and, in doing so, emphasises how case study is contained and limited in scope.

The second proposition stresses that case studies are rooted in reality and focuses attention on the learner's role as analyst, proposing that:

> *"A good case is the vehicle by which a chunk of reality is brought into the classroom to be worked over by the class and the instructor. A good case keeps the class discussion grounded upon some of the stubborn facts that must be faced in real life situations."* (Barnes et al., 1994:44 citing professor Paul Lawrence)

This highlights the idea that action in case studies revolves around discussion of a problem. The third definition provides an extended list of characteristics inherent in the case study approach as follows:

> *"A good case should (a) tell a story, (b) focus on an interest-arousing issue, (c) be current, (d) create empathy, (e) have dialogue, (f) be relevant, (g) serve a teaching function, (h) be conflict provoking, (i) have a dilemma to be solved, (j) have generality, and (k) be short. But we might add: be written with exuberance, charm, and wit" (Herreid, 2012:74–5)*

This definition emphasises the narrative properties of case studies It asserts that there should be some kind of emotional connection with people involved in the situation, and again underscores the problem-solving nature of the task involved. It provides a bridge to two models, drawn from the literature on simulation, which integrate case study, games and simulation, as outlined in the next section. This leads us to our proposal of the Mobius strip as a metaphor for the interconnectedness of case study, games and simulation.

Positioning Case Study as - and within - Simulation

The two models explored below are not definitive. Indeed, together they help demonstrate the almost limitless variety of options for describing both the various elements of case study, games and simulation, and their inter-relationships. However, they are particularly effective in helping both novice and expert users of all forms gain a better understanding of their characteristics and multiple uses.

The authors of the first model, Ellington *et al.* (developed during the 1980s; published in 1998), were particularly concerned to identify inter-relationships and draw attention to ways in which these allow the 'pure' forms to be adapted and modified for multiple purposes.

Figure 1 shows how Ellington *et al.* arranged what they considered to be the three pure forms of games, simulation, and case study into a Venn diagram. This creates three hybrid forms called respectively 'games used as case studies', 'simulated case studies' and 'simulation games' and a single hybrid form they called 'simulation games used as case studies'. Table 1 provides a list of key characteristics of each of the seven approaches identified in the Venn diagram and indicates how the analytical features of case study contribute to the other forms.

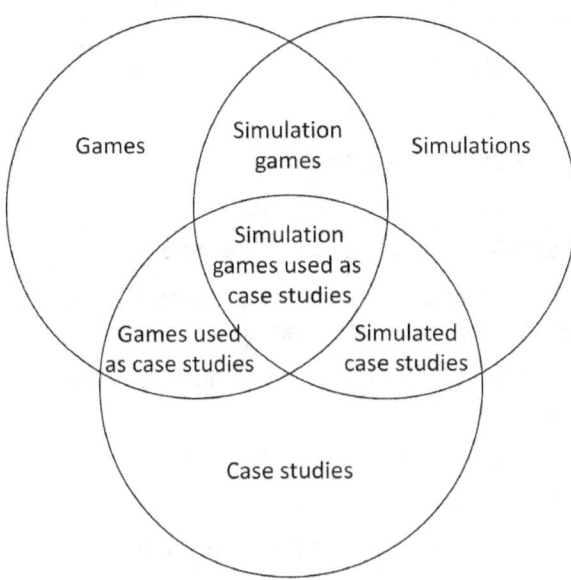

Figure 1: alignment of 'pure' and 'hybrid' forms of case studies, games and simulations (Ellington et al., 1998:3 in Leigh, 2003)

Ellington *et al.* do not consider that 'pure' case studies involve active engagement. This is because case study users are positioned as dispassionate observers removed from emotional and physical enactment of the events in the case study. In contrast, the unifying form – simulation games used as case studies – abstracts elements from a known context and arranges them in a scenario for re-enactment by learners who thus create a unique case study for subsequent analysis.

This physical and emotional immersion of learners in the action ensures highly personalised outcomes for post-action analysis. After experiencing a well-managed hybrid form, learners can use a range of analytical processes to unpack intentions and consequences of their actions, such that they become 'observers' of their own case study and can apply case-based methods to extract lessons from their experiences.

Activity	Characteristics
Games	• Three characteristics make an activity a game • Overt competition of some sort • Rules to guide the action • Time bound
Simulation	• A simulation also has three defining features • Representing a situation of some sort, drawn from real life, or conceivably so. • Operational - enabling participant/s to enact all, or part of, a process • Open ended – no pre-set time limit
Case Studies	• Case study • Accurate reporting of a problem/situation • Identifies characteristics of the problem • Passive – values dispassionate analysis
Simulation games used as case studies	Simulated games used as case studies 1. Utilise elements of play 2. Represent reality 3. Emphasise analyse the outcomes

Table 1: Essential features of 'pure' and 'hybrid' form of simulation-oriented activities (Leigh, 2003).

In comparison with simulation, case study positions learners as analysts of a case, not as protagonists within it. Taking on a role within a case study involves a minimal mental shift. The perspective is not that of responding 'as if' in the first person but rather as if undertaking an abstract mental speculation about what someone else might have been thinking. However, in simulation, and in the hybrid forms, learners must first collaborate to create events, physically adopt roles and move into a first person stance in order to re-create a scenario for examination during debriefing. Participants are not merely analysts of a case but are active creators of it, with profound impacts on learning emerging from the action and analysis.

We do not propose that either position provides a better or less or more effective learning experience but we do emphasise the nature of the different tasks facing learners and educators in each situation. Case study, however active the discussion, is always aloof from direct engagement and requires the educator to be guide, director and decision maker. Simulation and its hybrid forms re-locate these roles as the responsibility of participants for the duration of the action. The increased engagement may influence how comfortable educators and learners feel, especially in regard to learner/educator role reversals.

The second model was developed by Taylor (1977) with the goal of educating users about the degree of realism in case studies, games and simulation. He aligns them along a continuum from Reality to Increasing Abstraction in terms of the nature of the abstraction from a real-life system, operation or process. The extent to which activities are more/less real determines an activity's location on the continuum. Here 'real' refers to the extent to which an activity abstracts the reality of a genuine item/event. Intended as accurate (albeit condensed) reports of the real world, case studies shape facts and data into objective descriptions to generate analysis of events within the ambit of the case. They create a scenario that exists in Stopped Time which does not change. In contrast, games and simulations occur during Living Time where everything is uncertain and changeable.

← Reality				Increasing abstraction →	
Case Study <	> In-basket or In tray Method	Incident <-> Process	Role playing <-	-> Gaming <- simulation or game simulation	-> Machine or computer simulation
Observations on real world	Non-interacting one-to-one representation	Interacting one-to-one representation	Informally structured group portrayal	Structured group representation	All data and decisions embedded in a mathematical representation

Table 2: Simulation activities on a spectrum of most to least real

Case studies are most real since their content is fixed in time, so inventiveness ends with the writing of the scenario; the authenticity of the story, as told, is fixed and factual. At the other end of the spectrum are simulations using tools as highly symbolic representations of reality to generate entirely fictional 'as if' conditions. These demand that participants engage their imagination to make the scenario seem real – at least while the tools are in use. During action, simulations exhibit great faithfulness (fidelity) to the real. Yet when not in use, they may not exhibit any fidelity at all. For example a flight simulator does not need to look anything like a real plane.

Reality and Emotional Engagement					
Most real/least emotional					Least real/most emotional
Case Study	In-basket / action maze	Hypothetical	Role playing	Gaming simulation or Game-simulation	Machine simulation / Computer simulation
Observations of the real world. No expectation of emotional involvement	Non-interacting, one-to-one representation. Some emotional attachment to quality of decision making.	Interacting one-to-one representation. Emotional engagement limited to being a 'panel member'	Formally structured group portrayal using one-to-one interactions. Interactions have potential to be highly emotionally engaging.	Informally structured group or one-to-one portrayal of interactions. May evoke strong emotions because of intersection between prior events and current experiences	Data and decisions embedded in mathematical representations. May have group interactions about decisions. No emotional engagement with 'machine' but likely to be strong emotional reaction to decisions and actions required.

Table 3: Continuum of real/unemotional case study to emotional/ engaged simulation (Leigh, 2003 adapted from Taylor, 1977)

While investigating Taylor's continuum, Leigh (2003) added the dimension of emotion. Table 3 illustrates the progressive shift from most real + least emotional engagement, to least real + most emotional engagement. The shift from an absence of embodied action to increasing physical engagement parallels the increase in emotional engagement along the continuum.

The examination of these two models with Leigh's variation raises problematic issues about what constitutes active learning. The next section explores this concept further in relation to case studies, games and simulation.

What is Active Learning?

This term, also, is not easy to define and some of the debate surrounding it seems to stem from underlying values about teaching and learning processes. Sydney University defines active learning as involving:

> *"... students in doing things and thinking about what they are doing. This can include discussing, critical thinking, solving problems etc." (Sydney University, 2008)*

... while the University of Minnesota describes active learning as:

> *"an approach to instruction in which students engage the material they study through reading, writing, talking, listening, and reflecting. Active learning stands in contrast to "standard" modes of instruction in which teachers do most of the talking and students are passive." (University of Minnesota, 2012)*

When we observe students using these forms of active learning we see little more than sitting, talking and reading – a sedentary form of active learning. The University of Michigan's version of active learning comes closer to our own definition, including as it does, direct (albeit secondary) reference to case study and simulation.

> *"Active learning is a process whereby students engage in activities, such as reading, writing, discussion, or problem solving that promote analysis, synthesis, and evaluation of class content. Cooperative learning, problem-based learning, and the use of case methods and simulations are some approaches that promote active learning." (University of Michigan, 2014)*

In our opinion active learning extends far beyond the image of sitting, talking and speculating that predominates here. To be actively engaged in learning involves use of all the senses in physical engagement with the action. In conventional case studies time is stopped. The scenario is 'dead' and laid out, as if for dissection by learners and educators. Games in the form of simulations occur in Living Time and scenarios unfold spontaneously, brought to life by players' actions and interactions.

The term 'immersive learning environments' (ILEs) in Gartner's IT Glossary (2012) is closest to our understanding of active learning.

> *"[ILEs] are learning situations that are constructed using a variety of techniques and software tools, including game-based learning, simulation-based learning and virtual 3D worlds. ILEs are distinguished from other learning methods by their ability to simulate realistic scenarios and environments that give learners the opportunity to practice skills and interact with other learners." (Gartner's online IT Glossary, 2012)*

Here the focus is on practice of skills, interaction and embodied engagement in action. In what follows we describe how to evolve sedentary case study based learning into physical movement and emotional engagement. "Yuppies Go Home" is a specific instance of a case-based simulation promoting active, creative, emotional learning.

The Case of "Yuppies Go Home"

As an exemplar of such a case-based simulation, this activity demonstrates how the integration of case study, games and simulation enlarges the framework for learning by creating an immersive learning environment. Participants first engage in a game that introduces the case study, then in a variety of role-play activities prior to creating a simulation-based scenario. Finally they return to the case study for a final analysis of the entire experience.

> **Yuppies Go Home**
>
> Tension between local residents of Darlinghurst, East Sydney and the trendy newcomers to the area, is evident in the graffiti on the sides of houses. "Yuppies get lost", "Leave locals in Peace", are the messages that are being forcibly put across.
>
> Local residents are angry at the way new houses are being bought up and done up by the rich and trendy. Estate agents admit that prices are booming and business is brisk. Locals complain that they are being pushed out of an area that they have lived in all their lives by incomers who force up the prices in shops and restaurants and cause an increase in the rent of local accommodation.
>
> "We can't afford to live here any more," says one resident. Builders argue that if the market is there for renovated houses it's their job to make sure they provide them for customers regardless of what this might do to the local community. Restaurant owners and shops say business has never been so good and accuse local residents of whinging. Locals say the character of the area, and its community spirit, has been ruined by flashy upstarts and heartless profiteers.

Figure 2. Fictional article triggering action in Yuppies Go Home

This short newspaper article was devised as a stimulus for adult students in higher education to encourage them to explore current topics of social change, local politics and the role of the media in reporting controversial issues. It can be seen as a type of case study as represented in the definitions earlier in this chapter. For example, the article is an examination of a *"real life situation"* (Lawrence *et al.,* 1994); it tells a short, interesting story which includes engaging characters who are in conflict with each other and provides *"a dilemma to be solved"* (Harreid, 2012). There are many other kinds of stimuli that could be used in a similar way and characterised as forms of case study, ranging from newspaper articles, video, photos, cartoons, and spoken story.

The Yuppies Go Home article presents a complex problem to be solved. It highlights how different parties may view the same situation differently according to their background experience, ideology and personal interests. In addition the article allows students to examine the wider issue of how media stereotyping could affect the arguments presented. These are only two of the possible areas of interest to participants engaging in the newspaper activity; many other topics may emerge from the participants as they actively engage in the learning context. A time frame of one and a half to two hours is recommended for the facilitation of this activity.

It has been argued that the case study approach has many possible learning benefits. These include developing higher order cognitive skills such as *"problem-solving, decision-making and creative thinking"* (Ellington, 1979:5) and encouraging students to take a flexible rather than a polarised view of a problem (Garvin, 2003). This includes students learning to be open-minded, empathetic and appreciative of other viewpoints so that barriers can be broken down (Ellington, 1979).

The Yuppies Go Home case has similar learning interests to that of case studies in general but, as we will see from the way it is developed, it takes a different approach to active learning and interactivity. Rather than action being focused on 'summary discussion' (Hareid, 1999) and *"debating, oral and written presentations"* (Ellington, 1979:7) the participants in Yuppies Go Home play a game and engage in role play and simulation activities. These activities go beyond discussion to demand physical, mental and emotional involvement in the scenario.

The strategies used to transform the Yuppies Go Home case study into a game, and then into a role-play/simulation, are from "Structuring Drama Work" (Neelands, 1991) and are shown in Table 4.

- How Do You Like Your Neighbour?
- Collective Drawing
- Still-Image
- Caption-Making
- Overheard Conversations'
- Thought Tracking
- Role-on-the Wall
- Interview
- Role-reversal
- Teacher-in-role

Table 4: Activities and learning strategies from Neelands, (1991) and Brandes & Phillips, (1977) used with Yuppies Go Home

Specific strategies have been chosen and developed to be less threatening at the start and more challenging at the end. This means that opportunities are created for participants to move in and out of the activity so they are involved but remain critically aware. The idea is to avoid participants becoming lost in the activity and its emotional world as the action moves from the realism of the case study to the more symbolic and therefore less real role play and simulation activities as alluded to in Leigh's model (2003). Once participants lose their sense of being in a fictional learning situation they can find themselves identifying so strongly with a role that it is hard to separate it from reality. Some people will find this to be a disorientating and emotionally uncomfortable experience (Blake, 1987; Collier, 2005; Jones, 1997; van Ments, 1983).

The following section analyses how case study, games and role play simulation strategies are used together in practice.

Starting the Session

The session begins with a physically active game called "How Do You Like Your Neighbour?" (Brandes & Phillips, 1977). This energiser asks participants, in a light-hearted fashion, to say if they like their neighbours (the people sitting either side of them). Their answer will have implications for whether or not they move and get stuck in the middle without a chair.

The game is not only used as a fun energiser but is employed to raise themes or situations relevant to the drama. In this case it is to do with the issues of community and neighbourhood raised in the newspaper article. The game introduces the newspaper article and helps participants to move into the activity more smoothly.

The Newspaper Case Study Stimulus

Participants then read the article "Yuppies Go Home" (see Figure 2) and talk about their first impressions of it and the issues that it raises.

Co-operation is needed from the group to explore the case study further using a variety of different interactive strategies. This is why initially low risk activities are chosen which involve participants in doing a task collectively rather than being observed by others as they take on a complex role.

The second strategy after the introductory game is Collective Drawing. This activity requires participants to make *"a collective image to represent a place or people"* in the case study (Neelands, 1991:14). In this situation the group is asked to split into smaller groups of about four people and use large sheets of paper to draw the graffiti that can be found on the walls of houses around Darlinghurst. The graffiti paper is displayed on the wall and participants comment on the impression it makes and what points are being raised through it.

Moving beyond the Case Study

Leaving participants to work in the same groups, Still-Image and Caption-Making strategies are used to develop the context of the case study further. Still-Image requires participants to use *"their own bodies to crystallise a moment, idea or a theme,"* (Neelands, 1991). They create a physical still-picture: a frozen moment that represents something in the case. Caption-Making is about devising *"slogans, chapter headings of what is being presented visually"* (Neelands, 1991). Still-Image encourages participants to build up literally a picture of the case as they see it; Caption-Making is concerned with distilling the experience and finding the essence of the case. Caption-Making allows the action to be slowed down and gives space for participants to look at the case from the outside. It also encourages a move from focusing on contextual detail to finding the essence of a situation: its key motif.

In Yuppies Go Home, participants are asked to create the picture (using their bodies and any props at hand) that might accompany the newspaper article they have just read (Still-Image) and the title that might accompany it (Caption-Making). Participants look at the different pictures and titles that the group have created and read them, commenting on the meaning they have for the different observers. The group devising the pictures and headlines also have the chance to add their perceptions. At this stage the case and the issues raised within it should be a great deal more complex and detailed than was offered by the initial newspaper article.

Engaging with Physical Activity

Participants then return to their physically-created pictures and two more strategies are introduced: Overheard Conversations and Thought Tracking. The first strategy involves eavesdropping on short moments of conversations. The second strategy asks participants to talk their thoughts out loud: to verbalise what is going on in their heads at that time. This begins to get participants to relate to people in the case and represent their roles. This adds extra depth to the groups' understanding of the different issues under debate.

At this point in the activity the Role-on-the-Wall strategy is introduced to further explore some of the key people in the case study. An outline of a figure is drawn up on some butchers paper and put up on the wall. This is then identified as being one of the roles in the case under investigation: for example, the yuppie newcomer. Each participant is given a few Post-it® stickers and asked to put on these any qualities or characteristics that they have noticed about this role from their involvement in the previous activities. They allocate one quality/characteristic per Post-it and place them in and around the figure. These can then be used as a basis for discussion and can bring into the open different perceptions people have of the role. The Role-on-the-Wall can be left up and referred to regularly as the role-play activities proceed. Post-its can be added or subtracted from the drawing as more information is gleaned from the case.

Moving into Role Play

After this, participants work in pairs and begin the role-play simulation. One person in the pair takes on the role of a newcomer or a long-term resident, the other takes on the role of a journalist from a newspaper who is looking to follow up on the initial story. They engage in an Interview strategy and then reverse roles so they get a different perspective of the role they have just played. This Role-Reversal strategy allows participants to gain multiple perspectives and actively explore the essence of the roles represented in the case.

From Stopped Time to Living Time

It is apparent that, from the time of the introductory game and the initial graffiti exercise onwards, participants have moved from Stopped Time into Living Time. They are physically and mentally involved in the scenario and moving through 'real time space' where the experience is no longer bounded and frozen in time but unpredictable and spontaneous. In addition, if we define role play as responding 'as if' participants are specific people in a particular situation (Heathcote, 1984) then it could be argued that all the strategies used to explore the case study have been a form of role-play activity. When participants draw the graffiti on the paper they are responding as if they are disgruntled Darlinghurst residents. By physically creating in Still Pictures the newspaper photo and headline, participants are identifying with the people in the story, or even at another level with the photo-journalist who would have taken the picture for inclusion in a newspaper.

The concept of responding as if in a role-play allows for different physical and mental levels of involvement in any given situation. The case study approach requires, at most, that participants exercise a purely mental speculation about the roles indicated in the scenario. On the other hand, Yuppies Go Home requires participants' physical, mental and emotional involvement in their roles.

The scenario gradually develops into a full simulation in which participants take on the roles of specific people involved in the newspaper article and beyond. They become representatives in a fictional TV discussion programme – Issues for All – where disputing parties are brought together in a TV studio before a studio audience. The facilitator can take on the role (*Teacher-in-role*) of the program interviewer and lead the discussion, or give this role to another participant. Commercial breaks provide time out for participants and space to reflect on what has been learnt. Returning to the original case study after the simulation is completed provides a reflective prompt to help participants identify more clearly what the combination of the game and role play simulation strategies has added to the initial case and to the learning.

The activity as a whole provides participants with opportunities to manage uncertainty. Consequently the educator has to take on the lower status, less powerful role of facilitator who is the planner, host, moderator, devil's advocate, fellow student and judge. This requires the educator as facilitator to balance planning and spontaneity, to pursue opportunities and teachable moments that emerge through discussion and analysis, and to guide participants towards discovery and learning on multiple levels (Roland & Christensen, 2013b).

Comparing "Yuppies Go Home" and Conventional Case Study

The following list illustrates how Yuppies Go Home is different from the case study approach.

- Participants engage in face-to-face interaction as role players
- No background reading prior to engaging with the action
- Participants are unaware of what lies ahead
- Participants build details of the case, in real-time, as they go
- Case is co-built – everything is happening now
- Distractors occur via interactions - not artificially contrived
- Case studies are well written, inert stories. In Yuppies Go Home the case is negotiated in present time.
- Learners and teachers are co-authors/co-actors
- Learners are responsible for the consequences of the

outcomes/trajectories they generate through interaction
- Whole-body interaction invites risk and emotional investment
- Multiple and complex levels/contexts of connection

The following is a list of features shared by Yuppies Go Home with more conventional case study approaches.

- Requires teacher facilitation/guidance and planning
- Uses a pre-determined script and/or guiding questions
- Employs pre-determined principles
- Has a pedagogical purpose/utility/value in mind
- Takes time to write and prepare
- Is based on real-life contexts
- Is written for a particular audience in mind
- Is flexible and adaptable
- Is experiential learning, learning in action

Drawing on these lists and the preceding analysis we see the Mobius Strip as a metaphor for the way key elements of case study, games and simulation can be integrate to an create active learning environment.

Mobius Strip – a Metaphor for Alignment

Figure 2. A Mobius Strip showing the twist that turns a two-sided strip into a single sided and endless surface.

Imagine a continuous line drawn along one side of a long thin strip of paper lying flat on the table with the blank side 'face down' and the line 'face up'. Pick it up and make a half twist in its length, and then join the slightly twisted length. It is now a loop. This new shape has a surprisingly important topological property in that now it only has one side. There is no 'down' or 'up'. It has become a Mobius Strip – a closed loop with only one side.

This endless strip represents how we suggest case studies and simulation games are all on one side of an endless loop. While we believe we can still see two sides, the loop now only has one side when we trace a finger along the surface. This image is a metaphor for how case studies and simulations are distinct tools, yet parts of one field. Educators can design learning events beginning with a sedentary case study then move into a simulation game representing an aspect of the case and directly engage learners in an active experience. The entire process is then analysed in relation to their experience and the reality being represented.

In Yuppies Go Home, for example, learners receive a fixed, Stopped Time inert case study, to be analysed as a discussion piece. They are then shifted into action by adopting particular (and different) viewpoints, and they take action using their bodies through space and in 'now' time (Living Time). The case study is a fixed point that provides stability and focus for analysis as participants engage in active practice, gain new insights and explode the learning into new, unexpected areas.

While this later analysis is itself a case study, it is not a return to the beginning, nor yet a turning over of the strip; it is a continuation of the line of development. Objective analysis informs direct action and leads back to further analysis of what was created.

Conclusion

This chapter has explored the implications of positioning case study and simulation-games as sub-sets of simulation-based learning strategies within a Mobius loop relationship. Such a positioning can assist educators to develop closer links between their own and others' use of case study and simulation-games for learning. Both approaches are valuable educational strategies and they provide educators with appropriate means for encouraging learners to explore relationships between past and present knowledge. They also encourage engagement with future applications of new knowledge acquired through action, analysis and reflection. However, there are differences between case study, games and simulation and we argue that, despite these differences, their strengths as learning tools lie in their alignment rather than in their present artificial separation.

About the Authors

Elyssebeth Leigh is Senior Research Fellow, Faculty of Engineering and Information Sciences, University of Wollongong. She can be contacted at this email: eleigh@uow.edu.au

Kate Collier is an Honorary Associate at the University of Technology, Sydney. She can be contacted at this email: kate.collier@uts.edu.au

Chapter six

Case Based Learning Approaches Used in Business Schools in Western Greece: the Experiences, the Values, the Good Practices.

Ioanna Giannoukou and Chrysostomos Stylios

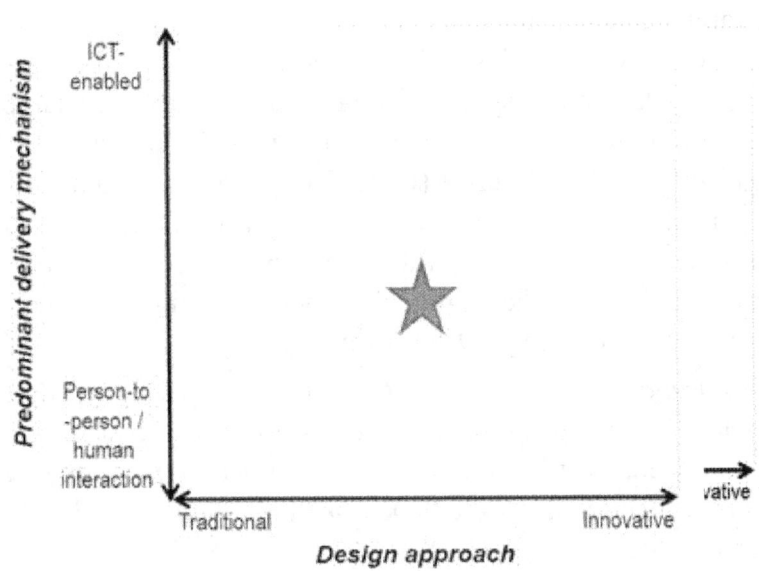

An Overview of the Case Based Learning Methodology

The globalisation that has characterised recent decades has been accompanied by the development in Higher Education of innovative teaching methodologies designed to improve the level and quality of student learning. Race (2003) observes that these new teaching and learning methods and approaches have been prompted by the need of teachers to 'refresh' teaching with methods which can remedy weaknesses that have been found in traditional methods.

Traditional methods tend to be teacher-centered – an approach which does not take adequate care of student-centered aspects of teaching and learning. However, they retain many strengths and Race's (2003) advice is that they should be applied in conjunction with innovative teaching methods.

Business schools in Higher Education Teaching have a long history of using case studies. Many of these are written by individuals or teams affiliated with the top business schools (including Harvard, INSEAD, Ivey, IMD) and are available direct from case teaching schools and from case clearing organisations such as The Case Centre (www.thecasecentre.org/) or journals like that of the North American Case Research Association.

These teaching case studies endeavour to describe actual business situations and detail some aspects of organisational life – for example a change programme or the behavior of a new CEO (Naumes & Naumes, 1999:13). They describe (Race, 2003) a set of circumstances faced by an organisation in its real world context (Bussière, 2005; Mauffette-Leenders *et al.*, 1997) where a decision is required (Lyford, 2000), or they are used to help students understand multiple issues in complex situations (Dewing, 1931). Typically they include:

> *"... a chronology of significant events in the organisation's development; summaries of important cost, financial and sales data; statements and opinions of employees of the company; and information about the competitors and industry" (Edge & Coleman, 1986:2).*

Although they may be fictionalised cases often build on real situations in the life of an individual, a profit-seeking company or a non-profit organisation (Feagin *et al.*, 1991).

Lee (1983), Piotrowski (1982), Westerfield (1989), Boyd (1991), St John (1996), and Jackson (1998) all provide definitions of case based teaching and learning whose key concepts overlap. Broadly, they see the case method as a technique based on analysis, discussion, and decision-making. In this process, students are presented with a record of a problematic business situation that an organisation has actually faced; they are then required to reflect, interact, take responsibility for, problem-solve, and determine possible courses of action and the consequences of implanting these (Esteban & Canado, 2004).

A typical teaching case will contain a combination of primary data (e.g. interviews with managers) and secondary data such as press releases, annual reports etc (David, 2003).

In management education there are different types of teaching case for application in different situations (Heath, 2002) but all are designed for use in the classroom; this approach is seen as an essential way for students to develop an appreciation of real-life management issues (Liang & Wang, 2004). This can help students to develop a range of learning outcomes and skills, such as knowledge application, analysis, synthesis and evaluation (Banning, 2003; Bloom, 1964; Hartman, 2006; Mauffette-Leenders *et al.*, 1997).

A case will tell a 'story' that can be used in the classroom as a basis for learning (Broder *et al.*, 2003; Patten & Swanson, 2003). Cases tend to be contextually rich in detail; students learn through the application and adaptation of theoretical concepts to specific business situations described in the case. Students develop judgement and reasoning skills by evaluating different options and focusing on complex problems which usually do not have 'one right answer' (BIM, 1960; Greiner *et al.*, 2003). In this way cases provide a classroom substitute for experience (Garvin, 2007).

Case based teaching (CBT) was adopted by business administration at Harvard Graduate School as long ago as the 1920s (Jackson, 1998; Kleinfeld, 1990) and has since gained *"a long and varied history as part of the curriculum of programs in professional education"* (Boyd, 1991). Its increasing popularity and effectiveness has led to its use in a variety of disciplines including medicine, social work, science, public administration, teacher training, demography and business (Kintner *et al.*, 1994).

Among all student-centred learning methods, the case method is particularly good at immersing each individual student into the case situation. This helps them to prioritise resources and identify and analyse relevant information in order to make decisions that would resolve the case (Wassermann, 1994).

Types of Case Study Method

Three main types of Case Method have been distinguished by a number of authors, including Westerfield (1989). One type requires the student to suggest a solution to a situation or problem which is faced by management and which has as yet not been solved. This, in Westerfield's opinion, is the most effective in stimulating discussion. The second type requires the student to evaluate an action that has already been taken the third type asks the learner for a general appraisal of whether a situation is proceeding as it should.

Lee (1983) also points to three main case study methods, namely; the Harvard Approach, where the student must consider a series of questions about a problem described in narrative form; the Abbreviated Case Approach, which condenses the problem situation and avoids the complexities inherent in the real situation; and the Incidence Approach, where it is the student's responsibility to look up any additional facts necessary to solve the problem presented.

The latter approach has much in common with what Mascolini and Freeman (1982) term the 'open case', since here the students gather information themselves, either through group discussion and direct observation or from newspapers and other library sources. The alternative is the closed case, where all the information is supplied.

Miles (1987) observes two distinctly different types of case: vignettes (see also Patterson, 1994) and the pre-structured case method. Vignettes are understood as descriptions of situations or problems written by a professional, along with a suggested outline and comments. The pre-structured case method refers to an outline written by the researcher prior to collecting any data.

Benefits of Case Based Teaching

According to Soy (1997), case studies *"excel at bringing us to an understanding of a complex issue or object and can extend experience or add strength to what is already known through previous research."* Another major strength of the case study method is that its focus encompasses richly detailed contexts (Feagin *et al.*, 1991). A further important benefit that appears to accrue from using the case study method is that it promotes Deep Structure Learning (Patten & Swanson 2003; Swanson 2005; Swanson & McKibben 1999), which is aimed at the development of critical thinking skills. Students view it more positively than courses not designed using this approach and they are more willing to participate and learn (Roberts, 2002; Swanson, 2005). Part of the reason for this may be that the deep structure learning approach naturally accommodates other features associated with the case study method, namely; the use of real world problems, the emphasis on concepts rather than mechanisms and on writing and presentation skills, active cooperative learning and the *"worthwhileness"* of a course (Patten & Swanson, 2003; Swanson 2005; Swanson & McKibben, 1999).

The flexibility and adaptability of CBT to myriad educational settings and purposes is highlighted by both Boyd (1991) and Jackson (1998) as one of its most notable advantages. In addition, it allows the learners to enhance their communication skills – listening critically, inferencing, and synthesising information – in an integrated manner (Grosse, 1988; Jackson, 1998). It also allows students to refine their interpersonal and teamwork skills by collaborating with classmates and working together towards the achievement of a common goal (Jackson, 1998; Nagel, 1991; Piotrowski, 1982; Westerfield, 1989). Furthermore, it helps students better to understand and articulate their own values and beliefs, making them more active, responsible, independent, and reflective as regards their own learning and helping them to develop effective leadership and managerial skills (Jackson, 1998; Kleinfeld, 1990; Piotrowski, 1982; Westerfield, 1989). In addition, it can help them to sharpen their analytical, problem-solving and decision-making skills by aiding them to differentiate fact from opinion, relevant data from irrelevant data, and trivial from vital information (Jackson, 1998; Piotrowski, 1982; Westerfield, 1989).

The analysis of teaching case studies offers us the opportunity to capture idiosyncrasies and complexity; it can enable the student to explore the idiosyncratic detail of the trees while generating an understanding of the background forest (Reddy, 2000). Broad fieldwork or ethnographic studies are often advocated because large samples can mask idiosyncratic details (Wassermann, 1994), but it is also argued that these methods, while providing depth, do not permit the verification of theories, and that sacrificing validity for richness could detract from the strength of the findings (Leenders & Erskine, 1989). Problems can arise because of the variability in the way data are collected and interpreted across the different teaching cases. However, such problems can be reduced by means of strict selection and coding criteria (Reddy, 2000).

Case studies also narrow the gap between theory and practice by enabling connections to be made between knowledge and practice, presenting relevant and fresh material, confronting learners with real situations, and fostering the skills and confidence which students will need in order to feel at ease in the community of Business English practitioners (Boyce, 1993; Jackson, 1998; Piotrowski, 1982). These considerations, together with the fact that case studies seem to work well with the learning style of most adults (Jackson, 1998; Piotrowski, 1982), make this method extremely motivating, interesting, intense, and engrossing (Mostert & Sudzina, 1996; Piotrowski, 1982; Westerfield, 1989).

Advantages of Traditional Pedagogical Approaches in Comparison with CBT

However, the advantages of case studies are only part of the picture; their drawbacks must also be examined. The literature on CBT agrees that its most noteworthy disadvantages include the fact that it is a difficult instructional strategy to use (Boyd, 1991; Grosse, 1988; Jackson, 1998; Kleinfeld, 1990; Westerfield, 1989).

Furthermore, the success of CBT largely depends on the teacher's role. This is a non-traditional one which may make some educators uncomfortable and some students hostile (Boyce, 1993; Jackson, 1998; Mostert & Sudzina, 1996; Piotrowski, 1982). In CBT, the instructor is no longer an expert who provides the right answers or solutions, but rather a facilitator or consultant who hands the responsibility of learning over to the student (Lee, 1983; Milheim, 1996; Paget, 1988; Smith, 1987). Welty (1989) qualifies this view when he suggests that, although this is the ultimate objective, it is not always the most suitable one for students who are not familiar with the discussion method.

According to Piotrowski (1982) even the physical learning environment needs to be modified for optimal results. Welty (1989) asserts that that the ideal physical environment should involve:

- a U-shaped arrangement (as opposed to a circle shape) because it facilitates visual contact and interaction among the participants in the discussion and provides space for the leader to exercise his/her authority and control)
- tables and swivel chairs (tables reduce the threatening nature of the exchanges while swivel chairs favour interaction and make for a freer use of classroom space)
- a small table in the front for the instructor (useful for placing outlines, notes, and handouts)
- board space on at least two walls (for a more versatile use of different parts of the room)
- enough space for the instructor to move around freely without stumbling over students or interfering in the discussion.

Such arrangements might be difficult and expensive to introduce. A further factor to be borne in mind is the unreported bias of the author of a case study and the potentially incomplete description of the situation (Jennings, 1997). Yet as a counter to this point it could be argued that there will be few grounds for suspecting deliberate bias on the part of the case writer. Publications offering teaching case studies explain that authors are meant to report the facts of a case objectively and that teaching cases are *"not supposed to be works of fiction; the literary license invoked by creative writers and film makers is not an option open to case writers"* (Swiercz & Ross, 2003:424). A case should be *"the vehicle by which a chunk of reality is brought into the classroom"* (Lawrence, 1953:215). And because it is *"describing real business situations that capture the complexity of organisational life, the case method gives participants firsthand experience in the analysis and evaluation of business situations"* (Liang & Wang, 2004:398).

As Miller and Friesen (1977:256) explain, teaching cases that supply published data on a firm avoid *"the subjective impressions of an executive of the company. It is more difficult to hide the real situation from a case writer who studies a firm in detail."* However, in the writing of teaching case studies certain issues or phenomena may be given more prominence than others as a means of highlighting a specific point to students (Liang & Wang, 2004). Furthermore, some teaching cases may be imprecise or incomplete due to the impossibility of providing exhaustive accounts of past events (Kieser, 1994), or because of the organisation's denial of access to some pieces of information. In addition, some teaching cases tend to be over-rationalistic, CEO-centric and instrumentalist (Liang & Wang, 2004).

Nevertheless, far from adopting a negative attitude towards the application of this method, authors such as Jackson (1998) insist that these obstacles can be surmounted given careful preparation, considerable practice, and clear explanation of objectives; they argue that *"in most situations, these disadvantages can be overcome with creativity, ingenuity, hard work and perseverance"* (Jackson, 1998:159).

CBT Usage in Business Schools in Western Greece

In preparation for this chapter, we interviewed professors teaching at business schools in Western Greece. We focused on professors who teach Business Administration, International Business and aspects of management such as Operation Management, Marketing

Management and Financial Management. For clarity, we excluded classes in Economics and only looked at university courses and not Technical School studies. The result was that we interviewed a total of 33 professors at the Department of Business Administration of the University of Patras and at the Department of Business Administration of Food and Agricultural Enterprises of the University of Western Greece.

Our inquiries concentrated on whether they practice CBT and, if they do, how they apply it in their classes. Twenty professors (60.6% of our sample) at the two Universities do not use CBT. They prefer the traditional methodology of teaching with speeches and open discussions on the theory and examples – although these do not include case studies. The remaining thirteen professors (39.4% of our sample) said they were enthusiastic CBT practitioners.

From the interviews and the literature used by the CBT practitioners we were able to identify four distinct approaches to CBT, characterised as:

1) the typical way
2) the historical narration
3) CBT to transfer specific skills
4) CBT to build decision-making skills (Patten & Swanson, 2003).

Approach 1: the Typical Way

The 'typical way' approach to CBT is applied by the majority of professors in the specific target group. What they do closely resembles the five steps documented by Mauffette-Leenders *et al.* (1999).

Step 1: Introduce the case. The professors present to the students a brief problem statement of the case. Each professor can choose a different format of case study – such as showing newspaper cuttings or role-playing – which can make the problem realistic and stimulate student interest. Then, the professor asks the students to read the problem statement carefully to get a sense of the case and its issues.

Step 2: Form groups and initiate discussions. The professor splits the class into several groups of four to six students so as to be an effective group. The group must work together, discuss and identify the issues and solve the problems. During these discussions students may be motivated by and discuss issues that are relevant but may not be the intended focus of the study. While teachers acknowledge the importance of these issues and recognise good ideas, they also help students to identify and focus on the key issues for solving the case.

Step 3: Identify the way forward. All students know the limitations of time and resources and must now prioritise the issues. Some sensible assumptions might have to be made and some details might have to be set aside. What is important is that students identify their own way forward, assign research tasks within the group for analysing the issues and resolving the case, and then engage in a variety of tasks or learning activities.

Step 4: Guide the learning activities. Students participate in different learning activities, such as information searching, literature review, data collection. Teachers provide guidance, and closely monitor the activities with a view to providing timely feedback so as to facilitate students' learning.

Step 5: Organise presentation, mobilise discussion and provide timely feedback. The professor, at the final step of this procedure, organises a session in which groups present their findings. When each group presents its ideas, the professor asks a representative from each of the remaining groups to ask questions or provide feedback. The presenting group is prompted to answer fully all requests for clarification. At the end of the Q&A session, the professor provides immediate feedback on the group's work, confirming the good points that were made, supplying any missing information, and clarifying any misconceptions.

Approach 2: the Historical Narration

Because a case tells a story, it can be used to teach an historical narrative; in fact, storytelling is increasingly becoming a taught subject in business schools (Patten & Swanson, 2003). Through historical narrations the student is expected to learn what has actually happened during the life of the subject entity in a case. This narrative method is especially appropriate for comparing the preconceptions that people may have about a particular subject.

Swanson and Morrison (2010) give the example of a Swiss manufacturing company faced with shrinking demand for its products. The company responds by changing the product design, thereby returning to profitability. The student reading this case learns how the company discovered and described the problem. S/he then evaluates the various actions the company contemplated taking and considers how and why the company finally responded as it did.

This kind of case gives teachers the opportunity to analyse step-by-step with their students the entire sequence of events and to cover the whole experience of the specific case. Also, they can focus students' attention on the alternatives and how they were formulated in order to highlight the relative importance of alternative strategies that a company might have been able to implement. Finally, the teacher can promote good practices resulting from the specific actions that returned the company to profitability (Swanson & Morrison, 2010).

The use of narrative in business studies helps students to understand how and why businesses succeed or fail. Storytelling by sharing of actions, views and opinions shapes a business's culture and may be a power for good or it may provoke division and subversion. The need for narrative understanding has increased in importance due to the rapid changes resulting from modernisation and globalisation. More importantly, the use of narrative in education provides a connection to experience and morality that captures the complexity and contradictions of life, and empowers the learner through caring interdependent relationships (Witherall & Noddings, 1991; Gilligan, 1988).

Educational critics such as Postman (1995) connect knowing through narrative to motivation. Postman states that a narrative of interdependence needs to be chosen above narratives of reason, science, economic utility and technology in order to give students a reason for learning.

Scholars agree that storytelling creates a learning situation (Mostert & Sudzina, 1996). It allows one to think 'outside the box' that defines one's own experiences and to develop creative ways to problem-solve. It also allows us to identify with the theme and character of the story and to perceive how others think. Through this process, one's own errors in thinking tend to be become apparent (Witherall & Noddings, 1991).

Narratives help build moral development and enhance verbal communication. They also enhance interpersonal communication. Narratives allow the student to look at life from different angles. They engage the mind and promote the development of critical thinking. When students start to look at a problem differently they begin to see how things could have been better – or worse.

Narratives offer an opportunity to look at new ways of processing things so when similar situations offer themselves in the future they can be processed more efficiently and effectively. Narratives provide a down-to-earth method of teaching case studies which might be foreign to the student. They activate the student's existing background knowledge and, because of this, the student is more likely to process information better and remember it better.

Narratives may invoke emotion, which is proven to help people to learn better and retain information. Besides, historical narratives can make learning fun (Witherall & Noddings, 1991). They help students put themselves in someone else's shoes and this assists them to see solutions and alternatives where past thinking patterns offered no alternatives (Swanson & Morrison, 2010). Also, narratives are less abstract and can be very powerful for looking at problems from other viewpoints. Stories about others show how others were able to overcome barriers and eventually succeed, and they promote critical thinking (Liang & Wang, 2004).

Approach 3: Transferring Specific Skills

This third application of cases enables students to acquire specific skills (Patten & Swanson, 2003). The typical format here is that instructor constructs a question which students must answer by conducting some sort of research exercise (e.g. downloading and assembling data and performing a series of calculations). In doing so, the student acquires specific skills by analysing the question and manipulating relevant data (Swanson & Morrison, 2010).

This approach has the advantage of using a real-life situation which helps to enliven the learning experience for the student and simultaneously emphasises the learning experience that the instructor wants to achieve (Swanson & Morrison, 2010). To illustrate, assume that a faculty member wishes to teach about channels of distribution; a case could be selected that describes a company and the product it manufactures. Information about the cost of manufacturing and the desired profit margin could be provided. The student could then be asked to identify possible ways in which the manufacturer could distribute its product to the consumer. This can be as extensive an analysis as the faculty member decides is appropriate given the level and objectives of the course (Swanson & Morrison, 2010).

Given a certain problem that the case has identified, the student then learns that s/he must now discover various alternatives to solving the problem (Swanson & Morrison, 2010). Since the alternatives must all concern distribution channels the student ends up acquiring a specific skill – in this case, knowledge of how distribution works.

As an example of this approach here is a brief description of a case approach that hones specific skills used in evaluating global consumer markets using data available from the U.S. Census Bureau and the World Bank. The prospect of rising incomes destined to transform massive populations into rapidly expanding consumer markets spurred a rush of U.S.-based corporations into China, India, and other markets during the 1990s. These expanding consumer markets continue to attract corporations whose present-day business derives largely from mature markets with limited prospects for further growth. In their efforts to globalise, corporations need to anticipate the future growth of these emerging consumer markets. Such markets pose distinctive problems amenable to applied demographic analysis. The case centers on a study to refine and expand a corporation's global view of the middle class consumer. In this case, the student is called upon to develop data on the preceding points and prepare an analysis to be presented to a client who is a builder interested in foreseeing future homebuyer preferences. This client is contemplating entry into one of several emerging markets and looking for guidance on the comparative demographic strengths and weaknesses of each market (Swanson & Morrison, 2010).

This third approach causes students to learn by engaging in problem-solving and other activities that motivate the need to learn. This gives students a chance to apply what is being learned in a way that affords real feedback (Kolodner, 1997; Kolodner *et al.*, 1996; Schank & Cleary, 1994). Students might engage in solving a series of real-world problems – such as managing erosion or planning for a tunnel or designing a software application – either for real or through realistic simulation. Each instance requires:

- identification of issues that need resolution and knowledge required to address those issues
- exploration or investigation or experimentation to learn the needed knowledge
- application of that knowledge to solve the problem
- generation and assessment of a solution (Kolodner *et al.*, 2003).

In the process students might engage in taking surveys and learning statistical concepts (sampling, averaging, probabilities) and social science concepts (question asking) (Kolodner *et al.*, 2003). Participation in design and problem-solving activity, especially when students must make something work, gives them the opportunity to work out what they need to learn, experience the application of that knowledge, and learn how it is best used (Kolodner *et al.*, 2003).

Approach 4: Fostering Decision-Making

The fourth instructional application focuses on the art of decision-making. How does one identify problems? What needs to be solved? How does one formulate possible courses of action? What criteria can be used in evaluating solutions or courses of action? Under this approach, the student must discover the problem – it is not identified as such in the case (Swanson & Morrison, 2010). This approach is very popular when teaching courses such as strategic management where it is desirable to encompass problems involving a variety of subject-matter fields.

The process of identifying the problem, enumerating possible solutions, establishing criteria to be incorporated in the solution that is selected, and selecting the solution along with the supporting rationale makes for an important experience. Case studies are particularly well suited to delivering a valuable learning experience in this type of situation (Swanson & Morrison, 2010).

A Bespoke Approach Developed in the Business Schools of Western Greece

During our research on the Business Schools of Western Greece, we elicited the following four discrete steps to promote decision making. They are:

Step 1: Identify/clarify the decision to be made. The case study will not specify the decision. It has to be identified by the students themselves. Not all students will succeed in doing so but the more discerning ones will lead the discovery process. A case containing multiple problems enables the instructor to focus on problem clarification as a key learning outcome. A brainstorming discussion in the classroom facilitates collection of all problems realised by each student. All problems revealed from the case study are displayed so that all students can have a clear view of the range of problems presented in the case.

Step 2: Identify possible decision options. This step requires the decision makers – at this point the students – to present, as clearly as possible, just what the decision alternatives really are. Again at this point a brainstorming discussion is initiated in the classroom in order to collect all possible decision options on each specific problem realised by each student. All decisions for each problem are collected and displayed so that all students can have a clear view of all the potential decisions.

Step 3: Gather/process information. Next, the students have to collect or process information that can help guide the decision. In some cases, all information necessary for the final decision is available in the case study itself. So the students must re-read the case study in detail and extract the information that will enable the decision to be made. A case might present no relevant information, or offer insufficient information. In that case, students have to search for and collect relevant information about the company featured in the case, or about suitable managerial strategies. They must also find and read handbooks on specific theoretical aspects that might be of great use in their decision-making. In doing this the students categorise the problems and prioritise the chief problem to be solved. The more significant the decision, the more rigorous must be the information-gathering process.

Step 4: Make the decision. During this step students can work individually on the case and document their ideas and solutions; alternatively groups of (say) 4 students can collaborate.

After the information has been considered according to its relevance and significance, and then discussed in the classroom, each student presents and explains his/her decision.

Good Practices of Business Schools in Western Greece

During our research into CBT as used by professors of the business schools of Western Greece, we uncovered a practice that the professors involved, and their students, felt resulted in better feedback and value. This method could be named Case Debates because it is concerned with comparisons between cases (Cinneide, 2006). Usually the cases used for this practice are different cases about the same company – often a multinational company or a start up.

This learning procedure has been used on the International Management course since 2008 to stimulate post-discussion learning among student cohorts. Case debates are organised in the course and administered to teams after three or four different case studies on a given topic have been discussed and analysed in the class. Emerging issues from all the cases are reviewed to develop analytical insights on the theme; these are then debated.

This process involves two phases. In phase A each group of students is separated in four subgroups each of which is required to examine a particular situation in each case study (eg: recognise the practices and critical situation; recognise the particular set of resources, practices and functional problems that seemed to account for company's performance; recognise the problem attributes or the success story and fixing flaws). In phase B the subgroups recombine as a group and they proceed to discussion: categorising critical issues; linking problems to critical issues; identifying major attributes to the problems; looking for appropriate solutions.

The students learning via this Case Debates method generally reported that it helped them to understand the anatomy of cases and gain deep managerial insights. This approach can enable the students to progress from study of a single case to comparison between different cases (Taousanidis & Antoniadou, 2008). Case debates are organised after one third and two thirds of the course contents have been covered. In the process students gain skills and become familiar with a wide range of management topics.

Clearly, the quality of a case analysis will depend on the information included in the teaching cases and available from other sources. Therefore there is no guarantee that all the critical aspects of each company will be captured. The complexity of some organisations and the unobservable nature of some resources would diminish any claims of a complete analysis of firm success (Ambrosini *et al.*, 2010).

Conclusions

Case-based teaching and learning has its roots in the well-proven apprenticeship method of learning by doing. It is a student-centered learning approach that allows students to take greater responsibility and play a more active role in the learning process than they do in traditional class learning (Christensen, 1987). CBT has been shown to be an extremely effective way of teaching business administration at Harvard Business School and other leading business schools.

In preparation for this chapter, we have interviewed a majority of professors teaching Business Studies on business schools in Western Greece. From the interviews and the literature used by the CBT practitioners we were able to identify four distinct approaches to CBT used by professors teaching business lessons in Western Greece, namely; 1) the typical way, 2) the historical narration, 3) CBT to transfer specific skills, and 4) CBT to build decision-making skills (Patten & Swanson, 2003).

The typical way approach is applied by the majority of professors in the specific target group following the four specific steps, avoiding any kind of differentiation from the typical kind of usage of CBT. Through historical narrations the student is expected to learn what has actually happened during the life of the entity. Narrative Method is especially appropriate for comparing the preconceptions that people may have about a particular subject. By the transferring specific skills approach, the instructor constructs a question which students must answer by conducting some sort of research exercise in order to acquire specific skills by analysing the question and manipulating relevant data. The fourth instructional application focuses on the art of decision-making. This approach is very popular when teaching courses such as strategic management where it is desirable to encompass problems involving a variety of subject matter fields.

During our research we uncovered the Case Debates methodology, a practice that the professors and the students involved felt resulted in better feedback and value. This learning procedure has been used to stimulate post-discussion learning among student cohorts.

Each method we have described contributes to student learning.

To a greater or lesser extent, each way of using case-based teaching and learning contributes to the appropriate organisation by students of information to be recalled later for use in reasoning. Furthermore it generates experience that students would not otherwise have, increases the visibility of students' reasoning processes, and increases students' confidence.

About the Authors

Ioanna Giannoukou is a Researcher at the Department of Business Administration, University of Patras, Greece and a business consultant. She can be contacted at this email: igian@upatras.gr

Chrysostomos Stylios is Associate Professor in the Department of Computer Engineering at the Technological Educational Institute of Epirus, Greece. He can be contacted at this email: stylios@teiep.gr

Chapter seven

Towards New Genres for 21st Century Business School Case Studies

Clive Holtham

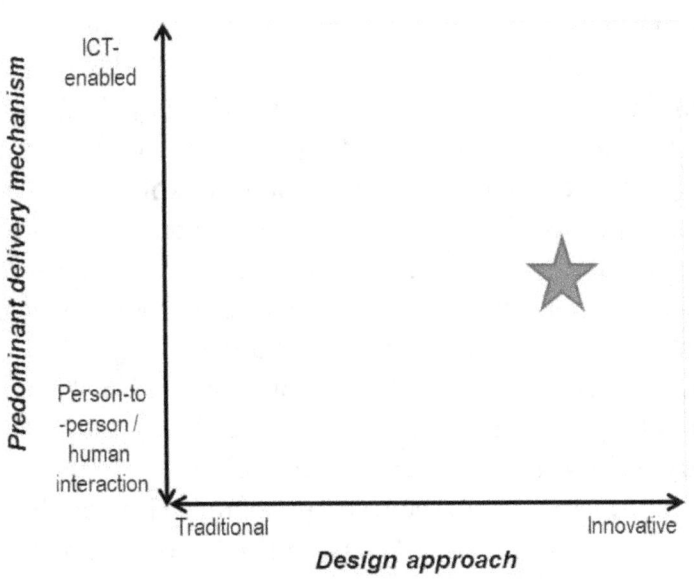

The Evolution of Traditional Case Studies

There are many different types of case study, and even more ways of using those cases, but much discourse about cases is centred on the traditional Harvard Business School-style case study. These are typically around twenty pages long, describing an organisation from a management perspective, and including background material in the form of 'exhibits'. All students read the case, which is then used as the basis of a discussion in class, usually in a horseshoe-shaped classroom.

My aim in this chapter is to suggest that whatever the merits of the traditional case study, it is an appropriate time to examine what might constitute a 21st Century rethink of this case study genre. A spectrum of approaches that can all be called case studies is emerging. This spectrum would include classic Harvard/Ivey-style cases, multimedia cases with minimal text, real-time hands-on cases (eg: featuring live visits; face-to-face interviews), simulations using data inserted into ERP-type software, virtual environments (eg: Shareville, Second Life), and fictional scenarios (eg: graphic novels, plays, movies, soap operas). For example, within this spectrum I would characterise the emerging genre of computer-based simulation as 'data rich, dramatically enacted'.

However, I also acknowledge that there are major barriers to innovation in business school pedagogy which may inhibit the evolution of such new genres of case study. On the other hand there is little dispute that the Harvard case method is explicitly derived from 19th century pedagogic thinking originating in the Harvard Law School (Garvin, 2003). It was then appropriated in the early 20th Century by the newly created Harvard Business School, for whom it has become a *"signature pedagogy"* (Schulman, 2005). Even in schools where the Harvard case method is not a signature pedagogy it is nonetheless a well understood pedagogy, fuelled by a steady supply of new, usually well-written, and relevant cases.

One factor in the longevity of the Harvard approach is undoubtedly that the traditional case study is also a vehicle for management research and for the acquisition and consumption of academic research resources. So the production of a case can draw from the intrinsic subject matter expertise of an experienced academic, as well as their scientific role in knowledge production. It can also utilise doctoral or post-doctoral researchers in its fieldwork and this helps to develop a virtuous circle of intertwined teaching and research.

By contrast, more innovative forms of case study or of experiential learning may place little or no value on conventional research resources and much more on expertise in publishing, media, storytelling and so on which, in some instances, may be completely absent from the roster of traditional university skills.

On its student recruitment web pages, Harvard Business School has a short summary:

> *"Over 80 percent of cases sold throughout the world are written by HBS faculty, who produce approximately 350 new cases per year.*
>
> *Simply put, we believe the case method is the best way to prepare students for the challenges of leadership". (Harvard Business School, 2014)*

There is a huge infrastructure supporting the production, distribution and use of business school case studies but, even though Harvard itself has become slightly more open to other forms of learning, its claim on 'the best way' appears not to be based on comparisons with other alternatives.

Grant (1997) outlines the benefits of using case studies as an interactive learning strategy, shifting the emphasis from teacher-centred to more student-centred activities. Raju and Sanker (1999) demonstrate the importance of using case studies in engineering education to expose students to real-world issues with which they may be faced. Case studies have also been linked with increased student motivation and interest in a subject (Mustoe & Croft, 1999).

In the context of engineering, Goodhew (2011) argues:

> *"In our experience of using case studies, we have found that they can be used to:*
>
> - *Allow the application of theoretical concepts to be demonstrated, thus bridging the gap between theory and practice;*
> - *Encourage active learning;*
> - *Provide an opportunity for the development of keys skills such as communication, group working and problem solving;*
> - *Increase the students' enjoyment of the topic and hence their desire to learn".* Goodhew (2011:47)

Case Studies in the Context of Simulations and Games

Modern decision makers contend with the twin pressures of ever greater information and diminishing availability of time. Learning to cope with these pressures calls for skills that combine dealing with rich information with the flexibility necessary to manage high-velocity decision making. The effective acquisition of these skills is usually the product of on-job-experience. But modern organisations expect young managers to possess these skills as soon as they enter the organisation (Woods & Dennis, 2009).

Effective learning requires rich knowledge structures with many links to help learners address and solve complex problems (Grabinger & Dunlab, 1995). In an educational context the transfer of learning is most effective in rich, complex learning situations where learners take an active role in forming new understandings. Skills and knowledge are acquired within realistic contexts where the learners can rehearse and learn the outcomes that are expected of them under realistic conditions.

Grabinger and Dunlap (1995) define *"rich environments for active learning"* as broad instructional systems that stimulate study and exploration within authentic contexts and create a feeling of knowledge building learning communities. Such environments utilise dynamic, interdisciplinary learning activities that promote high-level thinking processes through realistic tasks and performances.

Ellington *et al.* (1998) developed a framework (see also Leigh & Collier, this volume) for comparing and contrasting three types of experiential learning environments – games, simulations and case studies (see Figure 1)

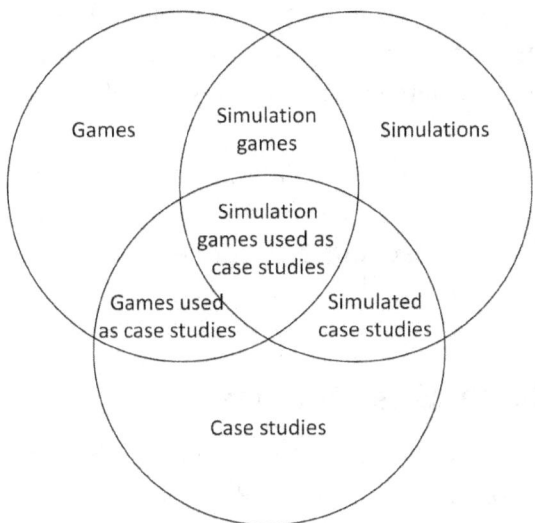

Figure 1: The overlapping sets of games, simulations and case studies. (Ellington et al., 1998:3)

Ellington (2002) has helpfully summarised the classic definitions of these terms.

A case study is "an in-depth examination of a real-life or simulated situation carried out in order to illustrate special and/or general characteristics". Thus, to qualify as a 'case study', an exercise must have two essential features, namely; in-depth study which is carried out in order to illustrate particular characteristics. These can be either characteristics specific to the case under examination or more general features of the broader set of which it is a member.

Ellington defines a game as *"any contest (play) among adversaries (players) operating under constraints (rules) for an objective (winning, victory or pay-off)"*. Thus, to qualify as a 'game', an exercise must have two basic characteristics, namely; overt competition and rules (arbitrary constraints within which the players have to operate).

On the other hand a simulation, according to Ellington, is *"an operating representation of central features of reality"*. Thus, to qualify as a 'simulation', an exercise must again have two basic characteristics, namely; it must represent a real situation and must be on-going. (Static analogues such as circuit diagrams do not, in other words, qualify as simulations whereas working models of all types do.)

In practice, case studies, games and simulations are closely interrelated, their sets overlapping in the way shown in Figure 1. We see from this that there are at least seven distinct types of exercises - three 'pure' types and four 'hybrid' types.

Alternatives to Traditional Case Studies

Alternatives have been available for some time – although take-up has also taken some time. For example, Zoll (1966) outlined a wide range of innovative experiential management education methods which, approaching 50 years ago, went well beyond the Harvard-style case study approach.

Two decades ago, Mintzberg (1990) was highly critical both of traditional case studies and their connection to what he dubbed as:

"... the design school of both management theory and practice. What effect has such case study teaching had on practice, on the generations of managers who have graduated from schools that rely on that pedagogy? If that has left managers with the impression that, to make strategy, they can remain in their offices with documents summarizing the situation and think – formulate so that others can implement – then it may well have done them and their organizations a terrible disservice, encouraging superficial strategies that violate the distinctive competencies of their organizations." (Mintzberg, 1990:188)

Mintzberg (2004) used his critique of the MBA once again to be particularly critical of both Harvard and its case study method.

The search for alternatives accelerated after the 2001 dotcom and governance crises, with the AACSB instituting a review of management education which concluded:

"The relevance of business curricula cannot be separated from

pedagogy. Preparation for the rapid pace of business cannot be obtained from textbooks and cases, many of which are outdated before they are published. Students must learn to use technology for managerial and strategic purposes through action-learning and technology-enhanced pedagogy, and faculty must be equipped to guide them in such learning." (AACSB, 2002:19)

After the 2007 global financial crisis there was another phase of review and critique, some of it again relating to case studies. Some now even came from within Harvard itself; Heskett (2008) identified four concerns that the case study method:

"(1) is time consuming.

(2) requires of students a great deal of synthesis of many individual decision making situations to form generalizations.

(3) is an imperfect way of teaching quantitative techniques.

(4) is based on the notion that there are no right answers, only some that are better than others." (Heskett, 2008)

However, the Harvard self-criticism may be partly fuelled by the innovativeness of competitors, for example Columbia Business School's development of greatly shortened case studies, called *"decision briefs"* (Gloeckler, 2008)

From Frozen Case Studies to Living Studies

The idea of being an actual player capable of actual experience has led to the development of live or living case studies, most notably via one of the most profound critiques of the Harvard-style case which comes from Stähli (1987; in translation 2006). Stähli's views seem to have attracted only a tiny amount of interest from academics outside German speaking countries – most notably and to the credit of Stumpf and Nevins (1999) – and yet Stähli developed the Zurich Living Case method which involves working with a real company in real time, with a very explicitly articulated approach to knowledge content supporting that practical activity.

Stähli's (2006) criticism of traditional case study methods has three dimensions. Firstly, they *"neglect to take into account the differing levels of education, age and experience of the study participants for didactic purposes."* Secondly, *"there is still a chasm between the learning environment (the advanced training institution) and the functional environment (the company), which is not bridged by traditional case study methods."* Finally, there is inadequate consideration of the time factor, with traditional methods favouring a situation-related decision based on a predetermined set of data. But in living cases, *"only the most current data can be used for analysis and planning."* Stähli (2001) also proposed a *"genetically growing case"*, where a single organisation is consecutively used in the teaching of different subjects, allowing students to understand that organisation more holistically.

However, in my own experience living cases involving direct contact with organisations do not scale very well – a key benefit of traditional cases. On the other hand, I observe a growing problem with classic case studies in that students seem to pay increasing attention to the date of the case study, and are increasingly questioning of the relevance of cases that are more than five years old … and sometimes even less.

A further and interesting alternative approach is explored by Griffin (2009) who reviews what she calls *"raw digital cases"*. Rather than involving the writing of a case study these involve curating links to the online resources of a real organisation, links to what commentators are saying about it, and perhaps brief video interviews of the instructors setting the scene. This approach has been pioneered by the Yale School of Management and attracts Griffin in part because:

> *"… the language of hypertext and the use of digital media have become essential competencies in today's business environment."* (Griffin, 2009:706)

Raw digital cases could not only scale well, they could be underpinned by a wider community of learning, perhaps along the Wikipedia model where successive waves of students would augment the initial teacher-curated link through their own co-production of knowledge.

The growth of Massive Open Online Courses (MOOC's) could even see such an approach institutionalised – MOOC student teams can be set the task of curating links to dozens or hundreds of organisations, which are then deepened, augmented, and corrected by subsequent cohorts of learners.

A second route to a lived experience could be to shift from a primarily cognitive approach to case studies, with the emphasis on rationality and 'right answers', to a much more subjective approach – perhaps most dramatically, in every sense, achieved through role playing cases. These are normally based on fictional case studies, albeit typically written by experienced professionals. They usually involve ambiguity, conflict and the lack of simplistic right answers.

An extensive range of role play situations is available in education from immersive environments such as Second Life (Gao *et al.*, 2009) to 'ad hoc improv', a form of improvisation originally developed for comedy, but now also used in business consulting. These typically diverge from traditional case studies in that they usually do not cite real organisations. In fact they may well cite fictional or even unreal environments – as in the case of Second Life (Jordan, 2009).

From Case Studies as Theory of Real Organisations to Case Studies as Fictional Role Play: an Example

With funding from the UK's Big Lottery Fund, Cass Business School and partners developed a pre-MOOC large-scale online learning environment to improve management in the charity sector. It is called knowhownonprofit.org, and now has over 40,000 registered users. At the design stage it was quite quickly realised that it would not be sufficient to transmit information to help managers solve challenging problems. So the project successfully piloted the development of a continuing, online, text-based management drama in the form of a soap opera named Millcaster Tales. It is based in the mythical, central English town of Millcaster.

The project recruited a professional soap opera script-writer to train the academic team in the craft of continuing drama. Britain's longest running radio soap opera, The Archers, is set in a country town surrounded by farms. From 1951 to 1972 it was part funded by the Ministry of Agriculture because it was used as an educational vehicle to promote modern farming methods to remote farmers through the vehicle of fiction. In Millcaster Tales, an unhealthy number of underperforming charities are located in Millcaster; its twelve published episodes all involve a messy and highly realistic management problem needing to be solved – for example, a missing laptop computer containing highly confidential information.

The creation of a standard soap opera 'setting', and a shifting cast of standard characters, greatly helped build emotional involvement for its audience in a way that is much more difficult to achieve via a traditional case study. Traditional case studies may be based on reality but they rarely deal in treachery, incompetence, malevolence or prejudice. A fictional approach actually needs some of these components to provide interesting stories, even including its characters saying the unsayable. All the episodes were actually written by academics, consultants or managers who had directly experienced senior management. Indeed we discovered that within the business school community there were a surprising number of talented writers, either novelists or playwrights, who normally would not have revealed that they had such skills. These people proved invaluable as writers of engaging stories that had clear educational aims.

From Case Studies of Real Organisations to Games which Emulate Reality

Traditional case studies could be said to incorporate elements of games in so far as they have a set of rules, a referee and, in some cases at least, a degree of competition between the participants to come up with 'good' if not 'winning' answers. There is a long tradition of war games in both the practise and the live evaluation of military strategy. In a similar vein, in competitive sports much of the preparation is not in playing the actual game but in carrying out exercises which involve enhancement of specific skills which may only be one tiny aspect of the actual game, and which do not need to be carried out in anything like the actual game environment. This involves emulation, rather than simulation.

Successful business games can be lightweight, compact or 'lo-fi', using cheap and simple technology such as cards or dice. They do not necessarily need high production values or to fill two hours of classroom time.

For example, at Cass Business School we have developed a board game called 'The Dean's Dilemma' to bring out key features of managing a business school. It involves a set of six players– typically deans designate and heads of department – who are allocated Higher Education Institution (HEI) roles and required to work through a series of difficult management problems. In each round the players change roles until each has experienced the role of Dean. The Dean picks up a card setting out the dilemma to be solved. The other players pick up a card describing the climate in their department and therefore affecting the advice they offer the Dean to help solve his/her dilemma. Though this is selective in relation to fidelity, and involves chance through the selection of cards from a pack, it enables participants in a very condensed period of time to feel some of the realities of being a senior manager.

More generally, I have observed the growth of various types of 'management gym'. In a real gym, very few people would use all the equipment on offer. They will instead be advised on a customised programme requiring the use of certain pieces of equipment in particular ways. This will take account of their unique physical condition and needs. It is interesting to see, for example, that the University of Mälardalen in Sweden has introduced an 'innovation gym' using a similar approach, but with the aim of enhancing personal and organisational innovation capabilities rather than physical capabilities.

From Case Studies of Real Organisations to Simulations of Realistic Organisations

The role play and the game approaches share common elements with the case study approach and with my final category, namely; simulation. The traditional war game has a set of rules, maps, models and so on. The modern war game is much more likely to be a highly sophisticated electronic multimedia simulation. This shift is similar to the way that paper-based business games evolved into 'first generation' electronic business simulations. These are often based around competitors in a market (eg: Markstrat) and, lattterly, to more comprehensive multimedia business simulation environments such as Simventure or products from Megalearning in Belgium.

In my observation the majority of business simulations are developed in a bespoke form; there has been a surprising lack of application of general purpose platforms. An exception is System Dynamics. One of the fruits of Jay Forrester's work on industrial and systems dynamics (Forrester, 1992), was the development of system dynamic modelling environments, first with mainframes and then with networked PCs. This has enabled the creation of non-linear simulations that have the potential to model real-world problems and explore alternative dynamics of the system under focus – particularly useful in education.

Proteus – a Pioneering Environment

A novel comprehensive learning environment might enable all the activities defined in Figure 1. However, it is challenging and costly and often impractical to include both real-life events and simulated events. I therefore foresee a simulated learning environment that excludes the 'pure case' studies but is flexible enough to enable the rest of the defined activities.

An early approach of this type is Proteus – a now largely forgotten 1980s initiative from the Manchester Business School that was extended by Nigel Howard at the Aston Business School. Gunz (1988) described the IBM-sponsored Proteus Programme as *"an attempt to simulate a real-life managerial environment in the classroom, designed to allow students to experience complexity and learn how to manage it"*. In concept, it resembled *"a cross between a flight simulator and an adventure game"*.

Proteus was an architecture through which the Proteus team could develop case studies and simulations, Protocomm was a specific case produced using a real medium-sized rainwear company and including at least 5 years' worth of real detailed financial and other data. Howard et al.'s (1993) contribution was then to augment Proteus with thinking from drama:

> *"The 'rational choice' paradigm underlying decision theory, game theory and mathematical economics is social sciences' most general mathematical model. Many have pointed out its limitations, but none has offered an equally powerful and wide-ranging deductive system. We propose a way of analysing emotional and political aspects of choice largely neglected by existing 'rational choice' models, yet maintaining a clear mathematical structure. As an integrating metaphor we propose to view situations not as games, but as dramas."* (Howard et al., 1993:99)

A researcher who is currently working on similar lines is Nisula (2012) who has deployed an open source Enterprise Resource Planning system, augmented by her own banking software module, to enable students to run a local marketplace of businesses in a realistic fashion. Interestingly, Harvard's Heskett (2008) also sees modern simulations as a competitor to the case study. In parallel there has been significant investment in the field of law in computer-supported role playing, most notably through the work of Paul Maharg (Barton et al., 2007). In education, Keeffe and Austin (2012) have managed to exploit the Moodle platform to create an anonymous role-playing environment for prospective school leaders.

Parallel Challenges to Business Learning Methods

Colby *et al.*'s (2011) very comprehensive critique of undergraduate management education provides a starting point for review. They have proposed four dimensions of liberal learning: analytical reasoning, multiple framing, reflective exploration of meaning and practical reasoning. Colby *et al.* are also specifically supportive of simulations *"to gain a heightened appreciation of the fast-paced, complicated, dynamic and competitive nature of business"*.

It is claimed that Higher Education produces graduates who have good theoretical knowledge but lack practical competencies (Martin & Chapman, 2006; Holden *et al.*, 2007). Despite long term efforts to bring education closer to the business, there still seems to be a gap between the competencies of business graduates and the requirements of business life. Jackson (2009) identifies disciplinary expertise as a required competence, but only one competence among many.

According to Pfeffer and Tong (2002) several business programs still have the incorrect assumption that good teaching equals more learning. Instead, they claim, there is an increasing need for experiential learning. Business schools need a larger practice component to provide graduates with lasting knowledge and competencies that improve performance. The requirements of contemporary businesses may be appropriately met with a simulation environment that provides learners with a dynamic, active learning environment.

Cases as Spaces for Learning

Apart from the outright critics of traditional cases such as Mintzberg and Stahli, and certainly relative to the widespread usage of the case, there has only been a modest amount of critical analysis of the case study method. In my wider research into knowledge creation, I have particularly drawn on the work of Lefebvre (1991), who identified three types of space:

Perçu – this is space as observed and experienced in an everyday sense
Conçu – this is the theory of space, for example as conceived by architects and planners

Vécu – this is the lived space, not just perceived by its users, but actively engaged with and changed by those users

I feel that the metaphor of space is surprisingly relevant for the pedagogy of case studies. If the 'reality' of any given case study is perçu, its writing and use by academics is undoubtedly conçu. That leaves the question of where students fit in by reading the case. They are not part of the everyday reality (perçu) and, even less, are they generally actively living the experience of the workforce or cast of players in the case (vécu). They can therefore only be part of the theory of the case (conçu), quite far removed from direct experience and, like Plato's unfortunates in the cave, not experiencing the real world, only what is indirectly communicated via the shadows being cast.

Discussion

Management educators need to consider 'exercise spaces'. These differ from the sort of place where people work; they provide an environment in which the focus is on coaching to augment intellectual agility. Athletes training for events do not prepare simply by running; they also exercise in a gym to develop specifics that support and enhance the final performance method.

In academic research in any subject the standard approach has been to sub-divide the field into smaller and smaller component disciplines. But this causes a particular problem for the profession of management. Although management depends on and is closely inter-related to every discipline of management – and to every 'technical profession' such as accounting, marketing etc – the profession of management is not, and cannot be, the domain of any one single research-based academic profession or any single technical profession.

This does not imply that business schools should only be populated by polymath academics, though a few of these are needed. In teaching, when cross-disciplinary team members are drawn from individual component disciplines (just as in business itself), so these teams as a whole can have a more polymath role and perspective than any given individual academic.

Even terms such as cross-disciplinary come with intellectual baggage. So too do inter-disciplinary, trans-disciplinary etc. Unfamiliar terms such as 'anti-disciplinary' or 'indisciplinary' would give a better flavour of my real intent.

I observe numerous efforts to build the ideal 'anti-disciplinary' curriculum. Capstone projects, service learning programs, multi-disciplinary case studies, general management classes and team teaching appear to be the most typical integration methods (Weber, 2011; Athavale, 2008). Enterprise Resource Planning (ERP) systems (Fedorowicz, 2004; Johnson, 2004) and simulations (Green, 2004), have been utilised as learning environments to underpin integration endeavours. Navarro (2008) presents features of an ideal business curriculum: in addition to the multi-disciplinary integration, learning methods should be experiential and promote soft-skill development. The curriculum should emphasise the global perspective and information technology as well as ethics and corporate responsibility.

Conclusion

I do not believe that the simulation-based case study will wholly replace the Harvard-style case study; they have different pedagogic aims and different cost structures. Indeed, in the short run the simulation-based case will struggle to make headway against the Harvard-style case study because of the huge sunk cost in this signature pedagogy. However, the simulation-based case approach has accumulated over 20 years of experience and is supported by accelerating technology trends. The time is right to capitalise on this by increasing R&D investment in the development of new genres of case study, both in schools themselves and from national and international funding sources.

About the Author

Clive Holtham is Professor of Information Management in the Faculty of Management at Cass Business School, City University London. He can be contacted at this email: C.W.Holtham@city.ac.uk

Chapter eight

Didactic Categories for Organising Dimensions of Case Based Teaching

Thomas Muschal

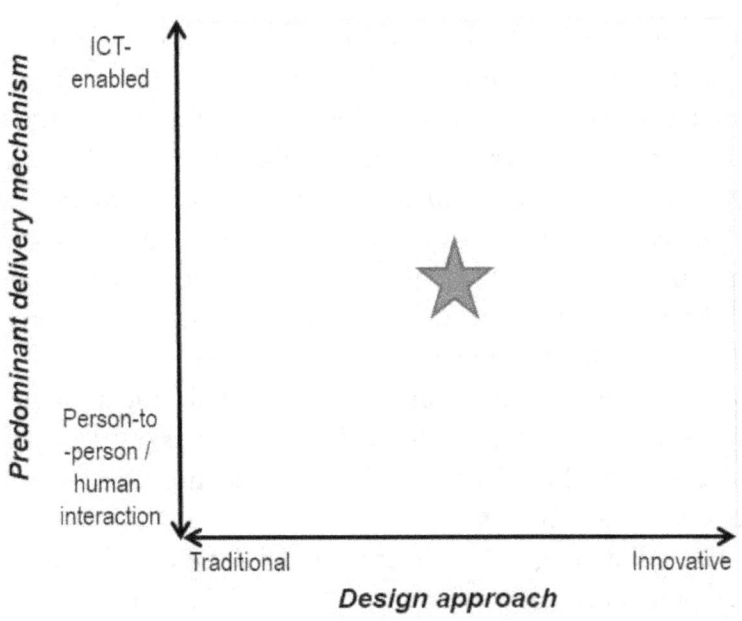

1. Introduction

The European Ministers responsible for Higher Education articulate the challenges of today's education in a European context. The intention is *"to enhance the employability and personal and professional development of graduates throughout their careers"*

(EHEA, 2012:2) to serve Europe's needs. Processes of globalisation and regionalism in economics, politics and society require a variety of skills to act creatively and effectively in situations where no adequate information is available or expected (Erpenbeck & Sauter, 2007). To prepare today's lifelong learners for such situations, the ministers:

> *"... promote student centered learning in higher education, characterised by innovative methods of teaching that involve students as active participants in their own learning" (EHEA, 2012:2).*

New situations in a globalised world require appropriate teaching methods to prepare today's learners with the necessary skills. In the learning process traditional communication methods are challenged by the application of new electronic communication tools. Another central challenge to education today is that a stock of knowledge is no longer a guarantee of competent performance.

In an educational context the term 'competency' can be defined as learning outcomes (e.g. Franke, 2005; Gnahs, 2010) for developing the *"capabilities of self-organised, creative performance when facing an uncertain future"* (Erpenbeck & Sauter, 2007:2, translated from German by author). According to these authors, competencies are capabilities to think and act in a self-organised way (personal competencies) with the focus on performance (activity-related competencies), based on subject-specific and methodological knowledge (specific and methodological competencies) by using social and communication skills (social and communication competencies) (Erpenbeck & Sauter, 2007:67).

Case-Based Teaching (CBT) is one potential method for students' skill development and may inform this debate. Within the context of constructivist theory, CBT is:

> *"... fundamentally student-centered [...], tending to focus on concrete, specific occasions [...] where the target knowledge is relevant [...] [and] contribute[s] to the development of thinking skills and an understanding of the nature of science, beyond the conventional conceptual content." (Allchin, 2013:364-365)*

To develop a wider understanding of CBT that acknowledges multiple perspectives I will combine theoretical and an empirical research. I will apply Baumgartner's (2011) model of didactic categories with its theoretical implications on teaching methods in general and combine this with a review of selected literature on CBT in order to develop and to structure a wide range of perspectives on CBT to facilitate a more integrative discussion. This may support the design process of didactic settings, particularly the design of learning material for CBT.

2. Defining Case Based Teaching

In research there are many theoretical and empirical perspectives on CBT that focus on very different didactic dimensions (Frank, 2003; Allchin, 2013). Guidelines for case development and reflection (e.g. Nelson, 1997; Herreid, 2005; Allchin, 2013) and best practices (e.g. Herreid, 1994; Hafer et al., 2010; Kerres, 2012) give insights into the application of CBT and lessons learned from it. But as yet there is no common theoretical perspective on systematic, didactic dimensions for CBT (Flechsig, 1996; Baumgartner, 2010, 2011). Terms like Case Method, Case Teaching, Case Study Method, Case-Based Teaching, Teaching Case, and others, address one specific didactic method which has many different variants and forms (Frank, 2003).

Empirically, the use of CBT is established in disciplines such as law, management and medicine where actions must comply with certain standards (Kerres, 2012; Carroll & Rosson, 2005). Peterßen points out that the use of CBT requires cases with realistic scenarios as well as didactic reduction: real-world settings are transformed to learning artifacts by reducing, simplifying and/or structuring the material (Peterßen, 1999:53; 92). While Carroll and Rosson present a paradigmatic definition of CBT as *"a brief but provocative story, sketching a problematic situation, and inviting the reader to elaborate missing or open details of the premise, and to construct possible resolutions"* (Carroll & Rosson, 2005:6), Kerres offers a helpfully broad definition of CBT as *"a sequence of learning based on working with (at least a part of) a case"* (Kerres, 2012:349, translated from German by author).

In this chapter I want to open up the perspectives to very different subjects and fields of higher education – including those which do not currently use CBT. Accordingly the intentionally vague proposition by Herreid (2005) on CBT as *"stories with an educational message"* will be used.

1. Defining the Level of Abstraction of Teaching Situations

Teaching and learning situations can be analysed from very different perspectives. I propose that Baumgartner's (2011) model of didactic categories offers an excellent way to examine and structure perspectives on CBT.

Basically, the development of theoretical scientific models requires abstraction of real-world phenomena. The level of abstraction depends on the context of use. In education science there are several levels of abstraction on teaching and learning situations. While best practices focus on a detailed description of a given teaching and learning setting (e.g. to illustrate the variety of elements), a more general examination of teaching methods tends to reveal patterns for analysing different situations. Applying these different perspectives to CBT is made easier with a well-defined model of different level of abstraction of didactic situations. As I shall explain, Baumgartner's thinking is helpful here.

To localise the necessary theoretical background of didactic categories as a framework for CBT development and reflection, the model presented in figure 1, derived from Baumgartner's (2011) work, embeds three different levels of abstraction that differ in the degree of detail. Let us look at each level.

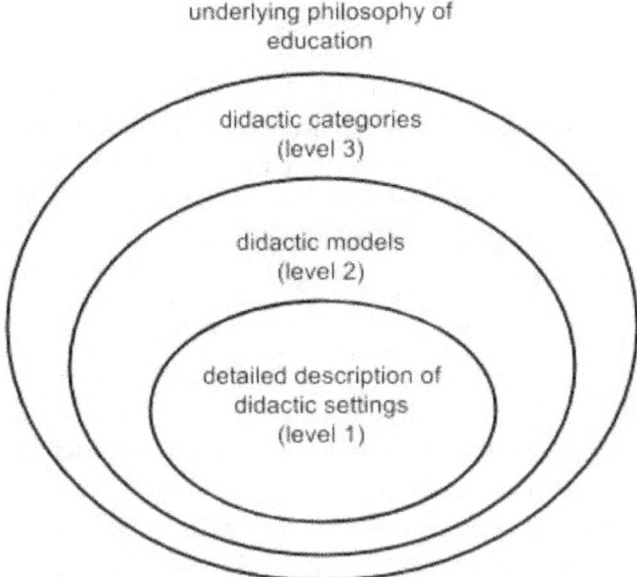

Figure 1: Three levels of abstraction (modified version based on Baumgartner 2011:72)

2. Level 1: a Detailed Description of Didactic Settings

Baumgartner proposes that, in a given educational setting, the detailed descriptions collected in notes of real learning situations are related uniquely to the perceiver and his/her mindset. Therefore it is difficult to apply the decisions made in this context to other situations. While 'lessons learned' by a small group of Bachelor level students on a business administration course might not be transferred easily to a Masters level in law, the strength of these realistic descriptions lies in the case itself. The decisions made in a specific situation are understandable to the reader.

3. Level 2: Didactic Models

Didactic models are generalised descriptions of real-world settings in education; so-called *"reconstructions of reconstruction"* (Baumgartner, 2011:70). Singular events are summarised in classes of similar structure. According to Baumgartner (2010, 2011) the theoretical focus on this level of description is mostly implicit, therefore the comparability of different descriptions and authors is difficult (Baumgartner, 2010, 2011). Baumgartner's central point here is that *"because of Popper's dictum, observation is only possible with theory, the focus of observation has to be confirmed on a higher [more abstract, theoretical] level."* (Baumgartner, 2011:71, translated from German by author) Therefore the observation of real world phenomena on level 1 is also influenced by theory.

Level 2 reconstructions are more abstract than those at level 1 and are based mainly on implicit theory. In turn, didactic categories (level 3) are viewed at a greater level of abstraction than level 2 phenomena.

4. Level 3: Didactic Categories

Didactic categories embraces the main aspects in learning situations. They implicitly present the theoretical framework for level 2 (didactic models) and therefore (on highly analytical consideration) also for level 1 (detailed description of didactic settings), all within a context of (mostly implicit) underlying philosophy.

In a generalised scientific perspective, reducing typical situations to categories that characterise a given scientific subject reveals a framework for theoretical reflection. According to Baumgartner, a *"model of didactic categories consists of a comprehensible amount of generic terms that designate the essential components of the didactic design framework"* (Baumgartner, 2011:75, translated from German by author).

To summarise, a certain level of abstraction of real world phenomena depends on both the more abstract level (as theoretical background) and the more precise level (as observation).

The application of Baumgartner's didactic categories (level

3) present a framework to structure selected dimensions on CBT presented in literature of (assumed) level 2 (didactic models) and level 1 (detailed description of didactic settings) research for CBT design. In this chapter I will consider CBT in terms of dimensions situated on level 2.

3. Baumgartner's Model of Didactic Categories

Didactic discourse employs models of varying complexity to identify relevant elements and theories for development of learning and teaching settings (Gudjons & Winkler, 2002). In my view, Hudson's (2011) Didactic Triangle model offers a helpful basis for understanding the evolution of Baumgartner's model of seven didactic categories.

1. The Foundation: the Didactic Triangle

One established model of didactic categories is the didactic triangle. This model illustrates a consensus in European perspective on education (Hudson, 2011). It focuses on the teacher, the student and the subject matter. Figure 2 presents a version of this concept.

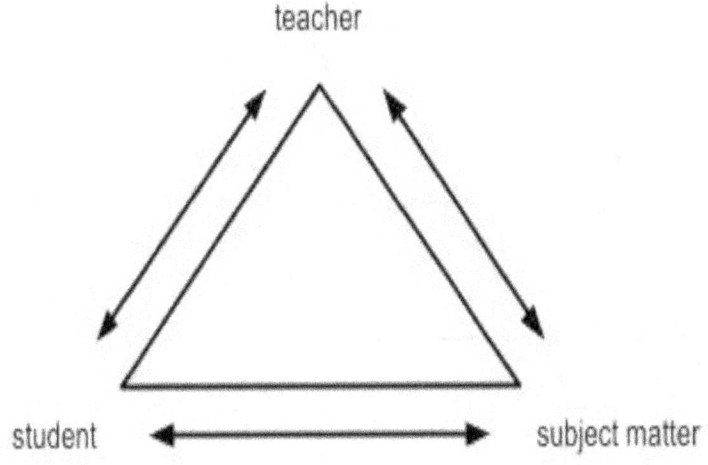

Figure 2: the Didactic Triangle (Hudson, 2011:19)

However, the high degree of abstraction in this triad makes it a rather simplistic tool (Schröder, 2001). Closer observation of teaching and learning situations requires a more detailed theoretical framework. While the three didactic categories presented in the didactic triangle illustrate basic interconnections in teaching and learning situations, the wide range of definitions of CBT rules out a fuller understanding (Baumgartner, 2011; Goodschild & Sriraman, 2012; Schoenfeld, 2012).

2. Baumgartner's Model of Seven Didactic Categories

To overcome the shortcomings of the didactic triangle, Baumgartner (2011) presents a model of seven didactic categories, inspired both by the didactic triangle and by Flechsig's model of four categories (Baumgartner, 2011:101-103). A review of the seven central elements of this framework, as presented in Figure 3, gives us a deeper perspective on learning situations.

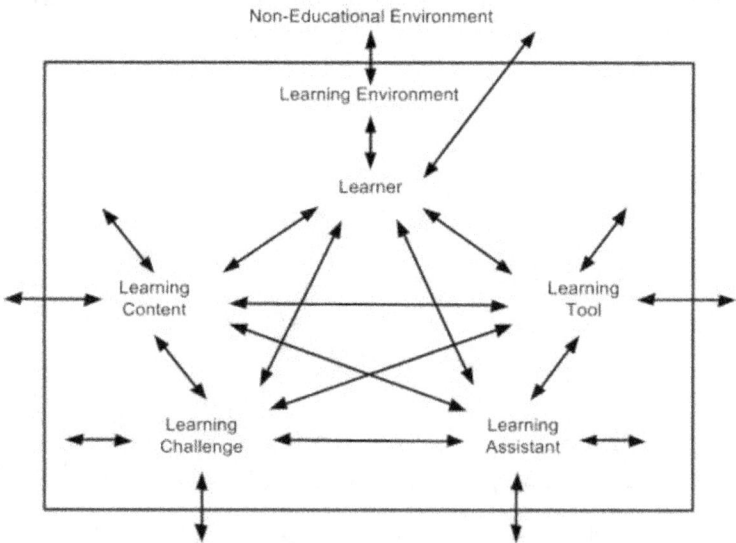

Figure 3: Baumgartner's model of seven didactic categories (Baumgartner, 2011, 2013)

The model of didactic categories by Baumgartner allows a useful reduction of learning situations while being complex enough to take a more precise look at detailed, differentiated elements.

In any particular teaching and learning setting the immediate importance of each category of Baumgartner's model may vary. Nevertheless, the interconnections between the seven categories continue even when some are muted. The relevance of each category for CBT will be presented in the next section.

4. Dimensions of Case Based Teaching Structured by Didactic Categories

A combination of Baumgartner's (2011) didactic categories (at level 3) and Herreid's (2005) intentionally opaque definition of CBT (at level 2) provides a useful way to address relevant aspects of CBT. This opens up a space which can be filled with empirical and theoretical perspectives described in the literature and so offer teaching professionals a way to identify relevant and available didactic choices and to make the optimal selection.

Because of the ever-increasing volume of literature on research and development in education the following outline does not pretend to be all inclusive. Nevertheless, it sets out to uphold and inform the central function of learning, namely; the individual development of knowledge, skills and competencies in a specific domain.

For the purpose of this chapter, the focus lies on relevant decisions on the learning content (category 7) influenced by the other categories. Because of the analytical fragmentation of integral situations (like CBT) the mapping of didactic elements to one specific category instead of relations between two or more categories may require consideration. Nevertheless, for the sake of clarity, the arrangement is designed to focus on the specific central category.

Note: The numbering sequence used here is purely for ease of reference and because the factors effecting categories numbered 1 to 6 all have a bearing on the optimal design and choice of learning content (category 7) for a particular learning setting.

1. Category 1: Learning Challenge

This category describes the learning task in general. It presents the central category for intentional didactic design. Typically, discussion of the learning challenge tends to focus on individual and personal learning outcomes. While CBT addresses higher and more complex skills (Kerres, 2012) a detailed consideration may help to identify central learning goals according to different dimensions of competencies (Erpenbeck & Sauter, 2007; Gnahs, 2010). Depending on the intended aspects of the learner's development – such as personal, activity-related, specific and methodological and/or social and communication competencies – preceding decisions become relevant. And it is important to develop a clear outline of learning outcomes by reflecting on: What are the central aims applying CBT in the learning setting? (For a case analysis see e.g. Carroll & Borge, 2007)

2. Category 2: Learner

Learners learn to perform new activities; they acquire qualifications, skills and competencies. This concerns concepts of learning theory as well as focusing on the individual person (Erpenbeck & Sauter, 2007; Gnahs, 2010).

Important decisions pertaining to CBT may include the level of autonomy the learner has in the process. Allchin (2013) highlights that selection of the problem, securing background information and resources, problem-solving activities, facilitating discussion and negotiating discussion should be considered in the perspective of learning outcomes. Depending on the learner's development the relevant facts as well as the definition of the problem may vary from predefined to unspecific (Erpenbeck & Sauter, 2007:200).

Allchin (2013) presents three distinct levels of problem clarity: a case problem is well-defined, ill-defined or unspecific. Jonassen points out that *"[i]ll-structured problems possess multiple solutions, solution paths, fewer parameters which are less manipulable, and contain uncertainty about which concepts, rules, and principles are necessary for the solution or how they are organized and which solution is best."* (Jonassen 1997:65) This may be a good starting point for reflecting on intended learning outcomes.

The choice of a meaningful topic with realistic challenges, including the aspect of collaborative work, is important for motivation (Allchin, 2013; Hakkarainen *et.al.*, 2007; Herreid, 1994; Jonassen, 1997) as well as for authentic activity and performance (Carroll & Rossson, 2005). For case design, aspects of having or denying predefined roles for student performance within a collaborative setting address skills that are important to social performance. This includes the nature of the perspective on a case – whether it is to have a single or multiple perspectives (Allchin, 2013).

While a range of information is given in a case, the learner separates what s/he feels is the important data in order to solve tasks. So a decision about the amount of irrelevant data presented in the case is necessary, especially in the context of a learning sequence. Frank found when offering more complex and less structured cases that *"the learner built up a framework of how to go about analysing the problem and finding a solution."* (Frank, 2003:96).

To summarise this category, considerations about the learner may include reflections on his/her experience and biography, motivation, emotion, autonomy, and social relationship.

3. Category 3: Learning Assistant

Although the learner is central to Baumgartner's model, the coach/instructor/teacher remains an important aspect in (most) learning settings. Within the differentiated framework this category clearly shows the relevance of the relationship both to the learner and to the facilitator to learning: e.g. when regarding feedback processes. According to Frank (2003) the central elements of the learning process are: decisions on mediation, guidance, organisation, and control. Within the didactic design, the learning assistant may include techniques of supervision and reflection into the learning process to support the development of meta-cognition (Erpenbeck & Sauter, 2007).

4. Category 4: Learning Environment

Didactic processes are, in a metaphorical sense, special 'spaces' of meaning (Hafer *et al.*, 2010) within which learning can emerge. In a learning context, this category describes the educational conditions for learning within a predictable framework that are in the control of the participants. This includes both the subjective and objective relationships between learners and their environment in terms of time, space, content and objects. Aspects like the magnitude of a given case, and the decision to deploy real cases as historic artifacts or as contemporary cases, become relevant (Allchin, 2013). Other factors that can influence management of the learning process and the selection of learning tools will include the learning setting, the size of the class and decision to deploy real or constructed cases. In each situation the historical and cultural background will affect the didactic setting and the way the cultural foundation of the case is perceived.

Thinking about the learning outcomes leads one to a decision in epistemic orientation (Allchin, 2013): typically, learners will use existing knowledge to interpret or solve a case. Focusing on the process of research in science may also include the building up of new knowledge to complete a given task. According to Allchin (2013) this is critical to develop ideas and mental models of epistemological understanding. The decision on grading a student's performance is also an important element of the learning environment.

Learning outcomes also influence how the epistemic process is reflected on. Open ended or close-ended cases may each *"shape student motivation and an understanding of science"* (Alchin, 2013:368). Close-ended cases focus on one correct solution. With the focus on higher learning outcomes, such as more creative skills, the decision on case design might tend towards open-ended cases with multiple correct answers. This more complex design may correspond better to real-world problems in science.

5. Category 5: Non-Educational Environment

The category of non-educational environment embraces the conditions that are beyond didactic control. These will include the subjective personal conditions of learners, the prevailing cultural system, and related subsystems. Reflection on any transitions between these areas will help to frame the non-educational environment. For example, the degree to which students engage in real world settings – such as interviewing relevant professionals – will impact on defined learning outcomes. Becoming part of a research project may have impact on student's motivation and may give important insights into professional culture, especially if it concerns the profession or discipline the educational setting is intended to prepare for.

6. Category 6: Learning Tool

The rapid development of technical tools for learning situations is strongly influencing current education discourse. The possibility of offering multimedia materials by means of synchronous and/or asynchronous communication is expanding the field for CBT. Elaborated forms of learning situation using technical tools such as blended learning or flipped classroom models may help to reach the learning outcomes (Häferle & Maier-Häferle, 2010; Kerres 2012). Hafer *et al.* (2010) point out that medial spaces generated by technical learning tools support learning in CBT – particularly in coaching processes and guidance.

Using multimedia structure, cases might be presented as hypertextual case studies (Carroll & Rosson, 2005). This may support the complexity of cases that might be non-linear rather than interconnected. Additionally, video-based material presents a primarily realistic vision of a situation because it is, by definition, closely related to perception (Sobchack, 1992). Therefore, even if the situation is technically mediated it can help to support understanding.

New tools also allow new options for monitoring and evaluating the learning process to emerge. The analysis of collected data can give important insights for modifying and supporting learning situations and providing more elaborated support to the student (Siemens & Long, 2011).

7. Category 7: Learning Content

When considering the application of CBT in any particular situation the outcome of reviews of Baumgartner categories 1 to 6 will shape the design and selection of the most appropriate learning material.

Table 1 summarises 27 of the factors which I have described above and thereby comprises a tool that can help with the learning material selection process.

Didactic category	Relevant didactic decisions to CBT on learning content/ material (7)
(1) Learning challenge	• definition of learning outcomes for skill development
(2) Learner	• level of autonomy in the working process • structured/ unstructured case material • structured/ unstructured problem • relevant/ irrelevant data • selection of meaningful topic • individual /team work • non- / predefined roles in the case setting • single/ multiple perspective on the case
(3) Learning assistant	• level of mediation • level of guidance • level of control • level of supervision & meta-cognition • dimensions of feedback process
(4) learning environment	• class size • magnitude of the case • historic/ contemporary case • fictional/ non-fictional case • intended epistemic orientation • intended epistemic process

Didactic category	Relevant didactic decisions to CBT on learning content/ material (7)
(5) Non-educational environment	• level of complexity • level of conceptualization • level of engagement in environment
(6) learning tools	• level of multimedia elements • types of communication tools • types of communication forms • level of supervision with learning analytics

Table 1: factors affecting the selection of CBT learning materials and setting

5. Conclusion

Case based teaching can be viewed from many theoretical and practical perspectives. However, Baumgartner's the seven didactic categories, taken together, present a powerful analytical fragmentation of real-world situations. They offer a framework for reflection, discussion and development of case based teaching. Consideration in detail of each category provides the basis for shaping appropriate learning materials and settings in order to improve the outcomes from case based teaching.

6. About the Author

Thomas Muschal is Researcher in Online Education and Instructional Designer at Lűbeck University of Applied Sciences, Germany. He can be contacted at this email: thomas.muschal@fh-luebeck.de

Chapter nine

Students as Collaborators, Contributors and Co-creators

Margrethe Mondahl, Lisbet Pals Svendsen and Daniel Horn

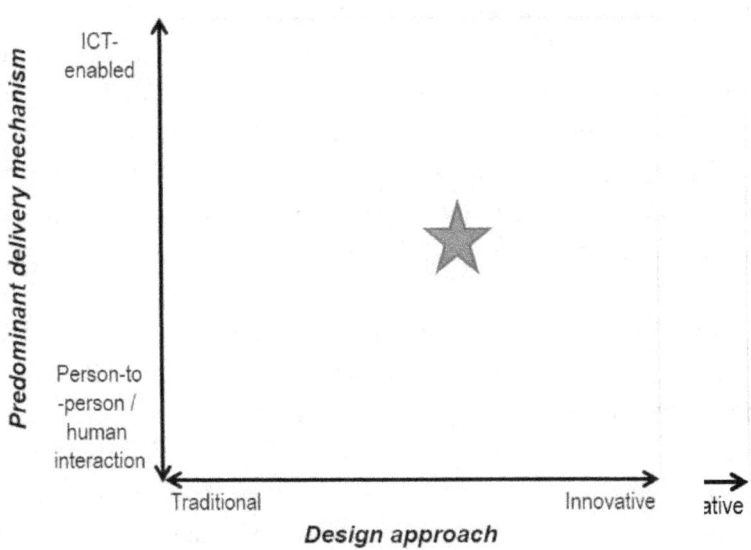

Introduction and Method

> "When students work with academic staff to develop pedagogical approaches, they gain a different angle on, and a deeper understanding of, learning." (Bovill et al. 2011:138)

ICT in the classroom changes roles. Educators will typically have a consulting and coaching role in contrast to educator authority in the traditional top-down, asymmetric teaching structure. *"The modern educator in the ICT era is no longer described as 'a sage on the stage' but a 'guide by the side'"* (Ghasemi & Hashemi, 2011:3100). This supports students' need for autonomy. According to Deci *et al.* (2001), autonomy is decisive and supports motivation, as students work out task solutions for themselves and take charge of their own learning. ICT's effect on student autonomy is supported by existing research (Duda, 2005).

This new, increasingly symmetrical, bottom-up teaching structure transforms students from passive recipients of information to active co-creators of knowledge – particularly in a case-based environment where solutions are negotiated between students. The didactic triangle is turned upside down as students actively research what needs to be learned in collaboration with other students (Mathiasen, 2008). It would appear that learning – in our case the acquisition of professional communication competences – is paradoxical in the sense that individual competences cannot be developed individually but only in interaction with others. Case-based learning and teaching (CBT) offers opportunities for active participation and ownership that distinguishes this learning format from other less student-oriented formats.

The aim of this chapter is to contribute an insight into student motivation and student learning processes based on data collected in the autumn semester 2013 at Copenhagen Business School.

The data sets stem from two groups of students at different levels in their education – (1) a group of first semester bachelor students and (2) a group of CEMS (Community of European Management Schools) masters-level students in their final year. The students in group (1) used an interactive learning platform (Podio®, at www.podio.com) throughout their course, which they used to chat with the educators with a view to solving pertinent questions in regard to their studies in order to support their learning activities. The students in group (2) used the same platform; they were invited to actively contribute to the co-creation of cases used in the classroom by means of targeted assignments in relation to a case. The role of cases was in both instances to involve students in knowledge building through active participation in order to support intrinsically motivated learning patterns.

Data Sets

Student group (1) produced two data sets: a primarily quantitative set of responses to a questionnaire regarding which course elements they considered motivating. Their responses were in some instances supported by a brief comment which constitutes supporting, qualitative data. The second data set from student group (1) consists of qualitative data from student-initiated, student-educator chats during the course. These data have been 'crunched' in a thematic analysis (Boyatzis, 1998).

Student group (2) provided a qualitative data set consisting of two elements: (a) A re-editing/co-creation activity of a case provided by the educators via the school's eLearning platform and (b) comments on the thoughts behind the re-editing/co-creation.

It should be mentioned that the student response rates are not sufficiently high to allow us to make generalisations about students' experienced motivation or interest in co-creation activities, yet the data give some indication of a direction, which may be further pursued.

Chapter Outline

The chapter falls into the following parts:

- a brief overview of current theories about student motivation, collaboration, learning and interactivity
- an outline of how interactive learning tools may be designed to facilitate student motivation, collaboration and learning
- discussion of the quantitative data collected from student group (1) in regard to motivational factors
- discussion of the thematic analysis drawn up on the basis of qualitative data from student-educator chats in student group (1), and
- consideration of students as active case co-creators drawing on two examples:

- one from student group (1) where a student with specific qualifications adjusted elements in a case used in class, and
- one from student group (2) where students re-edited a case used in class.
- summary conclusions that elicit learning points for educators in regard to the use of interactive learning tools in the adult learner classroom.

A Brief Theoretical Overview

Motivation is a well-researched area within education psychology. According to Dörnyei and Ottó: *"It is not the lack but rather the abundance of motivation theories which confuses the scene"* (Dörnyei & Ottó, 1998:118).

Dörnyei sees motivation, as expressed in the Dörnyei and Ottó's model, as a dynamic, process-oriented, time and context-dependent, psychological phenomenon (Dörnyei, 2005:84). In this, motivation is divided into three temporal phases (ibid):

- A *preactional stage* where motivation is created leading to the choice of target for the task (choice motivation)
- An *actional stage* where the target becomes concrete action (actional motivation) and the task is solved; motivation is maintained via regulatory mechanisms
- A *postactional stage* where the student looks back and evaluates how the task was solved (motivational retrospection).

Deci *et al.*'s (2001) Self-determination Theory is also relevant because it gives a general picture of the external and internal forces that guide student motivation. This theory introduces the concepts of extrinsic and intrinsic motivation as well as the three basic, inherent psychological needs: the need for autonomy, the need for relatedness and the need for competence (Deci *et al.*, 2001).

Clearly a given activity or course must make sense to the participants. If it makes sense to the student (at any given level), the student is likely to put in much more effort than if it makes sense to someone else than the student (parents, teachers etc.). We cannot of course ignore the fact that if a given activity makes sense to the parents they will have ways of encouraging or threatening the student into working. However, nothing beats the student motivation that comes from within because it makes sense to him or her! And this indeed leads to successful learning that may be repeated by the student.

According to Hermansen (2005), one dimension of student learning is the pair of concepts *"toil and exuberance"* (2005:60-70). This is also found with Dörnyei & Skehan (2003:614) who say that *"motivation is responsible for why people decide to do something, how long they are willing to sustain the activity, and how hard they are going to pursue it"*. Thus, in order to select the appropriate didactic tools, it is necessary to look at the students' motives for *why, how long* and *how hard*. Dörnyei & Skehan (2003) add that

> *"... motivation to learn in educational settings has another significant aspect, namely the important role played by 'time' in it. During the lengthy process of learning to master certain subject matters, motivation does not remain constant, but is associated with dynamically changing and evolving mental process, characterized by constant (re)appraisal and balancing of the various internal and external influences that the individual is exposed to".* Dörnyei & Skehan (2003:617)

Dörnyei & Skehan's point about constant (re)appraisal corresponds well with both the philosophy of learning loops (Nygaard & Bramming, 2008) and Hermansen's concepts of feedback/feedforward (Hermansen, 2005:43-47).

Dörnyei & Skehan's 'why' dimension points towards the types of learning that can be seen as instrumental in empowering the students: surface vs. deep learning (Biggs, 2003). Biggs (2003:11) states that students create knowledge via learning activities and their 'approaches to learning'. The outcome of the latter will depend on whether students aim at merely passing a particular test by being able to reproduce facts – surface learning – or whether they go below the surface to interpret and investigate – deep learning. From a motivation perspective we draw the theoretical conclusion that surface learning and extrinsic motivation go hand in hand, as do deep learning and intrinsic motivation.

As stated by Geyer *et al.* (2008), contextual collaboration seamlessly integrates content sharing, communication channels and collaboration tools into a unified user experience that enables new levels of productivity. Web 2.0 applications integrated into learning platforms may be used to develop innovative techniques for collaborative working processes and learning. This is in itself beneficial to student learning because it requires students to verbalise their understandings of a given topic being scrutinised. Additionally, empirical research (Barrows, 1998) has already emphasised that collaborative learning is beneficial because it leads to engagement in productive processes of knowledge construction.

Personal knowledge management becomes possible just as individualisation together with collaboration, whenever this is called for, becomes a motivating factor that enhances knowledge acquisition, deep learning and student performance. It enables learners to optimise their management of knowledge through reflection upon their knowledge during the creative process. Finally, it is particularly interesting in terms of the acquisition of communicative competences, because the acquisition of effective problem-solving, team skills and self-directed learning is probably more important than the content learned (Barrows, 1998:631).

Following Ryberg *et al.* (2011), we view learning in this context as falling into two competence dimensions – interpersonal and individual – depending on what competence areas are being acquired. Research in a previous project, where data was interpreted by means of a Categorical Principal Component Analysis (Mondahl *et al.*, 2013), documents that when it comes to communicative competence acquisition, interpersonal competences contain items of learning that are primarily acquired in interaction with others through negotiation, e.g. dialogue, cultural understanding and terminology. On the other hand, individual competences contain items related to correctness, which are primarily acquired individually. Between them, these two competence dimensions constitute the most significant ingredient in the concept 'action competence', This can be defined as the communicative language competence and (inter)cultural awareness, the speaker uses to participate in linguistic activities in a foreign/second language with a view to producing and/or receiving text in relation to themes within specific domains in such a way that the communication serves the purpose of the participants without significant misunderstanding. Therefore action competence enables students to navigate relatively seamlessly in intercultural contexts. Since the aim is to facilitate this seamless navigation, case based teaching (CBT) – with the ensuing possibility for individual as well as group-based work – serves as a vital tool in the development of action competence.

In connection with the use of interactive learning tools and Information and Communications Technologies (ICT) in the classroom, student comments point to the positive aspects of ICT that make themselves felt in knowledge-sharing and collaborative learning processes. These support the development of students' interpersonal competences, not only in class but also on a meta level, where the students learn to navigate in interaction with others and develop learning methods that are replicable in other contexts (Ryberg *et al.*, 2011).

Previous studies have shown that in the selection of ICT tools for use in the classroom, educators should strive to select tools that support students in their individual learning effort to allow them to function well in a collective process such as CBT:

"The focus on learning processes and the increased value given to students taking responsibility for their own learning processes, facilitated by the use of ICT tools, will give students a broader meta perspective on learning in general and their own learning processes in particular by enabling them to enter into collaboration with others in various settings and giving them the tools required to support their own individual learning processes. This means that they will be able to contribute higher quality input

into the collective knowledge construction, knowledge sharing and knowledge retention of the group of which they are part." (Svendsen, 2012:70).

Interactive Learning Tools Design

"Motivation is an issue that needs to be understood in order to be properly addressed in the classroom, e.g. via social-media enhanced learning platforms. Still, the introduction of such tools in the classroom inevitably leads to changing roles – a shift in the 'balance of power' where students are being empowered and [the] educators' role becomes more that of a mentor or coach as students are offered an increasing degree of personalization and individualization of the learning tools and processes." (Svendsen & Mondahl, 2013:262).

An e-learning platform needs to motivate the student to use it, and one way to do that is by making it attractive to use. A web based e-learning platform should follow guidelines by leading usability and design experts. Jared Spool is one of them.

According to Spool *et al.* (1999, 2004) and LeBlanc (2011), the basic principles for interactive learning tools design are that:

- Intuitive design is invisible
- Intuitive design is personal
- Intuitive design focuses on user experience
- Design should allow for embraceable change.

LeBlanc (2011) expands these points as follows:

"An important concept when striving for intuitive design is the Knowledge Gap. Spool said to imagine an escalator going up. At the very top are the people who actually built the tool in question. Beneath them is the point called the Target Knowledge, or what the user needs to know to get their tasks done in this tool. Below that are the users, who have what's referred to as their Current Knowledge." (LeBlanc, 2011)

Podio was used as the eLearning platform used in the two classrooms studied. We will therefore compare Podio to the above principles with a view to identifying the ways in which Podio handles the issue of intuitive design.

1. Intuitive Design is Invisible.

"The first is that an intuitive design lets users focus on a task, not the design" (Spool, 2011). Hence the essential point is to create a tool that is useful, which enables the user to accomplish the task at hand, not good looks.

Podio uses the same style all over the platform, but few colours. Also, Podio allows for some degree of individualisation of the screen, but not a complete remake.

2. Intuitive Design is Personal.

Users are different, and what might make sense for one user, might not make sense for the next.

Podio uses many elements from the social media platforms such as Twitter and Facebook, which makes it easy to understand for most people using these platforms already. Podio also allows to chatting and commenting and individualization.

3. Intuitive Design Focuses on User Experience

According to Spool (2011) it is important to focus on user experience instead of focusing on features. The problem with adding too many features is that the knowledge gap will be much wider than if the platform focuses on making few features work really well.

Podio has a core feature, the App Builder, which the developers keep on improving – this is a clear choice aimed at reducing the number of features, making the platform easier to understand and use.

4. Designing for Embraceable Change

Changes and updates to a platform are not always a good idea. As stated by Spool (2011): *"... a user's goal isn't a better system. A user's goal is to accomplish things."*

Podio's expressed mission statement is to offer a tool that enables users to *"Work the way you want"*. As Podio write on their website:

> *"You decide how to structure your projects, teams and workflows by creating your own workspaces and sharing them with relevant people. You also decide how to structure, create and present content and information that's linked to your work processes and interactions. You do this by choosing from hundreds of Podio's specialized work apps or creating your own to help you get the job done – whatever it is." (www.Podio.com)*

What Do Students Say about Motivation?

> *"If students experience engaging learning and study methods that facilitate student learning, rather than tests and exams, they develop a more comfortable role as partners in their own learning project. [...] This will lead to students defining themselves as community members rather than pupils or customers." (Löfvall & Nygaard, 2013:142).*

The quotation illustrates the ideal situations that most educators are striving for. However, reality is sometimes different from what the theory predicts.

Figure 1 below shows student responses to the questionnaire about motivating course elements given to student group (1). A total of 27 students responded, and the questionnaire allowed the participants to tick off all the elements that they found motivating (quantitative data). In addition to this, students were asked to rank the three factors they personally found most motivating and they could add comments (qualitative data).

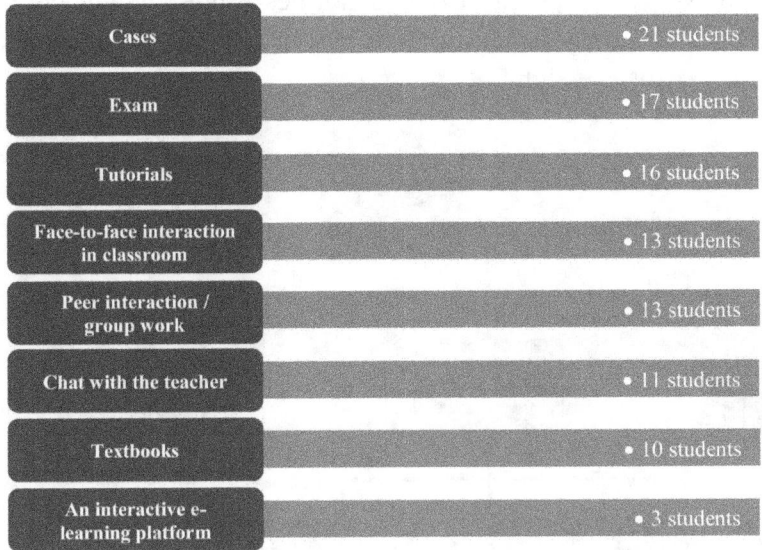

Figure 1: Student group (1), questionnaire responses, motivating course elements.

The figure shows that students rank case work as the most rewarding activity, closely followed by the exam and the tutorials - this makes sense since the tutorials were held as exam preparation. Peer interaction/group work and face-to-face interaction in the classroom rank as No. 4 with approximately half of the students finding these activities motivating. Chat with the teacher is ranked No. 5, whereas textbooks and the use of an interactive eLearning platform are the least popular.

These numbers fall well in line with Löfvall and Nygaard's (2013) observations of the use of engaging learning and study methods – to which category case-based activities clearly belong. However, an interesting (and perhaps slightly demotivating for the educators) point is that the respondents in this study rank the exam as No. 2. This could be interpreted as a conflict between intrinsic and extrinsic motivation, where case based work is usually seen as intrinsically motivating, whereas the exam is usually considered extrinsically motivated. This is illustrated in the below Figure 2, which is based on Deci *et al.*

(2001) and where we position the 'headlines' under which we can group the student responses to our questionnaire according to their intrinsic or extrinsic weight.

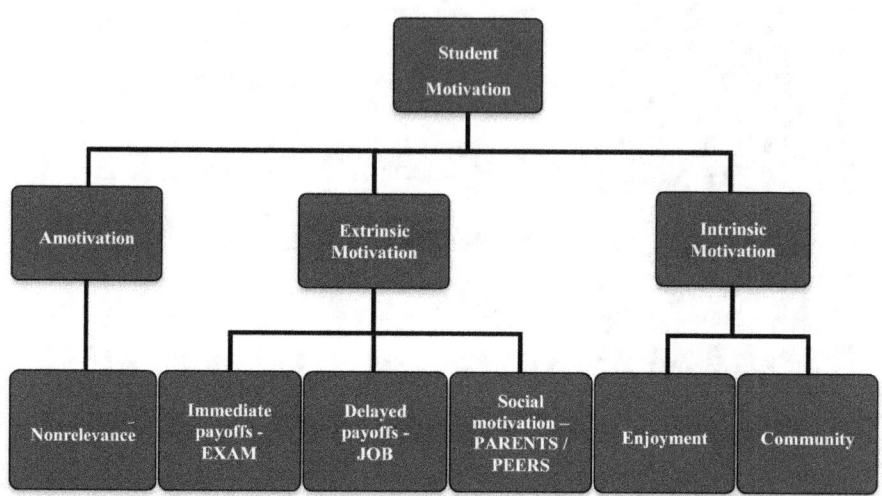

Figure 2: Student motivation (authors' design, based on Deci et al., 2001).

As illustrated in Figure 2, students may take different motivational approaches to learning in concrete contexts from amotivation to intrinsic motivation, where ludic elements of learning are in play and the community and involvement factors are prominent as levers in learning.

In regard to the students' weighting of the various motivational course elements, we note a certain balance between the extrinsic motivator – exam – and the intrinsic motivator – enjoyment and community. Here it could be argued that the extrinsic motivators are more an individual matter while intrinsic motivators are more interpersonal. This suggests that parallels may be drawn between student motivation and student learning aspects. In fact, this is supported by Löfvall and Nygaard (2013) when they suggest that students define themselves as community members rather than pupils or customers, just as it can be seen as a step towards the 'student-as-producer' role (Dobozy, 2011).

However, a methodological issue in the survey formulation of options arises here. We cannot know for sure that students interpret 'motivation' in the same way as Deci *et al.* (2001) and responses may therefore be less valid as regards students voting for 'exam' rather than 'participating in the case discussion'. That would mean that students are perhaps, after all, more intrincically motivated that the data set suggests. As one student in the data puts it:

"... the cases combined with group work are great factors of motivation, since you during the group discussions about the cases test your knowledge and figure out where you can improve your skills. Furthermore it strengthens your capabilities to actually apply the introduced theories in a practical perspective." (Student comment, BA student, questionnaire 2013).

Other studies (e.g. Sprogkernen II as reported in Mondahl *et al.*, 2013) support the above claim that interpersonal learning activities are intrinsically motivating, whereas individually orientated learning activities tend to be more extrinsically motivating in the context of exams and grades. As stated by Ashfield *et al.* (2013:76): *"Much student work is extrinsically motivated by compulsory assessment".*

A lesson to be drawn from this could be that in future educators will need to ensure a balance between extrinsically and intrinsically motivating factors and between interpersonally and individually orientated learning activities to support the 'student-as-producer' notion, thus moving learning outcomes from surface to deep learning (Biggs, 2003). This notion is supported by one of our respondents:

"The assignment - Look into a specific case and connect it to the theories we have learnt. This was very interesting and this was the part where I think I learned most. The exam - Preparation for the oral exams. Practice my communication skills and be able to speak, argument and discuss on behalf of my assignment is very motivating and exciting." (Student comment, BA student, questionnaire 2013).

Thematic Analysis: Student-Educator Chats

"Social media such as blogs, forums and wikis [....] can enhance the communication between students and teachers, and it can create an atmosphere and collegial workplace where teachers, researchers and students share ideas and knowledge with each other." (Löfvall & Nygaard, 2013:143).

"One of the things that I find most interesting and motivating is a course where it is possible to enter into a discussion with the instructors. Being able to interact in a personal discussion is an aspect worth taking into consideration." (Student comment to 'chat with the teacher', questionnaire 2013).

In an attempt to explore student motivation further we conducted a thematic analysis of the qualitative data in the student-initiated student-educator chats. This was to identify if student-educator dialogue facilitated through the chat can be considered a motivational add-on by clearing up points of doubt that students encounter and which could, if unaddressed, lead to amotivation. Figure 3 depicts this thematic analysis.

Figure 3: Thematic analysis of topics in student-educator chats, 2013.

Figure 3 shows that the most prominent topic is that of the case-based exam report (written in groups), closely followed by questions on the oral exam (individual defence of report), which shows us that the extrinsically motivated factor which is most prominent - the exam - triggers the most anxious questions in the students. This indicates that the students are proactive in terms of clearing away obstacles that they perceive as choke-points in their learning processes.

Overall, we can see from the thematic analysis that the questions raised by the students *vis-a-vis* the educators are primarily of a practical nature focusing on formal requirements and other questions about the exam as well as questions in regard to the use of the Podio interface. They do not to any significant degree pertain to course content or points of learning, except for very few questions/comments (represented by the Miscellaneous bullet in Figure 3).

Questions of this nature were primarily dealt with face-to-face either durings breaks between lessons or in the tutorial sessions. However, the quantitative data do point towards a different student perception of what contributes to their learning process; in short, that case work and face-to-face interaction are strongly motivating factors. Nevertheless, the student-educator chats are only part of the ICT-mediated learning processes because the educators do not have access to students' group chats and online discussions in online forums such as Facebook or GoogleDocs. Such private learning spaces may very well house in-depth discussions of case-related questions and problem-solving.

Case Co-Creation

> *"Firstly, students might experience increased autonomy and independence because social-media learning environments promote collaboration and group work, thus making the students engage actively in the teaching. Secondly, the passive learning structure will be limited or perhaps even absent. The students go from being passive recipients of information to active co-creators of knowledge." (Lenstrup, 2013:31).*

In an attempt to activate students as case co-creators, both student groups were invited to contribute comments and ideas and possibly re-written cases. In student group (1), only one student availed himself of this opportunity since he had prior, professional knowledge of the topic area of one case and was able to supplement some of the technical information in the case with more precise terms.

Student group (2) was given a case designed by the educators specifically for their course. One group of students took up the challenge and contributed a re-written version of the case. Here is what they said about their reasons for the changes (with keywords highlighted by us):

- *"When working on the case study in class we had the feeling that too much of the answer was already given away in the case. I.e., which problems the team members had with each other. Thus, we tried to make it more **challenging** and open the case for **more discussion** among the students".*

- *"We felt that it was difficult to relate to the characters, so we gave them **names**."*

- *"We tried to add a social network analysis dimension to the case, as we thought that this could be a **good tool** to 'map' the relationship between the team members. Here you could also introduce the students to social network theory in the class to give them (maybe) new perspective on how people work together and why there might be difficulties. (I had a very interesting class on social network theory with Louise Mors at CBS, maybe she would want to come to speak.)"*

- *"In the tasks given at the end we tried to force the students to engage in a role play. As the seminar is not graded we felt that <u>there needs to be a little more pressure to make the students engaged</u>."*

- *"In general, we thought that the first class of the seminar was not teaching us anything new. Thus, we tried to **add a different angle** to the case. The CEMS students that take*

> *the seminar are mostly in their 2nd master year and have heard about cultural distance many times. This is not to say that they cannot learn more, but **it should look interesting to them**."*

As can be seen from the student comments on the changes made to the case, also these students focus on the interpersonal learning dimensions/intrinsically motivating factors (highlighted in **bold**) as well as on individual learning dimensions/extrinsically motivating factors (highlighted in <u>*underlined italics*</u>).

Tying this to Lenstrup (2013) and Dobozy (2011), the outcome of our case co-creation exercise supports the notion that given the proper degree of autonomy, relevant input and a learning environment that supports and encourages interaction, students will progress from passively receiving a case assignment - student-as-customer - to actively revising, re-editing, adding and co-creating learning materials, and becoming students-as-producers. In this process, students draw on meta-knowledge from other learning situations, just as they are prompted to seek and process new knowledge in order to understand the problem at hand and contribute to the solution.

Going Forward

> *"Moreover, students need to be willing risk-takers, learn to cope with ambiguity and embrace the possibility of mistake-making as a necessary learning step. In this way they develop and practice a collection of skills and knowledge, assume identities and test personal values that form the transformative framework of the student-producer" (Dobozy, 2011:20).*

According to the theory, students will be motivated by peer interaction, autonomy, creating own learning trajectories and the opportunity to reflect on the knowledge taken in. However, our data suggest that parallel to these motivating factors, we should not ignore the fact that exams play a very important role in student motivation. From an educator's point of view this is unfortunate since in this situation the extrinsic motivation is dominant and takes away the focus from the whole point of learning – which in this context should be understanding, re-interpreting and re-using knowledge in new contexts in businesses and organisations.

Nevertheless, our thematic analysis pertaining to aspects of the exam report tells us that students want to know about formal requirements, problem statements, contents and subjects, theory and structure – all points of learning. So the lines are indeed blurred!

About the Authors

Margrethe Smedegaard Mondahl is Associate Professor, PhD, Department of International Business Communication, Copenhagen Business School. She can be contacted at this email: mm.ibc@cbs.dk

Lisbet Pals Svendsen is associate professor at the Department of International Business Communication (IBC) at Copenhagen Business School, Denmark. She can be contacted at this email: lps.ibc@cbs.dk

Daniel Horn is CEO at Phases, a Danish web and communications agency. He can be contacted at this email: dh@phases.dk

Chapter ten

Representation: Objectivity and Artistry for Trainee Lawyers

Nigel Duncan

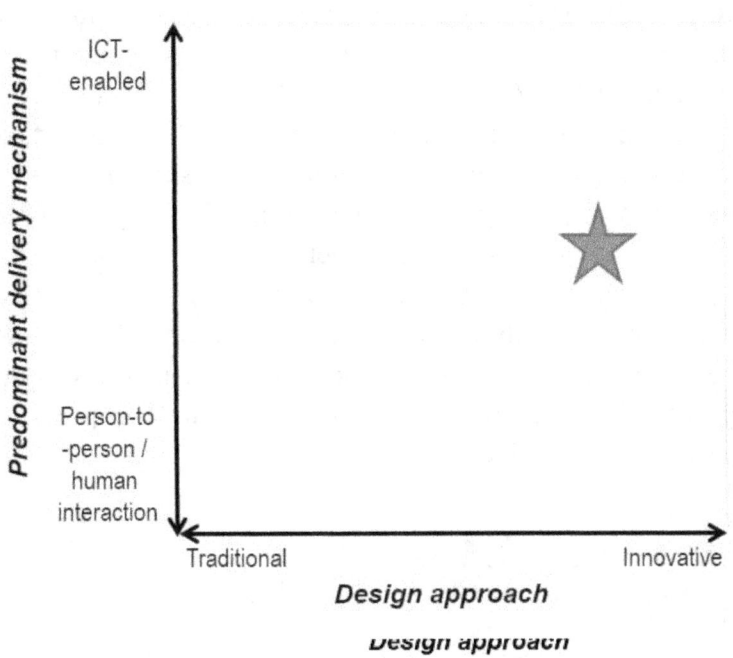

Introduction

Much of the academic study of law in the UK is based on the analysis of appellate court decisions, the rationale behind which constitutes the material of the developing common law. Students are asked to read legislation and the major cases which had interpreted it in order to develop their understanding of the law. They demonstrate that understanding either through essays – discussions of the principles engaged – or by answering problems. These are usually case studies with a given set of facts and instructions to advise one of the parties. This has been the main conventional use of case studies in legal education. They are used both as assignments and as topics for tutorial and seminar discussion.

This chapter will present a use of cases by City Law School, London (CLS), which seeks to take seriously the task of preparing students who have studied in this academic manner for the demands of practice. The case demonstrated is used on the Bar Professional Training Course (BPTC), the one-year postgraduate programme which follows the undergraduate degree and which is required for entry to the Bar of England & Wales (i.e. to become a barrister). The curriculum is tightly laid down by the Bar Standards Board (BSB, 2013). Students learn legal research and case analysis, foundation skills for a number of practice skills: advocacy, conference skills, drafting and opinion writing, all of which are assessed by practical case-based activities. In addition they learn the law of evidence, civil and criminal procedure, professional ethics and alternative dispute resolution, all of which are assessed by a mixture of multiple-choice and short answer questions. CLS is one of a small number of law schools offering this programme in an extremely competitive environment.

Approach to Use of Cases

Content

Factual situations are carefully designed so that the content draws out the issues and the challenges on which learning is to focus. This follows Shulman's (1992) definition of what a case is:

> *"To call something a case is to make a theoretical claim. It argues that the story, event, or text is an instance of a larger class, an example of a broader category. In a word, it is a "case-of-something" and therefore merits more serious consideration than*

a simple anecdote or vignette. It implies an underlying taxonomy or typology, however intuitive or informal, to which a given case belongs." (Shulman, 1992:17)

When used as simple individual assignments the case study relies on its content to enable learning. However, when used as a basis for class discussion its scope is greatly increased. Shulman, talking of the Harvard Business School tradition, notes that case studies in business education rely on the central role of the skilled teacher directing the discussion: *"There is no case method of teaching in the business school without group discussion conducted by a skillful teacher."* (Shulman, 1992:10).

Discussion

The discussion element of the use of cases is crucial to their value in student learning. Levin, writing in the context of teacher education, says:

"[w]e know that the discussion of the case is an important factor in promoting the development of teachers' thinking about cases. Case discussions appear to be especially valuable for student teachers and beginning teachers because they can lead to clearer, more elaborated understandings about the issues in cases. Furthermore, case discussions may be a catalyst for recognising the need to change or articulate one's thinking. For experienced in-service teachers case discussions also appear to have the potential to foster reflection and promote metacognitive thinking." (Levin, 1995:74)

Similar value may be expected in exposing the student lawyer to cases. There is also evidence to suggest that appropriate experiential learning methods may also encourage reflection in students as well as in experienced practitioners (Maughan & Webb, 2005:34-53). We can thus plan and design the class discussion with awareness of the stages of learning of our students and with different learning goals in mind.

Problem Solving

The practice of law is problem-solving. Kunselman and Johnson's research into the use of active learning techniques with case studies in the criminal justice field suggests *"the use of cases facilitates the accumulation of knowledge and allows students to progress from conceptualisation to application. Integrating case studies will provide well-rounded critical thinkers, which, in turn, will result in students becoming better informed."* (Kunselman & Johnson, 2004:92). Their techniques involved role-play followed by discussion and privileged cognitive development over skill development. Their approach approach – which effectively converts a case study (as defined by Schulman, 1992) into a teaching case study – is widespread in undergraduate legal education and, where effectively used, does develop the critical thinkers sought. The approach requires some development in its application to the professional courses and this is facilitated by the design of the case in the way presented below.

Role Play and Simulation

The role-play approach to active learning promoted by Kunselman and Johnson (2004:87-88) has been considerably developed in legal education. This is explained by Burridge, who describes the simulation clinic as *"a laboratory in which law in its practised and professional context can be studied."* (Burridge, 1998:181). This involves applying the insights of Schön (1987) that there is a false dualism between knowing and doing and that an approach that engages students in the complexities of practice will develop deeper and more contextual learning of what students need to understand (Burridge, 1998:181-2). For most law students *"the problem on paper is conventionally stripped of the uncertainties, emotions and interactions that arise in the lawyer's office, police station or courtroom."* (Burridge, 1998:181). The value of realistic activities is widely recognised in legal education. As Johnstone, using a social constructivist analysis, explains: *"To learn effectively students ... need opportunities to learn about law in 'real settings', to develop a personal interpretation of those learning experiences, and to collaboratively negotiate meaning."* (Johnstone, 2011:4).

Schön (1987) presents a process for developing 'reflection in action' through which we can learn from a realistic experience of legal problems. Through a reiterative process, we develop a degree of artistry, encompassing technical knowledge, experience, imagination and creativity. We can experience the consequences of failures of objectivity and empathy. This concept of artistry in legal education has been most fully explored by Webb (1995) and theorised by Maharg (2007). It can help to address the affective domain (Maharg & Maughan, 2011) and particularly its significance for developing ethical professional behaviour (Duncan, 2011). It leads us to develop case problems which engage students through different activities, sometimes working together, sometimes undertaking opposed roles, with opportunities for discussing the law, procedural, evidential and costs constraints, and for practising their developing skills.

Limitations of Case Studies

Limitations that are common to case studies are identified by Grupe and Kay. They may be summarised as:

- Cases may embed author biases so that one solution appears clearly to be the only one viable;
- Cases are limited in their scope, not providing the wealth of information which may be available in practice;
- Cases tend to focus on the perspective of one person, ignoring the interests of secondary players;
- Students tend to be given a neutral role and even where they are participants they are able to ignore the interests of others affected. (Grupe & Kay, 2000:123-4)

Grupe and Kay propose the use of incremental cases to address these limitations. This is the approach adopted both in the overall programme design and the design of the specific case presented below. The risk of author bias is addressed by the teachers working in teams to deliver the course to a cohort of some 350 students and meeting regularly to discuss all aspects of how the cases work, making revisions as appropriate.

Programme Design

The CLS BPTC is informed by constructivist design principles. Philips (1995) identifies three constructivist approaches: the active learner, the social learner and the creative learner. The first recognises that knowledge and understanding are best acquired actively; the second that they are best socially constructed; the third that they are created or recreated by the learner (Perkins, 1999:7). The design of the CLS programme adopts the first two perspectives more than the third, indeed, the social interaction embedded into its classes and learning method is integral to its approach to active learning.

The BPTC is highly integrated. Students have three or four Large Group Sessions weekly, but the core of their learning is through six streams of Small Group Sessions. Three of these address the skills and knowledge required for criminal practice, the other three similarly address civil practice. Each group sees the same tutor regularly for each stream, but classes in that stream may differ significantly from each other. In Civil Stream 1, in which the chosen case study is used, students learn the skills of legal research, analysis, drafting, opinion writing and advocacy, and to apply the procedural rules, rules of evidence and professional ethics. The course team decided to devise individual case studies which could be used for all these learning objectives over a sequence of classes. This was designed to achieve a number of goals.

At the simplest level we wanted to reduce the number of new fact patterns students had to learn. The workload on this course is heavy and we work with cases that are not pre-digested summaries of the relevant facts, but with realistic sets of papers that may be quite voluminous. The extra burden of working with four or more sets of papers each week was untenable. The positive consequences of this decision were, however, extensive.

Case Papers, not Case Studies

The decision to create cases provided with realistic bundles of relevant documents had been taken at the time the Bar course was first devised. Research had shown that the previous training for the Bar had not adequately prepared students for pupillage and practice (Johnston & Shapland, 1990). One element of that problem was the failure to ensure an experiential shift from law student to legal professional. Undergraduate law students focus on developing an understanding of the law itself. Where that is developed through problem questions, the facts tend to be given. They are not questioned. However, the reality of practice is that facts are slippery – partly because they are likely to be contested and partly because of the unreliability of those reporting them. Students must learn to inhabit the literary concept of the 'unreliable narrator'. Our concern was to develop students' understanding of that truth experientially.

The goals sought in the design of this programme can be summarised as:

- Introduction to the slippery nature of facts;
- Integration of a variety of skills with learning of law and procedure;
- Students develop objectivity by representing different parties;
- Students are faced with ethical dilemmas;
- Skills are developed in different contexts through a spiral curriculum;
- Learning is experiential and addresses both cognitive and affective domains;
- A high degree of constructive alignment.

The *Pemberton* Case

This is presented from the perspective of a student studying the course, with occasional comments from the tutor's perspective, shown in italics.

Analysis Class

We have been given a set of papers that we will work on over a period of several weeks. The dispute arises from a contract to replace the doors and windows in a large Victorian house. The Claimant, the owner of the house, had various discussions with the Defendant, who is a specialist designer and maker of doors and windows. Some of these were face-to-face and others on the telephone. Finally, an estimate was received from the Defendant that states the bare bones of the contract, but does not contain the detail of what was agreed orally. There is limited written evidence of what was discussed in the form of notes and diagrams. The Claimant and Defendant each have significantly different recollections of what was agreed orally.

We have been instructed to advise the Claimant, and the papers we have been given only provide his perspective on the case, but include a letter from the Defendant denying some of his arguments. In essence, the claimant is unhappy with a number of aspects for the work that was done and is refusing to pay the second half of the contract price. He also wants either to get his money back or to have the cost of putting right all the things he is unhappy with. The defendant denies that he is in breach of the agreement and he wants the unpaid money (nearly £50,000). We have been given blank grids to help us to analyse the facts, to link the factual issues with the legal principles and to identify gaps in the evidence. We were asked to come to the first class with completed grids and ready to discuss all the issues that arose. That did clarify some of the uncertainties so that we all had a common understanding of the facts and the law. We then had to go away and write our first barrister's Opinion, so that we could bring a hard copy to the next class. We had also received advice on opinion writing in a lecture and we have been given an Opinion Writing Manual (Duncan & Wolfgarten, 2012) and other guidance on Moodle, the online BPTC course site.

Opinion Writing Moodle Exercise

Before the next class we were directed to an exercise on Moodle *[Modular Object-Oriented Dynamic Learning Environment; our elearning platform]* that helped us with structuring our Opinion in a coherent way and with identifying the issues on which we should provide our client with clear conclusions. We were to use this exercise as a basis for writing our first full Opinion on the course.

Opinion Writing Class

This class started with discussion of how we might structure an Opinion. The tutor then spent most of the class taking our opinions in turns and projecting parts of them on the screen. This, while initially a frightening prospect, provides the whole class with the opportunity to learn from constructive peer critiquing. We were asked to give feedback to each other, the tutor sometimes agreeing and sometimes suggesting different ways of doing things. This addressed writing in good grammatical English as well as making sure we expressed ourselves concisely and did not include unnecessary material. The main focus was on giving clear advice and making sure that we stated clear conclusions and supported them by articulating the arguments we had developed. We were also expected to give practical advice such as what procedural steps needed to be taken and how gaps in the evidence might be filled. At the end of the class we were given a suggested Opinion that was colour-coded to demonstrate the functions of different sentences and paragraphs. It had a commentary which explained why each part was written as it was.

[Tutor's comment] *Thus we integrate students' learning of how to apply the law to a realistic factual situation with the skill of Opinion Writing, addressing not only analytical and writing skills but also encouraging them to think how they might give practical advice such as identifying gaps in the evidence and how they might be filled, and alerting the solicitor to procedural steps that must be taken.*

The discussion that takes place in these classes represents the requirement of discussion that was identified by Kunselman and Johnson (2004) as essential for the success of the case study method.

Conference and Mediation Class

The third *Pemberton* class was very different. The story had moved on. Half of us had to change sides. I was representing the Defendant, so for the first time I was thinking about the problem from his point of view. The aim was to meet the other side in mediation and try to come to a settlement of the dispute. We were told to prepare to play the role either of the lawyer, the client or the mediator. When we got to the class we were divided into smaller groups and assigned our respective roles. The clients and mediators were given fresh sheets of paper containing instructions personal to them. Initially the mediators went off in a huddle to work out how best to carry out their role. Meanwhile the rest of us carried out a conference with the client. The clients had new information that was not in our papers and details of their financial circumstances that we had not known. They were both pretty upset, for different reasons, and this made it hard to get the information out. Half way through the conference the tutor interrupted with a fax from our instructing solicitors telling us what costs had been incurred so far and how much it was anticipated to cost if we ended up in a full trial. The full costs were scary, providing us with a glimpse of the position that parties are in while contemplating the choice between Alternative Dispute Resolution (ADR) and litigation.

The tutor stopped us and moved to role-play a mediation. The initial session was in plenary, with the tutor taking the role of mediator and introducing the process. We then had to make opening statements. Most of the remainder of the class was then involved in our working in caucuses with the students playing mediators going between us and seeing if they could help us to settle. We managed to settle some elements of it but not all.

[Tutor's comment] *The mediation role-play is not, in the limited time available, fully realistic. However, it introduces students, in an experiential way, to the different types of oral communication they need to master: communication as legal representative with an upset client, with an opponent and with a mediator; and as a mediator to try to bring opposed parties together. Plenary reflective discussions through the tutor seek to draw attention to the differences involved and to bring students' attention to the importance of empathy and understanding the significance of the affective domain.*

Drafting Class

We did not manage to settle, so our next task, all acting for the Claimant again, was to draft Particulars of Claim. Drafting is incredibly precise and technical. You must pay great attention to structure, ensuring that you cover everything but also write concisely and include nothing that is not relevant. As with opinion writing, we have been given guidance in lectures, a Manual (Emmet, 2012) and exercises on Moodle to help us with structure. We have to bring printed copies of our draft to the class and, as with opinion writing, after some time discussing structure, the tutor put these up on the screen and we were encouraged to critique each others' work. At the end of the class we received a suggested draft with an explanatory commentary.

Advocacy Class

This is different again. The claim went in but it seems that the Defendant was suffering from depression and was in a clinic for help with it. So he missed the deadline for submitting a defence and the

Claimant has requested and received a default judgment in his favour. Now the Defendant has applied to get that default judgment set aside. The class is divided into two categories, those acting for the Claimant or the Defendant. I have been asked to exchange roles again, so I am representing the Claimant and trying to resist having that judgment set aside.

Before the class we have to draft a 'skeleton argument'. This is a document which we give to the judge and our opponent before the hearing so that they can see the essence of what we are going to present to the court and to help us to make a persuasive submission. We have to bring two copies along to the class, one for us and one for the judge. We also have to bring along a White Book (Jackson, 2013). This is the Civil Procedure Rules, plus a commentary. There are two volumes of it, each over 3,000 pages, and we are supposed to make active use of it as it lays out all the powers of the court and the criteria the judge should consider in exercising any discretion. We are advised to mark our copy of it up with tabs and highlighters so that we can easily find the material we need.

This is our eighth advocacy class if we include those in criminal and civil cases. We work in a half group of six people. We are each allocated a specific part of the argument to present and our performance is recorded on our flash drive so that we build up a visible portfolio of our advocacy work. The tutor takes the role of the judge and we have to persuade him or her to find in favour of our client. The most challenging part is where they make an 'intervention' in the form of a judicial question, mid-way through our submission. This is designed to see whether we can think on our feet as well as present a prepared argument and a lot of people find it particularly difficult.

One of us is asked to give peer feedback, normally focusing on some aspect of delivery. We then get the main feedback from the tutor. The recording runs throughout this time so that we can play it back later. We are encouraged to go down later to recording rooms where we can attempt the performance again (working with friends and playing the judge for each other) to try to improve on the particular issues that were identified.

[Tutor's comment] *Advocacy classes run throughout the programme across both criminal and civil streams. They total 24 in all and are of progressive difficulty across the whole year. Students are encouraged to develop a reflective practice whereby the reiterations in different contexts build a high level of competence. The e-portfolio described acts as a learning log to assist student reflection. All advocacy tutors are trained and accredited by the Advocacy Training Council.*

Tutors are required to make an appropriate intervention with each student. These are judged in the light of the level of competence (and confidence) of the individual student. Thus a student making a very basic error (failing, for example, to provide evidence to support an assertion of fact) the intervention may well be a simple request for that evidence. A student doing everything very well will face a much more challenging intervention. The goal in both cases is to provide appropriate stretching and to force the individual to think on her feet rather than simply presenting something prepared beforehand.

Advocacy from a Different Perspective

This is the final class in the sequence. I am representing the Defendant again, and this time there has been a dispute about the documents that are to be used as evidence in the case. The Claimant has applied for disclosure of a number of documents that my client either says do not exist, or has reasons for not wanting to disclose. My task is to resist that application for disclosure. Once again we have to prepare a skeleton argument (much better organised and written now – this is our fourth skeleton to draft and, with the third, tutors took them in and returned them later with detailed feedback).

[Tutor's comment] *This third 'submissions to the judge' class (using another case, not Pemberton) is dealt with differently from others. Students have individual appointments with the tutor and have a longer opportunity to perform than normal. They receive feedback and are also given an indication of how well their performance would have been judged had it been a summative assessment. Tutors take in their skeleton arguments and take the time to give students detailed written feedback on them with constructive suggestions as to how best to improve.*

The class operated much as other advocacy classes have done. This time, however, a lot of the basic issues, such as learning not to read a script and to make sure that you are maintaining eye-contact with the judge, have been addressed. We have learnt to think through what decisions the judge will need to take, the order in which s/he has to take them and the information required to take them. That helps with structuring the skeleton argument that then gives you the structure for your submission. I can annotate my copy of the skeleton argument to remind me of particular things I want to stress. The tricky bit is always when the judge stops you and asks you something you were not planning to deal with then. I have learnt not to blurt out the first thing that comes into my head. I stop and think and if it is something I have prepared for I can check where it is in my skeleton argument and take the judge there. I'm back in control again. Of course, if it is something I had not prepared for at all, it is one of those awful moments that the tutor calls a 'learning opportunity'.

Now that we have finished the whole series of classes on *Pemberton* I feel that I have a better idea of how a civil dispute operates, and why it can be so dreadfully expensive to allow it to go to litigation. We have had the costs aspects drummed into us throughout and I think that if I were to go back to the mediation session again after this experience, I would be much stronger in advising my client about the advantages of settling. Going through the different stages of the case has also given a better practical angle to our learning than if we were to deal with a set of papers for solely one class and then file it away.

[Tutor's comment] *You may recall that students may have several tutorials in a week, each involving work on different cases and problems. Thus we are able to emulate the work of a real practitioner who will be undertaking more than one case at a time. We are also able to integrate the work in the different streams to build skills, knowledge, understanding and the ability to combine them to achieve the best possible advice and representation for the client.*

A Spiral Curriculum

The *Pemberton* classes, integrated into the other streams of classes within the BPTC engage students in a reflective learning spiral where performance, peer review and tutor feedback are recorded and supported by providing students with opportunities to record repeat performances in which they address difficulties identified. (Maharg, 2003:16-18; Bruner, 1960:52-54). This contributes to the course's goal of encouraging reflective practice.

Constructive Alignment

The *Pemberton* case presented above addresses three skills and two of the knowledge areas in which students will face summative assessments. To the extent to which it is within our powers we ensure a high level of constructive alignment between the learning experiences students encounter and the nature of their assessments. This achieves its highest level in the advocacy assessment, is somewhat effective in the opinion writing and drafting assessments, but is less so in the 'professional ethics' and 'civil litigation and evidence' assessments. The limits on our ability to ensure constructive alignment are largely a consequence of decisions of the professional regulator, the BSB.

Advocacy

Through their series of advocacy classes students have become accustomed to preparing skeleton arguments and using them as support in seeking to persuade a judge to come to a decision that is in their client's interest. They are accustomed to having their advocacy recorded and to facing interruptions by the judge that push them beyond their prepared comfort zone. These are all characteristics of the summative assessment.

They prepare a skeleton argument submitted in advance of the assessed advocacy itself. This is given to a tutor who will act as assessor/judge for prior reading and assessment. Their performance is recorded and they will face an intervention by the judge. The criteria on which they are assessed are identical to those that are used to structure the feedback they receive regularly in class and in the formative feedback exercises they undertake in each of these skills.

Opinion Writing and Drafting

The opinions and drafts that students bring to relevant classes and which they submit for detailed feedback in the formative assessments are similar in nature to the task they will face in their summative assessment. The feedback they receive in class and on their submitted opinions is organised around the same criteria as those on which they will ultimately be assessed. In this way a degree of alignment is achieved. It is limited, however, by the BSB requirement that the summative assessment be undertaken under time constraint (3½ hours) in a conventional examination situation. The impact of this is mitigated by their being given advance notice of the legal issues that will arise in the papers that they will receive in the examination, and the exam being open-book in nature.

This requirement has the advantage of preventing any risk of collusion or plagiarism, which would always be present with a take-away assessment. However, it is not what students have been accustomed to doing in most of their classes, nor does it represent the subsequent reality of practice.

Professional Ethics, Civil Litigation and Evidence and ADR

These areas are required by the BSB to be assessed in closed-book examinations based on multiple-choice and short answer questions. The School addresses constructive alignment by running series of classes addressing these issues and preparing students for these assessments. By contrast, the *Pemberton* case is designed to embed them with the goal of preparing students for practice. Thus ethical issues may be designed in (for example, where a client is less than frank about the existence of relevant documents), inherent (as where the best outcome for the client involves the barrister in less lucrative activities) or serendipitous (as where an opponent in advocacy has misunderstood a legal precedent to his client's detriment). Tutors will be at pains to ensure that any ethical issues arising are discussed by class members and that they are alerted to issues that they may otherwise have missed. A case-based teaching approach to assessing these issues is adopted to the extent that where students behave unethically they will lose credit and, if the failure is serious enough, will fail the assessment.

Evaluation

A student evaluation of their experience of learning through the *Pemberton* case was conducted immediately at the end of the series of classes. This took the form of an electronic survey instrument seeking responses to a series of questions on a five-point Likert scale and offering opportunities for comment. 83 responses (24% of population) were received. The results were generally positive, indicating that the *Pemberton* case study is effective in reaching its learning goals. However, there were interesting variations that are presented and discussed below.

Fig 1   **It helped me to develop the ability to analyse a case**

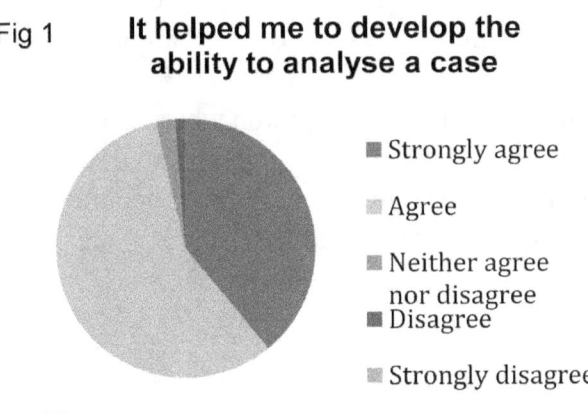

n= 83

Regarding Figure 1: There is no doubt that students recognised the value of the case for their analytical skills. Comments included:

> "My work from the first classes on Pemberton and the last ones we've had could be like the work of two different people."

And:

> "The addition of new material over the weeks was good because it made you return at times to re-evaluate all the evidence available."

Fig 2 **It helped me to develop written skills**

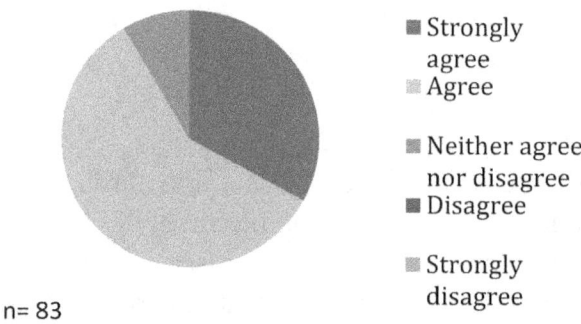

n= 83

Regarding Figure 2: The value to students' development of written skills was nearly as widely-recognised.

One student thought that a more gradual approach might help. "I think that, if possible, portions of the writing could be divided up further. For example, in tackling the Body, perhaps we could have the opportunity to rewrite it following a view of the Sample, without copying exactly."

'Body' here refers to the main part of an opinion where the detailed analysis and advice is presented to the client. In fact, students who are clearly having difficulty with writing opinions are encouraged to make a second attempt once they have read the School's suggested opinion.

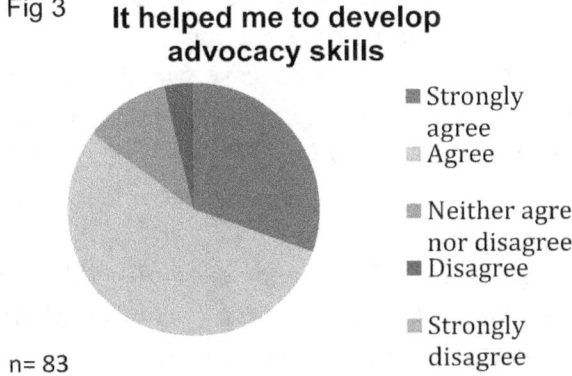

Fig 3 It helped me to develop advocacy skills

- Strongly agree
- Agree
- Neither agree nor disagree
- Disagree
- Strongly disagree

n= 83

Regarding Figure 3: This still represents strong support. However, it may be surprising that support here is not as strong as in written skills given that more attention is paid to advocacy. Most comments were positive, but one student said: *"The Singh papers helped me more on advocacy skills."*

This suggests that students may be responding relatively here, as the *Pemberton* papers form only a small part of the overall advocacy training.

Another comment, which the course team will consider in its annual review, was: *"I don't feel we did consistent levels of advocacy with Pemberton, it was somewhat piecemeal"*. It is true that the two advocacy tasks are separated by a lot of activity in the case. However, this is often true of litigation, court appearances often being analogous to the tip of an iceberg of legal activity.

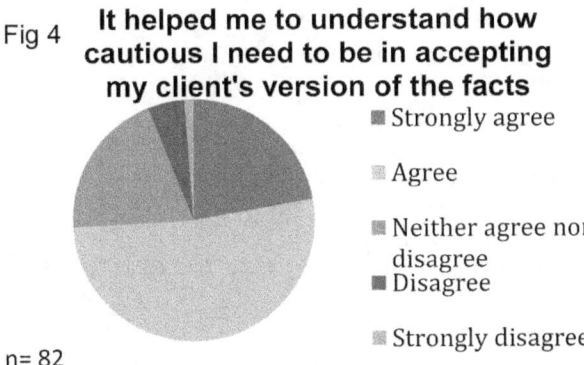

Fig 4 It helped me to understand how cautious I need to be in accepting my client's version of the facts

- Strongly agree
- Agree
- Neither agree nor disagree
- Disagree
- Strongly disagree

n= 82

Regarding Figure 4: Even though there is nearly 75% agreement with this proposition, this is the first indication of significant disagreement. Most students understood the way in which the case was designed to push them out of their initial comfort zone: *"In the early stages of the course, it was easy to accept what was said by Mr Pemberton as the complete facts of the case, which became a pure learning curve when reflecting upon the assertions of Mr Short."*

Those who did not recognise the point may be exemplified by the student who made this comment: *"I struggle with the wording of this question. Client's instruction and version of events is what forms the basis of my submissions. Cautious?"*

This student understands the responsibility to represent the client, but may fail to recognise the importance, if giving effective advice, of considering the client's instructions critically. What is more, ethical issues arise because a lawyer is not permitted to make assertions about, for example, the dishonesty of the opponent unless there is evidence to back it up. A mere assertion by the client, based on his own assumptions, will not suffice.

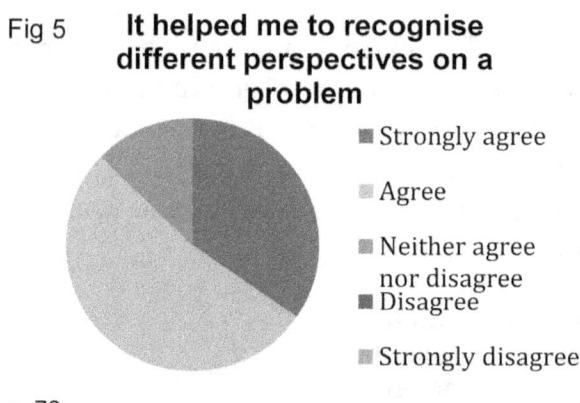

Fig 5 **It helped me to recognise different perspectives on a problem**

n=79

Regarding Figure 5: Most students clearly understood what this question was intended to address. Comments included:

"Changing what side you were on helped to view the case from all perspectives"

And:

"In particular the difference between litigation and Alternative Dispute Resolution proceedings."

Others, however, had not internalised this element of the aims of the exercise. One comment was: *"Not sure what you mean..."*

This raises some concern and may suggest a need to develop our existing encouragement of students' reflective practice. This currently focuses on the skill development, although at a reasonably sophisticated level. It may be worth-while prompting student reflection on specific factors such as whether they have recognised the perspectives of the different parties, the mediator, or the judge involved with the dispute.

Fig 6 **It helped me to recognise ethical dilemmas**

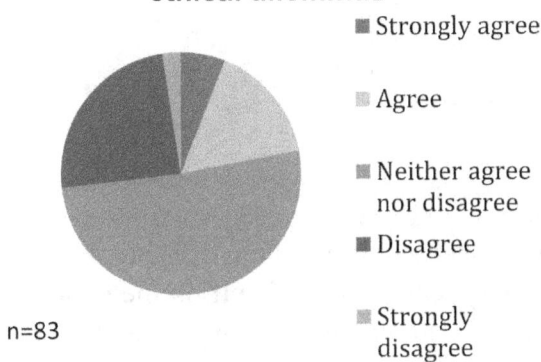

n=83

Regarding Figure 6: This was the only question that received, on balance, a negative response, albeit those expressing a view were marginally outweighed by those expressing none. The probable explanation is that ethical issues are not a strong focus of this case compared with others used on the programme. One comment was, however, worrying: *"did not present any ethical problems"*.

Although this student may mean that the ethical issues were well understood and not a problem, it may be that s/he simply did not recognise them, or the degree to which ethical issues are inherent in legal practice. A more positive light is cast on this question by responses such as:

"Other than mediation and confidentiality issues I didn't find that ethics was a huge factor"

It is certainly the case that if students perform correctly, the ethical significance of particular inappropriate actions, statements or decisions will not necessarily arise in the class and attention will not be drawn to them. It should be remembered that there is a discrete series of professional ethics classes in which students receive focused attention on a wide variety of ethical dilemmas that arise in both civil and criminal practice.

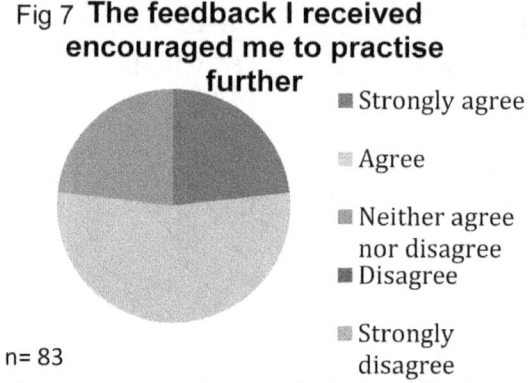

Fig 7 **The feedback I received encouraged me to practise further**

- Strongly agree
- Agree
- Neither agree nor disagree
- Disagree
- Strongly disagree

n= 83

Regarding Figure 7: Here again there was no dissent, which is gratifying to the extent that the School prides itself on the quality of the feedback provided. Only one comment gives any insight into the reasons for those who did not agree.

> *"However, more needs to be done to give feedback on work to get an idea of how you would have done, had it been the assessment."*

This reflects the fact that, for selected classes, students receive detailed one-to-one feedback with an indication of the likely grade. This is clearly motivating. However, there is evidence to suggest that where students receive both feedback and a grade for their work they tend to check the grade and to ignore the feedback (Parker & Baughan, 2009 citing Duncan, 2007:271). We intend, therefore, to continue our practice of only giving a suggested grade in a limited number of formative assessments while maintaining the practice of giving feedback on every formative activity the students engage in.

Fig 8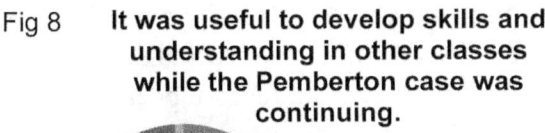

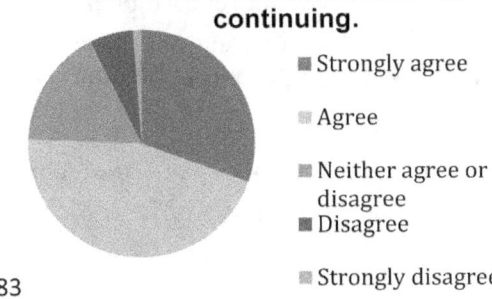

n= 83

Regarding Figure 8: Most students appreciated the integration of the classes using the *Pemberton* papers with others.

> *"A multiple of case studies is a positive system because it allows for sensible narrative in each while still covering the topics and skills required."*

And:

> *"Pemberton v Short really brought together all of the core courses that we study in the BPTC - including drafting, opinion writing, civil advocacy and practice and ADR."*

Others recognised that there was a degree of efficiency in using the same papers for a variety of different learning purposes:

> *"Using the same case in different classes allowed me to understand it in greater depth and concentrate on skills & analysis rather than spending time learning new facts".*

Fig 9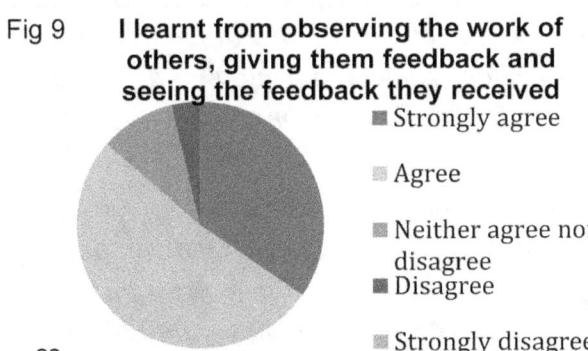

n=82

Regarding Figure 9: There are two issues raised by this question. One is whether it is useful to observe others' performances and the feedback they receive; the other is to give and receive peer feedback. On reflection it might have been better to separate out these issues. It is clear that there was some dissent from this statement and it may be explained by the following comments:

> "I was able to discover things in my own work that could be improved upon while not requiring the lecturer or lesson convener to repeat themselves."

And:

> "especially in the group advocacy sessions, skills are developed very quickly."

One student separated out the two:

> "Observing others and the feedback they get from the teacher is very helpful; the feedback from others in the class less so."

In my view, the value of peer feedback lies more in the learning that comes from considering and feeding back on the work of one's peers than in receiving it. However, it is important not to allow too much class time to be devoted to it.

Finally, students were invited to respond to the question: 'Please explain what features of the Pemberton papers had most impact on your learning'. This produced 66 responses, some of which are particularly helpful in identifying which characteristics of the case study are most worth preserving and developing.

> "I liked how long and complex it was, particularly that it was a practical and realistic case involving several different aspects to gauge my knowledge on. For example, having a go at mediation, and further oral hearings for application for specific disclosure."

And:

> "It helpfully brought together lots of different areas of the course, such as opinion writing, ADR, advocacy and civil litigation. It was useful to see a practical illustration of how these inter-relate and also meant that these areas could be learnt without having to analyse a fresh set of facts each time."

The mediation session was particularly popular:

> *"The mediation was probably the most useful experience overall, since we had to tie together all the groundwork on liability and quantum with a degree of realism/practicality, and think creatively about settlement options."*

And:

> *"I thought the practice mediation was very helpful. It put the issues into practice and made me really evaluate clients' aims and how to best achieve a practical solution as well as considering legal arguments."*

There was a degree of recognition of the value of dealing with slippery facts and different perspectives:

> *"The narrative of the case history helped to build a picture as the weeks progressed, which then caused you to re-evaluate earlier conclusions, and search for all the facts and information to come up with a practical solution. Furthermore, familiarity with the case in later weeks allowed me to focus on the technical and legal skills required of me in each class, because I was not grappling with brand new facts as well as procedures."*

And:

> *"I think the fact that it appeared in so many different instances and we had to look at different sides of the case made it a very useful and nuanced case to deal with. Also it felt good to be dealing with one case all the way instead of only picking at a small part of it."*

Some students recognised its value in the fundamental object of the progamme, to assist students to shift from the academic perspective of undergraduate studies to the professional perspective they will need to apply in practice:

> *"This is one of the case bundles that helped me to understand the practical features of different legal documents with appropriate applications."*

One negative comment addresses an issue of real concern to the School. *"The ADR, while interesting, was in light of the exams, pointless."* This refers to the mediation exercise, found so valuable by others. It confirms the point made above in the Constructive Alignment section. The School's response – the highly experiential programme described in this chapter – goes as far as it can to prepare students for practice, but at some cost in constructive alignment, with the result that, for a narrowly goal-focused student, some activities may be seen as pointless.

Conclusion

The student evaluation of the *Pemberton* case study confirms its fundamental effectiveness in achieving most of its aims through the device of a spiral curriculum. This flows not only from the design of how the case is used, but the way in which it is integrated into the remainder of the course. The use of realistic bundles of papers rather than partially-digested fact patterns is strongly supported. The experiential approach appears to be effective in developing a variety of student skills and also in helping students to understand the interaction of their different developing skills and the substantive and procedural rules within which they must practise. Likewise, the way the papers required students to shift perspectives was effective in developing their understanding of clients' perspectives and in ensuring they retained a view of the proportionality of the legal action in which they were engaged in terms of costs. The need to retain a critical distance from the client's version of the facts was not universally recognised. There appears to have been a reasonable degree of development of a reflective practice in their learning. The minor role given to ethical issues in this particular case reduced their significance as perceived by students.

Tutor feedback was valued, although that given by and to peers was not perceived as particularly useful. The learning method achieves considerable constructive alignment with the skills assessments, although less so with others. However, a reasonable balance is probably achieved given the complex outcomes of the programme which is seeking to prepare students for the experience of practice as well as for the specific BSB assessments. Certainly, the mediation class was well-received and clearly placed what was being learnt in the ADR classes in a more realistic context.

The lessons from running and evaluating this case have been valuable and will be transferable to students who are being prepared for a variety of professional and other responsible roles. It contributes to the possibility of their developing artistry in their practice.

Acknowledgements

Julie Browne, Barrister and Deputy Course Director on the City Law School BPTC, is the author of the Pemberton case papers. She also designed the integrated learning exercises undertaken by students using these papers. My thanks also to Pem Tshering, BPTC student, for her contribution to the student perspective presentation of the experience of working through this case study.

About the Author

Nigel Duncan is Professor of Legal Education, City Law School, City University London. He can be contacted at this email: N.J.Duncan@city.ac.uk

Chapter eleven

Real World Cases in Virtual Environments: Blending Environments, Bringing Teacher Training to Life

Graham Lowe, Dario Faniglione,
Mark Hetherington & Luke Millard

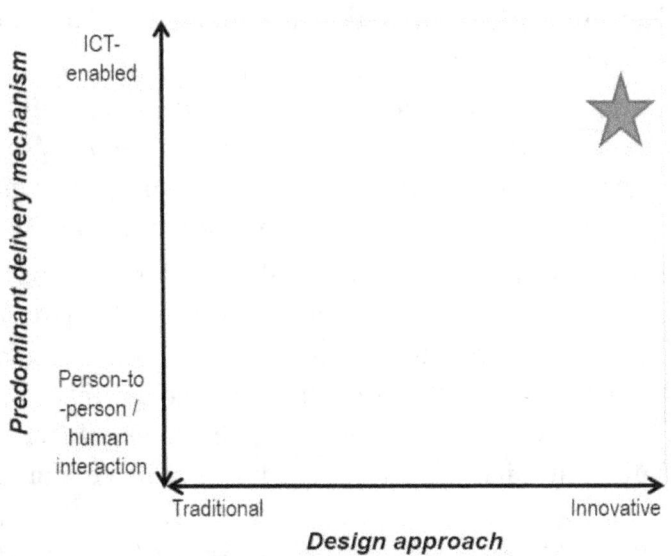

Introduction & Background

This chapter reports on a project involving simulation-based case studies and the emerging and experimental field of computer simulation in Initial Teacher Education (ITE).

Throughout the chapter the terms 'simulation-based case study', 'simulated case studies' and 'simulation' are used interchangeably. However, according to the definition presented by Leigh and Collier (this volume), the simulations being discussed here would fit their definition of simulated case studies.

By virtue of being a simplified yet realistic model of the real world, a simulation *"can support authentic enquiry practices that include formulating questions, hypothesis development, data collection, and theory revision."* (Rutten et al., 2012:136). Note the use of the word 'authentic'. The key to the success of any simulated activity is the authenticity of the responses elicited. This is related to, though not solely dependent upon, the authenticity of the presentation of the simulation (Bland et al., 2011; Pike & O'Donnel, 2010). Although popular in a range of professional training situations, in particular Initial Nursing Training (Berragan, 2011; Garrett et al., 2011; Hope et al., 2011; Ricketts, 2011), simulation as a tool in ITE has its roots in the work of Kersh in the 1960s.

"The shortage of qualified teachers, limited training facilities, and too few expert supervisors dictate that new methods [sic] to be found to provide systematic practice teaching opportunities for beginning teachers." (Kersh, 1962:109 cited in Tansey, 1970:283)

This work was started long before the use of computers was a possibility. Much of Kersh's work involved students observing 16mm projections of filmed incidents involving a fictitious class, accompanied with contextual information in the form of paper notes. In these cases, students would discuss and debate appropriate approaches. Other early simulations also included a mix of film and paper documentation including simulations related to behaviour management (Cruikshank & Broadbent, 1968) and teaching styles (Garrison & Kersh, 1969).

In a review of the literature of the time, Cruikshank (1971) sums up the prevailing view that simulation would become an increasingly important part of ITE. Indeed, it was predicted that *"It can be assumed that vastly superior, more sophisticated simulations can be developed as computer availability for training purposes increases."* (Cruikshank, 1971:200).

In reality there was very little move towards increasing the use of simulation, and the use of computer simulations in particular, in ITE during the next forty years. The underlying reasons for that, whilst interesting in themselves, lie beyond the remit of this paper. Rather, this article reports on the early stages of a recent move at Birmoingham City University, UK, to find ways to use more sophisticated simulations in its ITE provision.

The use of computer simulation in ITE is a relatively new and under-explored phenomenon. Yeh (2004, 2007) reports on using computer simulations to develop critical thinking skills. Passig and Moshe (2008) have used a simulation to enhance pre-service teachers' understanding of pupils' test-anxiety. In both cases the researchers, using control groups, found evidence for the success of the simulations. However, in both cases there is also a sense in which assumptions are made regarding the transferability of the skills from the simulated world to the real world. In the case of Passig and Moshe's work, subjects use Virtual Reality helmets to create a truly immersive 3D environment. However, rather than find themselves in a school hall taking a test, as might be expected from the subject matter, the subjects find themselves in *"the entrance to a small, dark, narrow basement, whose walls are made of tightly packed dark red bricks"* (Passig & Moshe, 2008:264), and are expected to complete a task relating to the appearance of some bouncing balls. The aim of the simulation is to give the student *"the experience of wandering aimlessly while under pressure of time"* (ibid). Whilst the metaphor is easy to appreciate, it is not clear to what extent the ability to understand or interpret the metaphor impacts on the efficacy of the activity. Although less extreme in nature, Yeh's work requires participants to consider that a computer screen with twelve cartoon-drawn faces represents the reality of teaching a class of children. We have found from previous work (Lowe, 2011) that the willing suspension of disbelief by participants is an important issue. Trainees generally found it easier to see the value in a simulation, and treat it as though it were real, if they considered it to be realistic; the more real it seems the more likely the reactions are to be authentic.

Although computer simulation in ITE is very much at an embryonic stage, in the last ten years or so simulation has become ubiquitous in the training of pre-registration nurses. In some respects, nurse education and teacher education are similar. In both cases practitioners are now expected to be educated to degree level where previously they were not. Both types of training programme involve a mixture of faculty/classroom based work and on-the-job training. Both require trainees to engage in reflective practice and both involve an element of caring for people in one's charge.

An examination of the literature surrounding the use of computer simulation in nurse education has provided a starting point for its consideration in ITE. For example, Bligh and Bleakley's (2006) description of simulation as 'the third place' that helps students see the link between faculty and work based learning is a useful way to conceptualise the simulations being discussed here. The view amongst trainees that there is little connection between theory and practice, commonly called 'the theory-practice divide', is just as common amongst trainee teachers as it is amongst trainee nurses (Hatlevik, 2012; Allen, 2009). The idea that simulation work can help bridge the divide and help trainees see more value in faculty-based learning has helped to inform both the type of simulations developed and the way in which they are presented.

Rationale for and Brief Description of the Simulations

The rationale for developing these simulations was essentially twofold. Firstly, through analysis of the literature and discussion with colleagues working in both education and nursing, it had become increasingly clear that the 'ethical driver' behind the use of simulation in nurse training is largely absent from ITE. One reason for developing the simulations was to give trainees the opportunity to fail, and learn from that failure, in a way that does not cause harm either to children, parents or the trainee themselves, as might happen should they fail in the real world. Secondly it had also become clear through discussions with colleagues in schools and the trainees themselves, that although trainees on ITE course are spending increasingly more time in schools, they are often protected from certain events. Simulation enables the trainees to encounter a range of experiences related to planning, teaching and assessing children that they would not see in school. Situations such as dealing with an angry parent, writing reports that are actually sent home and meeting parents at parents evening are not something that the trainees can expect as part of school experience training.

The simulations used in the research project reported here were therefore all connected with working with parents. The simulations formed part of a taught module on a post-graduate Primary ITE course. In each case the teaching involved a mixture of direct input (lecture), use of the simulation (individual) and discussion (small group).

The simulations are situated within a virtual primary school, Green Moor Primary, which exists within Shareville©, a virtual environment created at Birmingham City University. Shareville hosts an increasing number of realistic locations and simulation-based case studies, organised as if they were existing in a real town's districts. It is accessible over the Internet and presents users with a simple navigation system. Using a mouse, a left-click and drag navigates around computer-generated images and 360° panoramas, whilst left-click hot-spots give access to the simulations, other resources and provides a mean to jump between locations.

Green Moor Primary has been created as a 3D environment (see Figure 1) based on 360° panorama photographs of a real school.

Figure 1: Shareville's Green Moor Primary School is a 3D Virtual Training Environment.

Digital models were then made of those panoramas to create a realistic setting including entrance hall, classrooms, playground, Physical Education (PE)/dining hall etc. In order to populate the school, volunteers act the parts of key roles such as parents, teachers and other adults. Scenes are filmed against 'green screen' backgrounds and 'dropped in' to the 3D environment. Additional realism is created by giving the school appropriate documentation such as school policies and an Ofsted report (Ofsted is the Office for Standards in Education, Children's Services and Skills, and produces accreditation reports for the UK government).

There were three simulations used as part of this module and referred to in this research.

Simulation one: 'The Angry Parent'

In this simulation the trainee takes on the role of a teacher witnessing a confrontation in the playground between a parent and the head teacher. The action freezes at a certain point and the trainee is asked to select a response from the head teacher. The trainee then witnesses the results of that approach. As well as the initial confrontation, four different endings were filmed based on four different responses. The trainee can see the consequences and back track and see the results of other approaches. In group discussions the trainees can debate which approach was the most appropriate and why.

Simulation two: 'End of Year Report and Parents' Evening'

In this simulation the trainee takes on the role of a newly qualified teacher. The trainee is presented on screen with a basic end of year report pro-forma divided into sections (see Figure 2).

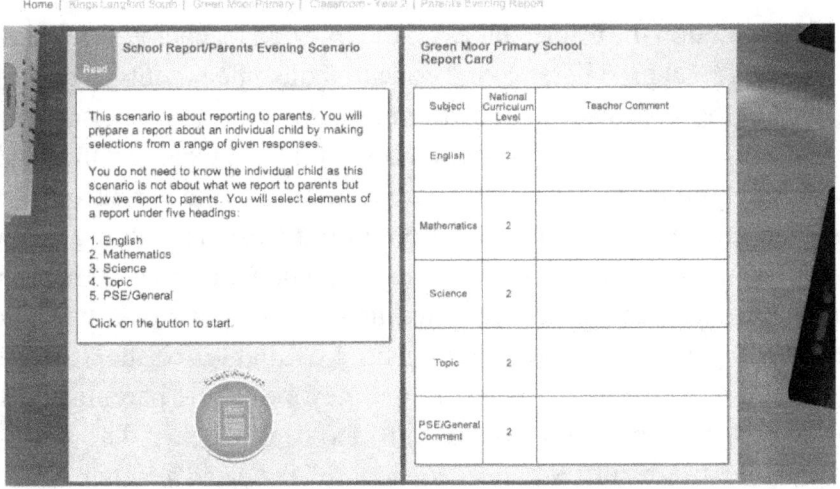

Figure 2: Interactive School Report form in Green Moor Primary School.

For each section the trainee is also presented with three versions of the same written report section. It is made clear to the trainee that this scenario is not about the content, which would relate to assessment, but about communication. The trainee selects what s/he considers to be the most appropriate version and drags that text into the named section. Upon completion of the report the trainee is able to print out the report and bring it o the discussion group. The trainee will then witness a short filmed scene set at the start of parents' evening where the parents have just sat down to discuss the report. Five versions of this scene were filmed with responses ranging from being quite angry to very positive depending on the amount of educational jargon and spelling mistakes included (parents are happier with less) and the extent to which the language is specific and supportive (parents are happier with more). Following the group discussions, trainees are able to repeat the process using their new understanding to improve the response from the parents.

Simulation three: 'Parental Opinions'

In this simulation the trainee takes on the role of a teacher who is asked by the head teacher to listen to the concerns of some parents regarding changes in the way the school swimming pool is used. In the scenario the school is required to find more money for the upkeep of the pool, which was built through funds by parents as part of the Parent Teacher Association. Several potential solutions are suggested including taking money from other curriculum areas such as Mathematics and English, hiring the pool out in the evenings, and allowing other schools to use it during the day thus reducing time available for the school's own children. The trainee listens to the views of some parents and is required to make a recommendation to the head teacher. The trainee is then told the results of the decision by the head teacher. In all cases the trainee is blamed for suggesting a solution that has angered certain parties. The trainee is able to try again but following group discussions should realise that this simulation is designed to show that it is not always possible to please everyone; sometimes the reality is that difficult or unpopular decisions have to be made.

Method

A cohort (n= 190) was selected of students following a Postgraduate Certificate in Education Primary ITE course. These trainees used the three scenarios described above as part of a course module which concerns the following issues related to working in partnership with parents:

a) Managing situations involving angry or upset parents

b) Communicating in writing through the annual report to parents

c) Taking into account individual parental concerns when making decisions affecting groups of pupils.

In each case the students were exposed to the virtual simulation on an individual basis followed by a group (approx. 30 sub-divided into smaller groups of six people) seminar to discuss the issues raised, their responses and the outcomes and implications.

A mixed methods approach was taken and students were invited to complete questionnaires before and after the module with the aim of uncovering both their attitudes towards the use of computer simulation and the degree to which they considered their skills and understanding had been affected. 184 students completed the initial questionnaire and 123 completed the follow up questionnaire. Where appropriate and possible, questions on the follow up questionnaire mirrored questions on the initial questionnaire. Data was collected anonymously so it is not possible to track individual changes in perception of changes to skill levels and understanding of the issues.

Both questionnaires were similar in presentation with two main sections. The first set of items consisted of statements that the students needed to respond to using a 5-point Likert scale graded from Strongly Agree to Strongly Disagree. In the initial questionnaire, students were given the option to expand on the Likert scale questions, particularly if they wished to explain any strong responses.

The second section set out the three main issues being focused upon and asked the students to write comments regarding their concerns and/or feelings of preparedness to face these issues in the real world. These comments were subjected to an iterative, free-coding process aimed at determining common themes or issues.

Students were also asked to grade their feeling of confidence by giving themselves a 'score out of 10' whereby 0= very nervous/worried and 10= totally confident and prepared.

Based on several comments presented during the initial questionnaire, a short section was added to the follow up questionnaire to elicit the student's understanding of the drivers behind this project.

Results

Several items were completed before the scenarios were created (as shown in Table1) and after the scenarios were created (as shown in Table 2) with the aim of eliciting the student's attitude towards computer simulation in ITE in general. In some cases exactly the same questions (with appropriate changes of tense) were asked to see if exposure to the scenarios had had any significant impact overall.

Initial Questionnaire (n=184)	Strongly Agree	Agree	Neither Agree nor Disagree	Disagree	Strongly Disagree
The use of computer simulation can help support my professional development.	42.9	52.7	4.3	0.0	0.0
Computer simulation should be an important part of ITE	29.3	53.8	16.8	0.0	0.0
Learning by 'Trial and Error' is the best method for developing new teachers.	29.9	48.4	16.3	5.4	0.0

Initial Questionnaire (n=184)	Strongly Agree	Agree	Neither Agree nor Disagree	Disagree	Strongly Disagree
Virtual professional experiences may supplement but never replace real experiences.	49.5	45.7	3.8	0.5	0.5
Ability to 'perform' during virtual experiences should be assessed before students are allowed 'do it for real'.	6.0	29.9	31.0	29.3	3.8
The development of Virtual Professional Experiences should be a priority for those delivering ITE	6.0	42.4	40.2	10.3	1.1

Table.1. Initial Questionnaire: Likert scale values presented as percentages to one decimal point

Post- Scenario Questionnaire (n=123)	Strongly Agree	Agree	Neither Agree nor Disagree	Disagree	Strongly Disagree
On the whole, this use of computer simulation has helped support my professional development and ability to work with parents.	37.4	56.9	4.1	0.0	1.6
I feel more confident now, as a result of these experiences.	22.8	57.7	13.8	4.1	1.6
These simulated experiences had greater value than I was expecting.	38.2	40.7	18.7	1.6	0.8
Using these simulated experiences was engaging and enjoyable.	39.0	48.0	10.6	1.6	0.8
I would have preferred a more traditional approach (more lectures, academic readings, watching videos etc.) to this aspect of my development.	1.6	4.9	21.1	53.7	18.7
I would have preferred to be, 'thrown in at the deep end', and learn these skills by trial and error with real parents as and when they arose.	0.0	5.7	8.9	56.1	29.3

Post- Scenario Questionnaire (n=123)	Strongly Agree	Agree	Neither Agree nor Disagree	Disagree	Strongly Disagree
Simulated experience is a 'Third Place' that links Faculty Based Learning and Real World Learning.	13.0	56.9	27.6	1.6	0.8
The use of simulation, where mistakes don't have real consequences, is more ethically sound than trial and error.	18.7	51.2	22.8	6.5	0.8
Computer simulation should become an increasingly important part of Initial Teacher Education.	19.5	61.8	15.4	1.6	1.6
The development of virtual professional experiences such as these should be a priority for those delivering Initial Teacher Education.	13.8	49.6	29.3	4.9	2.4
The ability to 'perform' during virtual experiences should be assessed before students are allowed 'do it for real'. (As is required by aircraft pilots for example)	6.5	33.3	16.3	34.1	9.8

Table 2. Follow-up Questionnaire: Likert scale values presented as percentages to one decimal point

Just under half of the students (n= 70) wrote at least one comment in the space provided to expand on the Likert scale items. These comments tended to be related to one of four types:

a) Generally negative – 'cannot replace real life' (n= 15)

b) Mixed – some value but not as useful as real life (n= 15)

c) Wait and see (n= 4)

d) Generally positive (n= 36)

Students understanding of the drivers of this use of computer simulation are shown in Table 3.

Post- Scenario Questionnaire (n=123)	A 'Main Driver'	Important Consideration	Valuable Point	Not Important
It might make learning more enjoyable	32.5	50.4	16.3	0.8
It could save time	10.6	43.9	35.0	10.6
It could save money	8.1	34.1	43.1	14.6
It is more ethically sound	19.5	43.1	33.3	3.3
It might develop trainees' skills more effectively	43.1	43.9	11.4	0.8

Table.3. Student perceptions of drivers for development of simulations (values as percentages to one decimal point)

The students were asked to quantify their confidence and skill level by giving themselves a 'score out of 10' in each case (Table 4). Minimal guidance was given as follows: 0= very nervous/worried, 10= totally confident and prepared.

Student estimation of self-confidence in each area; 'score out of 10'. Figures in parenthesis represent the Standard Deviation.	Before (n=184)	After (n=104)
School Reports and Parents Evenings	5.2 (1.9)	7.1 (1.3)
Angry or Upset Parents	5.0 (2.2)	7.2 (1.4)
Considering Parental Opinions	6.4 (1.8)	7.0 (1.6)
Total (to one decimal point)	5.5 (1.5)	7.1 (1.0)

Table.4. Student quantification of confidence and skill level (values as percentages to one decimal point)

Some (n= 77) students added comments to the follow-up questionnaire and these which were coded as previously described. The results are shown in Table 5 in which only issues raised by 2 or more students are included Numbers are given to indicate how many students gave comments relating to that issue.

Code	Description	Notes
U+	Skills/ Understanding increased	Some (n=30) students felt the scenarios had improved their understanding of 'how to' engage with parents. A smaller number (n=4) felt more confused and less sure as a result.
U-	Confusion	
R+	Reflection	Some students (n=27) commented on how the scenarios had given them the basis for reflection on the issues raised and that this had supported their development.
S-	Too Short	Some students (n=17) commented that the scenarios were either too short or needed to be developed further and include more information or higher levels of engagement.

Code	Description	Notes
T-	Technology	Some comments related to technological aspects, in particular difficulties with Internet connections and bugs in the software (n=13). Where technological issues were raised this was generally in a negative context.
C+	Confidence Increased	Some students (n=9) reported that their confidence had been positively affected by the use of the scenarios. No student's commented that the scenarios had knocked their confidence.
W	Missing the point	Some comments (n=9) clearly indicated that students had 'missed the point' of a scenario. The most common example related to not being able to find 'the right answer' when the point was to make them realise that there are some situations where one cannot please everyone.
P+	Sense of 'Practising'	Some students (n=6) commented on the simulations in terms of practising. Where students considered the scenarios to be a type of 'teaching practice' they tended to be positive. No students specifically commented that this was not a form of practice, although other comments implicitly indicate that some do not recognise it as such.
A+	Good level of Authenticity	The degree to which the scenarios felt 'real' was commented upon. In general positive comments (n=5) were related to a strong feeling of authenticity whereas if students felt the scenario was not authentic (n=4), this was seen as a negative thing.
A-	Poor level of Authenticity	

Table.5. Issues arising from follow-up questionnaire qualitative responses

Discussion of the Findings

The first conclusion to be drawn from the data is that, overall, student perceptions of their own self-confidence in dealing with parent-teacher relationship issues has increased through the use of these simulated experiences. It is, of course, not possible to determine the exact relationship between the students' perceptions of their own abilities and their actual abilities, but the nature of the reflective comments of many students following the module indicate that a degree of professional development has indeed taken place. In the following commentary the evidence we offer typifies the student's anonymised responses about each issue.

Firstly, when the students were asked to quantify (Table 4) their own self-confidence before and after use of the simulations this elicited a clear and noticeable increase In fact, expression of improved confidence was the most common issue to emerge from the coding of the qualitative data:

"This was good. I didn't expect parents to become that angry in the playground – I feel more prepared now."

"I definitely feel more confident with writing reports after this scenario."

"I understand the value of parental opinions now & feel more confident to take these into account."

Secondly, the next most common type of qualitative comment following the module related to how the simulations had given them a useful experience to reflect upon. With the emphasis placed on reflective practice in ITE, the fact that many of the students applied the language of reflection to these simulations can be seen as a positive indicator. Comments such as the following indicate the value this gave to these students.

"I thought that this highlighted the difficulties well and gave me lots to consider."

"Really helped me to think about my own practice and how I would deal with a real situation."

"Good scenarios and got me thinking ... "

An important point to note is that the value attributed by the students to these simulations is often related to a sense of authenticity. Before the students used the simulations a very common point raised was that it could not be as real as real life. In previous work, Lowe (2011) has shown that where students become engrossed in simulated experiences they are able effectively to suspend their disbelief and treat the simulation as if it were real. The number and type of comments requesting that the scenarios should be extended further indicate that authenticity is important because many of the comments made relate to developing a sense of reality by providing a greater breadth of experience. The following examples typify the feedback.

"Very useful responses to have available to me. Very beneficial. Maybe as a development, have further discussion options?"

"Could have been developed further in responses. Overall, very good nonetheless.'

"This was a valuable experience, but it might have been more worthwhile if it could have been extended further. So if we could have read more about the child, seen marks etc."

Both positive and negative comments relating to authenticity indicate that some students see that as being a very important consideration:

"I did not think all reactions were entirely true to life."

"Very useful due to visual responses of parents."

"Good scenarios – realistic."

However, there is evidence from the follow-up questionnaires that deficiencies in the technology are potentially a major hindrance to this process. Where technology was mentioned at all it was almost always in a negative context. Comments such as the following were common amongst those few who did discuss the technology:

"Difficulty navigating around scenarios – not very user friendly to find options."

"The report based one was not as effective and the video clip took over 1 hour to load."

"Computer kept crashing."

It was also noted that although students often gave multiple comments relating to different issues, the coding process found no student who had both positively commented on authenticity and negatively commented on the technology.

Ethics is an important issue that has emerged from the research and this warrants further research. The drive towards the use of computer simulation in other spheres of initial training (particularly medical and transport) is largely an ethical one. It is clear that the welfare of the patient or the passenger is paramount and the use of simulation means that mistakes have no consequences other than being learning experiences. As previously stated, a review of the literature in Initial Teacher Education reveals little discussion of the ethical considerations of an approach to training teachers. Indeed, recent developments such as Teach First and School Direct seem to run counter to any consideration of the ethics of having teachers trained 'on the job'. Perhaps one should consider whether one would be happy with a hospital that ran an 'Operate First' training programme, or an airline with a 'Fly First' policy for its pilots!

The initial questionnaire deliberately omitted use of the word 'ethics' in the Likert scale statements (see Table 1). The intention was to see if any student would recognise the relationship between the virtual simulations and one of the key drivers of their development. The fact that initially 78.3% of students agreed or strongly agreed that trial and error was the best way to train teachers, that only 35.9% of students felt that simulations should be used as an assessment before being allowed to practise in real schools and that no students made any qualitative comments at all about ethical matters, indicates that such ethical considerations are not something many of the students were concerned with.

To see whether such considerations might be drawn out from the students if prompted, potential ethical considerations were made purposely more explicit. in the second questionnaire. Firstly, ethics was presented as one of the potential drivers, along with enjoyment, money saving, time saving and efficacy and students were asked to decide which they felt were most significant (as shown in Table 3). Secondly, next to the Likert scale item about the use of simulation to assess trainees before real practice, the words 'As is required by aircraft pilots for example', were added (Table 2). Even with such prompting, understanding that ethics might be the main driver was limited. Although an ethical driver was considered to be more important than savings in time and money, efficacy and enjoyment were seen as more important.

With regard to using the simulations as part of an assessment, there was little change in the overall number of students agreeing. However, the number of undecided students decreased and the number disagreeing increased (see Figure 3).

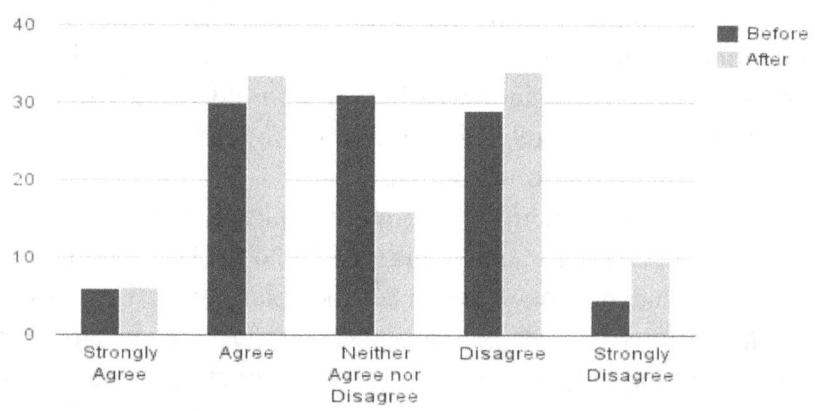

Figure 3. Change in student opinion in relation to simulation as a pre-'real world' assessment

It is interesting to note that the use of the simulations as part of the training has produced quite a polarised view amongst this cohort of ITE students. This suggests that, if a proposal was made to include the use of simulations in a summative assessment, it is unlikely that a consensus view amongst trainees would emerge that this was a useful and valuable thing to do. Whilst the designers have no intention of using the simulations as part of a summative assessment framework, the small number of students whose comments indicated that they had missed the point of the simulation does give the designers pause for thought. Comments such as the following perhaps indicate the potential for problems to arise when these trainees are faced with the same scenario in the real world:

"This was good – but why wasn't there a final overall solution?"

"I found it difficult to listen to all the parents opinions and make a decision that would please them all. PTA meetings would mean parents can vote and the majority would get the vote."

"Have more options – a scenario that you can have a positive "WIN" in, rather than you always fail."

In such cases it might well be considered that the simulations have highlighted significant issues that ought to be addressed before the trainee meets a similar situation in the real world.

Conclusions and Recommendations

Simulation, through vehicles such as Shareville, has the potential to change the way students engage with case studies. There is the potential for multi-agency, interdisciplinary simulations that really challenge students in situations that they may only encounter infrequently and would certainly not see during their placement experience. Students are no longer simply observers; they become a virtual party to the case study, interacting with various components that are brought to life through the use of crafted characters, businesses and environments, enclosed in an episodic-style narrative.

"Shareville attempts to ameliorate against [the student being on the periphery] by showcasing a multi-agency approach, particularly in the areas of Health and Social Work. The initial philosophy behind the development of the environment was that of seeing

resources that already existed online in a number of areas within the university, in a more realistic context." (Hollyhead, 2010:14)

We believe that there is a need for future development of case based teaching innovations like Shareville to focus on character-driven cases that are holistically embedded within learning activities shared across faculties and schools. Further research is needed to evaluate the effectiveness of this approach in encouraging students to engage with their own subject, enhancing their understanding of how their field of study fits in with the bigger picture, and allowing for the collaboration with other students from different academic studies as we seek to help shape student experiences that result in them becoming better professionals.

About the Authors

Graham Lowe is Lead Academic for Technology Enhanced Learning and Teaching in the School of Education, Birmingham City University, UK. He can be contacted at this email: graham.lowe@bcu.ac.uk

Dario Faniglione is a Senior Lecturer in Learning Technology, Centre for Enhancement of Learning and Teaching, Birmingham City University, UK. He can be contacted at this email: Dario.Faniglione@bcu.ac.uk

Mark Hetherington is a Senior Lecturer in Learning Technology, Centre for Enhancement of Learning and Teaching, Birmingham City University, UK. He can be contacted at this email: Mark.Hetherington@bcu.ac.uk

Luke Millard is Head of Learning Partnerships at the Centre for Enhancement of Learning and Teaching, Birmingham City University, UK. He can be contacted at this email: Luke.Millard@bcu.ac.uk

Chapter twelve

Benefits of the Use of Video in Case Based Teaching

Christian Poulsen and Steffen Löfvall

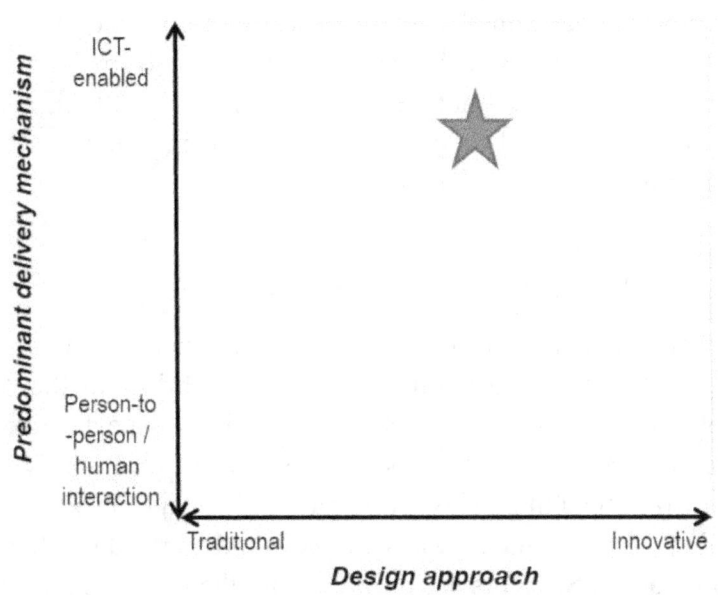

Introduction

This chapter reviews the use of video in education and specifically in Case Based Teaching (CBT). It compares the didactical benefits of using video in education at large and in CBT. To conclude, it gives guidelines on where the use of video could be most effective in terms of student learning and ultimately which aspects of the use of video in CBT need further attention.

Following Kay's (2012) example we browsed publications in journals and books for empirically-based contributions to the field of video and CBT. A majority of Kay's results were examples of receptive viewing and fewer were student-generated video podcasts or concerned with problem solving. It is fair to say that there is a lack of studies with an experimental design on the use of video in CBT. Nevertheless, the search query *"video case teaching"* resulted in 30 relevant articles from the library data bank Libsearch™. Libsearch is a search engine that queries all books and journal articles dating back 20 years from editorials such as Cambridge, Elsevier, Emerald, OECD, Oxford, Sage, Springer, Taylor & Francis and Wiley. The relevancy was determined on the basis of empirical evidence of videos being used in CBT. The period queried was from June 2013 to March 2014. The articles that were found were screened and analysed for empirical findings of the pros and cons of using video in the case teaching approach.

Video in Education

The use of video in education has a 30-year history. In the 1980s it slowly began to replace films as a way of bringing the outside world into the classroom. Production and equipment costs have fallen dramatically since then and this has resulted in an increase in the use of video in teaching. The ever-faster and cheaper production and distribution of video material has allowed students and teachers alike to be co-creators. Students are moving from the role of consumers of video towards potentially becoming co-producers of video material. Initially the hosting of videos was expensive in terms of hardware (video cassettes and -discs, TVs and video players) but is now literally free via on-line platforms such as Vimeo™, Youtube™ and university portals (Wiley & Hilton, 2009) as well as an integrated part of video case-based books (Smithenry et al., 2013). The high speed and low cost of video production and distribution is also making it easier for teachers to use recordings of small group discussions (Dede, 2009).

Previous Reviews

Kay (2012) identifies three different pedagogical strategies for involving video in education, namely; receptive viewing, problem solving and created video podcasts. Within these three categories there are both didactical and pedagogical pros and cons of using video in teaching.

Receptive viewing of videos. These occur when the student views the video content with the aim of receiving information in a passive way. In Kay's review this accounts for 95% of the papers examined. In this category, by far the least used are video-recorded lectures – also known as 'lecture capture'.

In general terms, receptive viewing is reported to be a good supplement to traditional lectures but less of a substitute (Copley 2007; Schreiber *et al.*, 2010; Walls *et al.*, 2010). When students are asked to report on their own impression they say that repetitive videos helped them a bit more than text-based supplementary resources (Walls *et al.*, 2010). Pursel and Fang (2012) review 47 journal articles on lecture capture. The majority of these articles conclude that students find that lecture captures have a positive influence on their educational experience. It is reported that video in itself does not improve student learning outcomes but can do so when accompanied by a proper learning design (Sung & Meyer 2013; Zottmann *et al.*, 2013). Most students do not watch the entire recorded lecture but prefer to watch segments – especially when preparing for exams (Pursel & Fang, 2012; Marchussen, 2013). Although these studies report that students perceive lecture captures to be helping them in their learning, studies directly linking viewing lecture capture and performance are absent (Pursel & Fang, 2012; Whitley-Grassi & Baizer, 2010).

Problem solving videos. Kay (2012) characterises these as explicitly aimed at helping students in their aim of problem solving. Such supporting video material is specifically designed to address the problem at hand and is not of a generic kind.

Created video podcasts enable students themselves to create video content. This allows them to learn while collaboratively designing and creating videos.

Kay found that these last two categories, taken together, account for only 5% of papers concerned with video in education (Kay, 2012). In the following section we will consider whether these insights are similarly found in the narrower field of video-supported CBT.

Video in CBT

The central idea behind our use of case-based teaching is to allow students to engage in contemporary real-life situations of firms and organisations. This practice-oriented ambition indicates that CBT builds on the same core learning assumptions that we find in problem-based learning (Zottmann *et al.*, 2013:2101) and situated learning theories.

A study by Austin *et al.* (2009) suggests that CBT can improve a student's learning by providing both the experimenting and reflecting parts of the Kolb learning cycle (Kolb, 1976). Theoretical-reflective learning is however a difficult task if the learner has little empirical experience in the subject at hand. Nevertheless, the CBT method helps to situate the learning in a specific empirical context and, thereby, to foster reflective observation. Videos are an aid in this process, making the problem more situated, while helping to put the student 'in the shoes of the decision maker'. It is important to add that this reflection should be a result of an open dialogue. Accordingly our definition of CBT would echo others in this volume and emphasise that CBT should always contain a case discussion. Furthermore, an instructional video could not be a teaching case unless it leads to some kind of public dialogue between learners.

Traditional versus Creative CBT Approaches

Following the typology developed in the introductory chapter to this anthology we have divided CBT-approaches into 'traditional' and 'creative'. We define the traditional case approach as concerned with cases with a fixed or closed ending. The CBT planning process is often very detailed in this approach. Typically, the questions and case elements are presented to the student within a pre-defined theoretical framework that will only allow them to choose between a small number of possible solutions. If the teacher can control the possible solutions or the relevance of theory in this way, then it is possible to steer the case discussion in particular directions.

Cases with closed endings are often accompanied by a large amount of pre-prepared material and this may be re-usable in new educational settings. On the other hand, the students will also have high expectations of structured case discussions. The closed-ended approach will demand that the teacher guides the discussion towards a reasonable decision that will leave the case 'solved'.

In open-ended CBT, the case material (videos, text, still images etc.) will not restrict possible reactions and the questions that the teacher will ask students about the material and this will allow for many possible solutions or threads of discussion. The open-ended CBT approach requires the teacher to be self-confident and courageous because discussions might take many practical or theoretical directions which will need to be supported.

Both approaches are time consuming and may or may not be embraced by the students. Factors influencing this include the work experience of the students, the subject matter and the time and resources allocated for feed-back.

Practice-based versus Theory-based CBT Approaches

A further, empirically based division of CBT approaches contrasts practice-based and theory based.

The practice-based orientation should illustrate *praxis* and generate interpretations of that praxis by the students. This is an orientation that is popular in several forms of professional education including nursing, medicine, and teacher training.

The theory-oriented approach is centered on presenting case material that allows the students to test theories in an effective way. Hence, the case material, including videos, is designed to inform and allow an analysis of specific theories. The approach is popular at business schools and engineering schools and somewhat popular in the social sciences. This approach could also include supplementary interventions about theory – for example, a video-recorded explanation of a theory or concept to accompany the case. This is a logic that is mirrored in the so-called 'flipped classroom' teaching methodology. The flipped classroom allows the instructional design to be flipped so that the learner would watch a video-recorded lecture at home and the classroom activities would be organised so that the student takes an active role as the discussant or participant in exercises etc. (for more information on flipped class room in general see Strayer, 2007; Bergmann & Sams, 2012).

Contrasting and Comparing the Two Spectrums

Juxtaposition of these two approaches – closed v open-ended and theory v practice – allows us to identify four ideal types of relationship between students and teachers in the CBT method (see Table 1).

Practice oriented cases	**Model 2: The Mentee** Cases where text and video content are constructed to introduce students to a specific practice. Example: chemistry and computer laboratory video tutorials (Cambell Stevens, 2004; Nemirovsky & Galves, 2004)	**Model 4: The Reflective Practitioner** Cases where text and video content are constructed to invite students to discuss different conclusions on observed practice. Example: ethnographic video case material used in teacher training (Beck et al., 2002; Abell & Cennamo, 2004; Koc et al., 2009)
Theory oriented cases	**Model 1: The Decision Maker** Cases where text and video content are constructed according to certain theoretical perspectives and debates. Example: Managerial decision making video case material (Austin et al., 2009; Zottmann et. al., 2013)	**Model 3: The Illustrator** Cases where text and video content are constructed to invite students to discuss different theory-based conclusions and analytical strategies. Example: Student's own production of video case material applying/illustrating theory (Hakkarainen & Saarelainen, 2005; Hakkarainen et al., 2007; Llinares & Valls, 2009)
	Traditional / "Closed-ended" cases	Innovative / "Open-ended" cases

Table 1: Typology of CBT based on the degree to which they are open/closed and their practice/theory orientation.

In the following section we will set out the positive and negative empirical experiences reported in the articles we have reviewed. They are arranged according to how close they come to the four ideal types described above. Neither the order nor the naming should be taken to indicate any priority but merely to show the vast range of possibilities made available by the use of videos with CBT.

Advantages and Disadvantages of Using Videos with CBT

Model 1. The Decision Maker

This model involves cases with video elements designed to help students to reach a decision based on reasoning and theory-infused discussions. For this type the student will be trained in the application of theories and the art of argumentation.

One of the advantages of this design is that it brings authenticity into the classroom and engages students (Mattisson & Ramberg, 2013; Beck *et al.,* 2002; Hakkarainen *et al.,* 2007; Austin *et* al., 2009; Brunvand, 2010). Furthermore it supports individual meaning-making from the discussion of video cases (Copeland & Decker, 1996). The use of video enables simple heuristic decision matrices to gain realism and emotional complexity. Realism would help any student to step into the shoes of the decision maker. Adding emotional complexity, however, might not suit students who are unfamiliar with case teaching pedagogics or who have little experience from organisational life (Mattisson & Ramberg, 2013).

Model 2. The Mentee

This is a design that puts the student in a position to learn from examples of mastery in relevant situations. A case study by Campbell Stevens (2004) describes how a software platform can be used successfully in different CBT settings. The software would allow 'teacher-students' and their instructors to present a mini-case on the left side of the screen, while the themes that the teacher-students should identify and explain to the instructor are displayed on the right side. This arrangement allows the instructor to control the case discussion in terms of solutions and themes to elaborate on. The advantages of using video cases in this way is that they show the complexity of a classroom environment by capturing emotions, gestures and body language for the viewer to engage in. Students generally view realism of video cases positively (see also Nemirovsky & Galvis, 2004 for *"situated generalisations"*).

Nemirovsky and Galvis (2004) argue that, in development programs, video cases about teaching style accompanied by certain questions can lead to reflections on one's own teaching practice. Video cases in such settings would significantly improve students learning of *"technological and pedagogical learning"* according to Han *et al.* (2013).

The disadvantages of using videos are chiefly concerned with the time and effort costs inherent in making video cases – especially for editing, booking and authorising classroom filming. Nevertheless these efforts would be a one-off because one can re-use the cases in subsequent years. Nilsen and Baerheim (2004) report another downside of using videos in their article on video-recorded doctor-patient interactions. In this instance, the medical students in particular showed resistance before the project started because they feared they might lose face in front of other students.

Model 3. The Illustrator

This type requires the student to role play the instructor who sheds light on different aspects of theory. By grasping different case and theory combinations the student will gain expertise in the analysis and comprehension of abstract knowledge.

Llinares and Valls (2009) used video-filmed lessons as cases for discussion in an online forum for pre-service and practising teachers. The forum showed that the videos served as a basis for student-driven discussions that were informed on a practical, a theoretical and a meta-theoretical level. The forum was set up so the students could be asked guided questions after watching a video. The questions triggered various peer-discussions where theory was used collectively to create meaning. One of the advantages in this case was that the videos served as an artifact to foster discussions on specific classroom practices. The discussion and synergistic interaction based on the videos stimulated higher order thinking among the students. On the other hand, it was only when the themes in the videos were personally involving for the students that they felt encouraged to participate in the forum discussions.

Hakkarainen *et al.* (2007) performed an action research case study of eight students who were preparing a video for the purpose of illustrating some of the dilemmas on a Network Management course. The video was going to be used in a subsequent e-learning course on the same subject. The study indicated that producing videos for cases had a positive effect on the student's emotional involvement in the learning process. The satisfaction of students was related to the opportunity to construct a local case, to being active with their study group, to being able to produce learning material for others, and to the case approach itself. In the case-writing and selection phase, the fact that the students were highly engaged enabled the teacher to revert to the role of guide (Hakkarainen *et al.*, 2007).

Further studies suggest that student-driven, video-supported case production can be beneficial in education programs where observations are important, such as in policing and nursing (Beck *et al.*, 2002).

Another advantage identified by Beck *et al.* (2002) is that students enhance their ability to identify, interpret and analyse situations if they construct their own video cases. Planning, producing and reviewing the cases all led to improvements in the quality of the case discussion. The study showed a statistically significant learning advantage for the group of students working with video cases compared with a control group that based their discussions on pre-produced case materials. Beck *et al.* also observed that class discussions on the basis of video recordings of formal learning activities (such as group presentations, fieldwork, and counselling) have strong learning potentials. Video-recorded counselling offers possibilities for the students in a specific case setting to reach deep reflections on their own experiences and on theory (Brubaker, 2011; Poulsen & Löfvall, 2014). Based on an empirical studies among students being trained as teachers, Baran (2006) asserts that video-based instructions have a positive impact on learning processes compared to more traditional lecture-based instructions.

Model 4 - The Reflective Practitioner

The Reflective Practioner is a design which employs video case material to help the student to generate empirically-based, *ad hoc* theories.

Abell and Cennamo (2004) used highly-edited videos for teachers-in-practice training. The videos contained filmed science classroom interaction between pupils and teacher as well as brief interviews with the participating teacher. The videos explicitly served as a case for reflection and the course was designed so that the video cases opened up discussions. The cases provided context that assisted the teachers in practice to uncover their own theories about teaching. The authors observed that students used the video cases as a standard to follow, as a component of self-regulated learning. Other advantages were that the videos were realistic; they helped students visualise the operationalisation of curriculum theories because of the rich nature in which the video allowed for multiple modes of representation and flexibility of use. The authors warn that using these video cases required a lot of class time and preparation. They were designed not to cover themes in a linear way but to cause students to reflect on themes as they occurred. The meta-theoretical learning that the videos afforded was one of the reasons for requiring a lot of classroom time even when the students viewing the videos were familiar with the science that was taught in the videos.

Koc *et al.* (2009) provides evidence that a problem-solving video helps students bridge the gap between theory and practice. Their study involved a long mathematics video case for use in elementary school and an online forum for discussion of the case. In the forum the teacher participating in the video case is responding to the questions and suggestions of the course participants. This case is thus a mixture of live case and video case in which the teacher from the video can provide a 'reality check' of learnings from participants in the forum. Such an on-line forum based on video cases of teaching activities can also serve as a place for peer learning between pre- and in-service teachers (Liu, 2012).

Occasions for Introducing Videos in CBT

In all four of the case model types described in Table 1 and above, videos can be introduced throughout three phases in CBT, namely; before class, during class, and after class (Poulsen & Löfvall, 2014). These are summarised in Table 2.

	Video components	
Practice oriented cases	Before: Videos with fixed questions to students' preparation; Practitioner's video tutorials During: Videos that introduce assessments questions and supplementary case data on-the-fly during class After: Video based teaching notes and recommendations	Before: Ethnographically-inspired videos of practitioners' situated practice; Videos on different analytical strategies; Videos of teacher feedback to students analytical drafts Student's own video recordings of situated practice and experiments During: Video recordings of students' role play (documentary videos) After: Students' own unstructured video diaries
Theory oriented cases	Before: Video case material with fixed working questions; Focused theoretical video lectures; Videos that introduce pre-class tests During: Video recordings of students' role play (documentary videos) After: Teacher's pre-produced video feedback on certain theoretically and analytically issues; Video based teaching notes and recommendations	Before: Video case material with open working questions; Ambiguous theoretical video lectures (addressing competing theoretical perspectives) During: Videos with supplementary case data; Video recordings of students' theoretically discussions (documentary videos) After: Teacher's retrospective video feedback on student presentations; Video based teaching notes and recommendations
	Traditional / "Closed" cases	**Innovative / "Open-ended" cases**

Table 2: Video components of CBT for use before, during and after class.

Before class, teachers design their cases to accord with course plans, personal and institutional teaching traditions. In this initial phase, teachers can be inspired by previously recorded student presentations on the case as well as watching video-based teaching notes (Nemirovsky & Galvis, 2004; HBS, 2013).

In designing conventional cases, videos with fixed questions for students' preparation, video tutorials, focused theoretical lectures and pre-class test videos can be a good supplement to the text-based case material. In more innovative examples, videos that both illustrate the practitioners' situated practice and invite the discussion of open questions lend themselves to ambiguous theoretical and analytical strategies. Video recordings of the teacher's counselling talks with student groups about their analytical progress (Bechman & Frankel, 1994; Brundvand, 2010), and students' own video recordings of situated practice and conducted experiments, can also be an effective learning component (Hirschel *et al.*, 2012).

During class videos can be used in different ways in conventional and innovative CBT. Firstly, the teacher's case presentation can be video recorded, stored and reviewed as a supplementary learning resource. Video that introduces assessments, questions and supplementary case data on-the-fly can also serve as a tool to engage students. Secondly, students can record their fellow students' role-play and theoretical discussions (Elliot, 1986; Brown et *al.*, 1997; Yamkate & Intratat, 2012). This documentary material can be used in the preparation for exam and, in some cases, as part of the course assessment (Nilsen & Baerheim, 2005). In addition to this, students can record their own individual and group-based working activities for individual reflection purposes and for class discussions if the material is shared properly (Stokoe, 2000; Nilsen & Baerheim, 2005).

In the *after class* evaluation phase, teachers can distribute to their students either pre-produced video feedback on certain theoretical and analytical issues or more retrospective feedback on previous class discussions. Teachers can also produce video teaching notes and recommendations about a specific case to make it easier for fellow teachers to use it. This can also stimulate the introduction of CBT via educator training programs (Beck *et al.*, 2002). From the student's viewpoint, structured and unstructured video diaries can be a good supplement to written study notes.

Conclusions

Based on a review of scientific articles about the use of video in education and specifically in Case Based Teaching, this chapter describes the potential didactical benefits and ways of using video in CBT. Our review leads us to the strong conclusion that the use of video in CBT can benefit from experiences gathered in the general field of teaching and video. It also confirms the hypothesis that video in itself does not improve student learning outcomes but can do so when accompanied by a proper didactical design. In addition, video can certainly improve the motivation of learners to learn more.

In this chapter we have argued that video in CBT can be described by four different types of relationships between students and teachers. Video has a documented track record in the *reflective practitioner* and in the *mentee*, where teacher training courses in particular have showed that the use of video reinforces CBT. However, the *decision maker* relationship needs more empirical studies of the use of video with case teaching.

In developing this relationship framework, we have argued that video can be used before, during and after class. Before class, video can be used in several ways. Teachers can be inspired by previously recorded case presentations and can deploy videos as a part of the case content. In more innovative CBT settings students can produce their own videos as a class preparation. During class, case presentation can be video-recorded and later reviewed and analysed by students and teachers. As a part of the final evaluation phase, video can be used in feedback processes regarding previous class discussions.

We are in no doubt that the introduction of video as a visual and realistic component in CBT makes it possible to enhance student learning. It is our belief that video has the potential to benefit students' learning and modernise the field of case based teaching in general.

About the Authors

Christian Poulsen is PhD and external reader at Copenhagen Business School, Denmark. He can be contacted at this email: cp.ioa@cbs.dk

Steffen Löfvall is Senior Advisor and PhD at Copenhagen Business School, Denmark. He can be contacted at this email: sl.edu@cbs.dk

Chapter thirteen

ICT Tools and Approaches to Support and Enhance Case Based Learning

Stefanos Petsios, Petros Karvelis and Chrysostomos Stylios

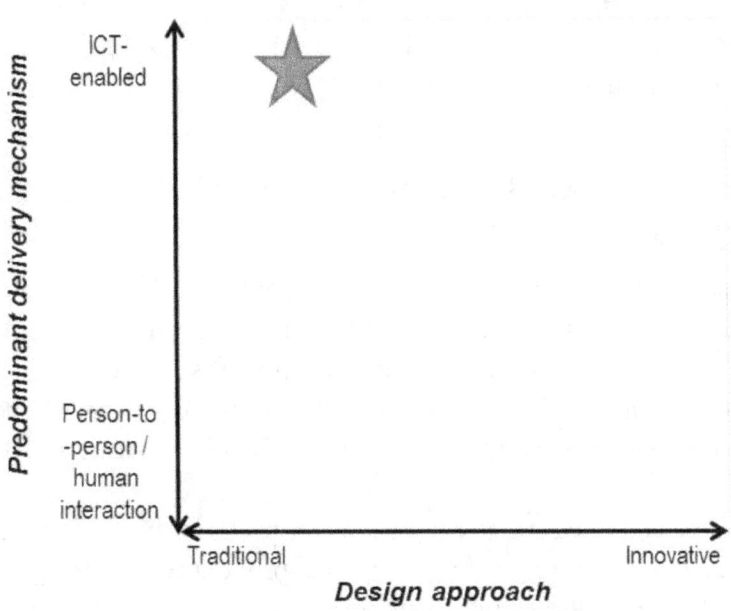

Introduction

Information and Communication Technology (ICT) tools are continuously and increasingly used for learning and educational procedures. Many educational platforms have been proposed to support learning and today these typically take advantage of wireless communications and the Internet to enable online learning. Although such ICT tools and participation technologies could enable these educational platforms to be used for Case Based Learning (CBL) relatively few have been specifically developed for this purpose. This chapter considers the extent to which pedagogical needs are met by the existing educational platforms and their tools.

Most features of educational platforms give the opportunity to create online student/teacher communities whose participants can link variously via PCs, mobile phones, tablets, web TVs etc. The generally accepted pedagogical model today offers a combination of off-line teaching methods and real time participation and interaction with the e-students. In this chapter we will describe the most representative educational platforms that support CBL. We will categorise them according to their features and their capabilities to fulfill pedagogical requirements and instructional strategies.

Pedagogical Model Requirements for Case Based Learning

A case based pedagogical model incorporates the possibility of working with more than one problem at a time. In this approach the students have to combine, choose and prioritise different disciplines and problems. CBL promotes the development of a collaborative, personal or team-based teaching approach suitable for any education field.

Case based learning is similar to problem-based learning but it is also considered as an iterative procedure covering problem orientation, problem solving and innovation. Important characteristics of CBL include hypothesis generation and the integration of learning activities. In the case based pedagogical model every case aims to teach specific attributes. In the field of business studies these will typically include organisation, risk treatment, risk management, and communication – in short, management that is faster, cheaper, better and easier. However, case based learning is not limited solely to working with cases (McNair, 1954; Bolt B, 1998; Flynn & Klein,

2001; Yadav, 2007; Zbylut, 2007; Bradley, 2004; Crawa, 2006; Lombardi, 2007; Iacono, 2011).

Instructional Strategies for Case Based Learning

Advances in ICT are having a major impact on the way people do business, access and share information, and create and transfer knowledge. Teaching and learning strategies and their procedures have to be updated to prepare students to cope with these new situations. Students need to be able to pose questions, seek and find appropriate resources for answering these questions, collaborate and co-work with others, and then to communicate and present their solutions effectively to others.

Duch *et al.* (2001) offer extensive descriptions of the desirable skills that should flow from a problem based learning strategy. In particular these include the ability to:

- think critically and be able to analyse and solve complex, real-world problems
- find, evaluate, and provide appropriate learning resources
- work cooperatively in teams or small groups
- demonstrate versatile and effective communication skills, both verbal and written
- use content knowledge and intellectual skills acquired during higher education in order to become continual learners.

Consideration of Alternative Instructional Strategies

Various instructional strategies have evolved which can complement or offer an alternative to CBL. The following examples set out key aspects.

Problem based learning (Srinivasan, 2007) is both a teaching method and an alternative to the traditional curriculum. It includes carefully designed problems that challenge students to use problem solving techniques, self-directed learning strategies, team participation skills and discipline-specific knowledge. Problem based learning can be very effective in the learning process concerned with the natural sciences.

Challenge based learning (Challenge Based Learning Organisation) has its roots in the problem based learning approach. There is a redefined approach which focuses on increasing student engagement, especially for students most at risk of dropping out. In challenge based learning a collaborative learning experience is performed where teachers and students work together to learn about compelling issues, to propose solutions to real cases and to take action. This approach requires students to reflect on their learning and the impact of their actions, and then publish their solutions for the benefit of learners anywhere in the world.

The *Role play and debates* approach is usually a real-time teaching interaction. Fortin (2012) promotes it as one of the best ways to educate people – and, in particular, students who are potential future teachers. The real time interaction accelerates learning of the skills of speed and real time adaptation. Achieving real time online teaching and learning through synchronous web-based conference platforms is an essential component of any e-education platform – especially when there are high levels of demand but limited hardware resources and network infrastructure. When the online teaching is delivered asynchronously it often deploys text-based chat or forum platforms to enable debates about matters of relevance to the course.

Virtual Environments and Simulation of real cases can be particularly effective when training students to deal with 'close to reality' situations. This is a novel and emerging approach with many possible expansions and features that may be escalated to provide virtual worlds for educational and skills training purposes. The technological trends in portable devices and upgraded metropolitan infrastructures enable the use of augmented reality tools that simulate the real world.

Analysis and reflection are capabilities that are prioritised in many

Higher Education institutions. However, the scope of the analysis stage is often very wide and under-specified and this can make it very hard for students to discern and address the real case problems. To remedy this, tutors may have to gather the students' reflections and motivate them to perform new and better analysis.

Long term projects can be a highly effective teaching strategy for team building and for developing skills to work collaboratively. Learning and working in groups involves shared and learned values, resources and ways of implementing tasks. Teams learn how to succeed by combining these factors. The effectiveness of a team – and of its individual members – will depend on their ability to respect differences within the team.

ICT Tools for Case Based Learning

There are many learning platforms offering a variety of features and specifications, The main criteria for selecting the platforms are that they should be used by a large number of users and should to be actively supported.

There is a recent trend on web-based education platforms towards having an up to date web browser as a minimum client requirement. In the following section we envisage the set of features that would make an ideal platform focusing on Case Based Learning.

A Review of Representative E-Learning Platforms

Numerous ICT tools and platforms are available for tutoring that their vendors claim have features for case based learning. Table 1 (below) presents in alphabetical order a representative sample of the currently available platforms that are providing CBL tools. The key characteristics of these are then summarised and evaluated. Table 2 then compares the reviewed platforms on the basis of the features and functionality offered.

Platform	Web Page
ATutor	http://www.atutor.ca
Dokeos	http://www.dokeos.com
dotLRN	http://www.dotlrn.org
ILIAS	http://www.ilias.de
LON-CAPA	http://www.lon-capa.org
Moodle	http://www.moodle.org
OpenACS	http://www.openacs.org
Sakai	http://www.sakaiproject.org
Docebo	http://www.docebo.com
Claroline	http://www.claronie.net
SLED	http://www.secondlife.com
Shareville	http://www.shareville.bcu.ac.uk

Table 1: Platforms provided features for Case Base Learning

ATutor is a standards-compliant, Web-based Learning Content Management System (LCMS) developed by the Adaptive Technology Resource Centre of the University of Toronto. It is open-source software compliant with the GNU Project Standards. This means that course content created in ATutor and other compliant packages can be exported/imported from one to the other.

Dokeos (Scalise & Gifford, 2010) is a platform for distance learning (ie an e-learning platform) which is intuitive and easy to use mainly by trainers, learners and continuing education auditors. Dokeos allows trainers to focus on creating scenarios and content by freeing them from any technical aspect. It also provides collaborative tools: videoconferencing, forums, blogs, and wiki etc. Dokeos includes four main components, namely; AUTHOR to build e-learning content, LMS to handle interaction with learners, SHOP to sell a course catalog, and EVALUATE for assessment and certification.

.LRN (pronounced "dot learn") is actually a global community of educators, designers, and software developers who partner together to drive educational innovation. This software is open source and this enables organisations to invest in people and curriculum development instead of expensive licensing and support fees.

ILIAS is an open source web-based learning management system (LMS). It supports learning content management and tools for collaboration, communication, evaluation and assessment. The software is published under the GNU General Public License and can be run on any server that supports PHP and MySQL.

LON-CAPA (Learning Online Network with Computer-Assisted Personalized Approach) is an e-learning platform which possesses the standard features of many learning platforms (user roles, calendar, e-mail, chat rooms, blogs, resource construction, test grading, etc.). The main advance of traditional e-learning platforms is that the web servers can communicate with each other. Consequently, the term LON-CAPA also refers to the LON-CAPA network, i.e. the entire set of LON-CAPA web servers and the specific implementation of an internet protocol that connects these web servers.

Moodle (acronym for Modular Object-Oriented Dynamic Learning Environment) is a free software e-learning platform, also known as a Learning Management System, or Virtual Learning Environment (VLE).

Moodle has several features considered typical of an e-learning platform, plus some original innovations (like its filtering system). Moodle is very similar to a learning management system. Moodle is widely used in a range of environments such as education, training and development, and business settings.

OpenACS (The Open Architecture Community System) is an open-source web application framework.

The Open Architecture Community System provides:

- A set of applications that are used to deploy web sites and are strong on collaboration. Some of the applications are Workflow, CMS, and Messaging, Bug/Issue tracker, e-commerce, blogger, chat and forums.
- A sophisticated application development toolkit that provides an extensive set of APIs and services to enable quick development of new applications. Features include sophisticated permissioning, full internationalisation, Ajax, form builder, object model, automated testing, sub-sites and a powerful package manager.

Sakai is a community of academic institutions, commercial organisations and individuals who work together to develop a common Collaboration and Learning Environment (CLE). The Sakai CLE is a free, community source, educational software platform distributed under the Educational Community License (a type of open source license). The Sakai CLE is used for teaching, research and collaboration. Systems of this type are also known as Course Management Systems (CMS), Learning Management Systems (LMS), or Virtual Learning Environments (VLE).

Docebo. The Docebo suite is a completely free content management (CMS) and e-learning (LMS) platform released under Open Source license.

Claroline is a collaborative eLearning and eWorking platform (Learning Management System) released under the GPL Open Source license. It is used in hundreds of organisations worldwide ranging from universities to schools and from companies to associations to create and administer courses and collaboration spaces over the web. Claroline is used in more than 100 countries and is available in 35 languages.

Second Life (SLED) is an immersive, online, simulated environment, with 3-D graphics that allow users to interact by means of an avatar – a virtual embodiment of a person (or oneself) that mimics real-life interactions. SLED has a user base of thousands of registered avatars. These avatars can be used for many different purposes such as gaming, social networking, marketing and commerce and real world business. The software incorporates a three-dimensional modeling tool based on simple geometric shapes that allows avatars to build virtual objects.

Shareville is a backronym for Shareable, Holistic Assets and Resources, Existing in a Virtual Interactive Lifelong Learning Environment (Staley & Faniglione, 2010; Lowe *et al.*, this volume). The hardware specification required to run the environment is minimal and, being web-based, it works on a variety of computer platforms. Shareville provides an approximation of the socially and ethnically diverse city of Birmingham, England, and many of the local areas and landmarks within the city are parodied in the names used within Shareville.

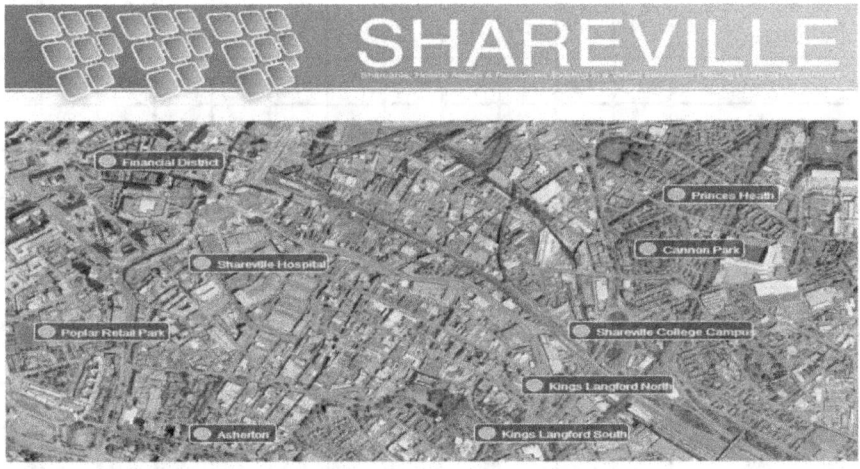

Figure 1: The Shareville Map.

Navigation within the Shareville environment is possible through 'point and click'. At the top of each page there is a breadcrumb trail to improve accessibility, alongside quick navigation to the locations. There is no 'full screen' mode or fully immersive environment. The perspective of the student is always 'first person', so there is no requirement for an avataristic representation on screen. Whilst not a JISC-sponsored project, the Joint Information Systems Committee has demonstrated interest in Shareville, including presentations at online conferences (Staley, Mackenzie, Hetherington & Faniglione, 2009).

Table 2 presents a comparison of the reviewed platforms based on their provision (or not) of features or attributes which we consider to be essential.

	ATutor	Dokeos	dotLRN	ILIAS	LON CAPA	Moodle	Open ACS	Sakai	Docebo	Claroline	SLED	Shareville
Available free of charge	✓				✓	✓	✓	✓		✓		
Platform		✓			✓	✓	✓	✓	✓	✓		
Interface		✓			✓	✓	✓	✓	✓	✓	✓	✓
User Account		✓	✓		✓	✓	✓	✓	✓	✓	✓	✓
Email	✓	✓	✓	✓		✓	✓	✓		✓		
GradeBook	✓	✓	✓	✓	✓	✓	✓	✓		✓		
FAQs	✓		✓	✓		✓	✓	✓	✓	✓		
File Storage		✓	✓			✓	✓	✓		✓		
Forums	✓	✓			✓	✓	✓	✓	✓	✓		
News	✓	✓				✓		✓	✓	✓		
Survey	✓	✓			✓	✓		✓	✓	✓		
application for Android Devices									✓			
application for iOS Devices									✓			

	ATutor	Dokeos	dotLRN	ILIAS	LON CAPA	Moodle	Open ACS	Sakai	Docebo	Claroline	SLED	Shareville
Web TV or Smart TV												
Real time participation and interaction												
problem based learning	✓	✓				✓	✓					✓
challenge based learning	✓	✓				✓	✓		✓			
role play and debates												✓
simulation												✓
analysis and reflection	✓					✓	✓					
group projects	✓					✓	✓					

Table 2: Comparison of the features provided by learning platforms reviewed

E-Learning Platforms which Support Case Based Teaching

A successful e-learning platform has to satisfy certain rules in order to be effective and able to respond to a well-defined scenario. The main requirement of a web case based platform is to support the authoring of cases and to provide and elaborate different types of learning activities based on cases. In our view the essential components of a case based teaching platform are:

- Users: The personal profile of the user.
- Articles: The abstract and the analytical description of the case.

- Keywords: Each case should be described by a number of keywords.
- Forums: A place where the users can communicate, collaborate, chat and ask questions with other users.
- Questionnaires: online tests where questions and multiple choice answers are presented to the student.
- Administration of each case.

Table 3 presents a comparison of the case based features for different e-learning platforms. In order to compare and grade each platform we have introduced the following formula which reflects the value of adoption of the different case based teaching features mentioned above:

$$\text{Grade of Platform} = \frac{\text{number of Case Based Features}}{\text{total number of Case Based Features}} * 100.$$

Platforms	ATutor	Dokeos	dotLRN	ILIAS	LON-CAPA	Moodle	OpenACS	Sakai	Docebo	Claroline	SLED	Shareville
Users	-	+	+	+	+	+	+	+	+	+	+	+
Articles	+	+	+	+	+	+	+	+	+	+	+	+
Keywords	-	-	-	-	+	+	-	+	+	+	-	+
Forums	+	+	-	-	+	+	+	+	+	+	-	-
Questionaires	+	+	+	-	-	+	+	-	+	+	-	+
Administration	+	+	+	+	+	+	+	+	+	+	+	-
Grade	67%	83%	67%	50%	83%	100%	83%	83%	100%	100%	50%	67%

Table 3: Comparison of the reviewed e-learning platforms based on the features provided for case based teaching and learning

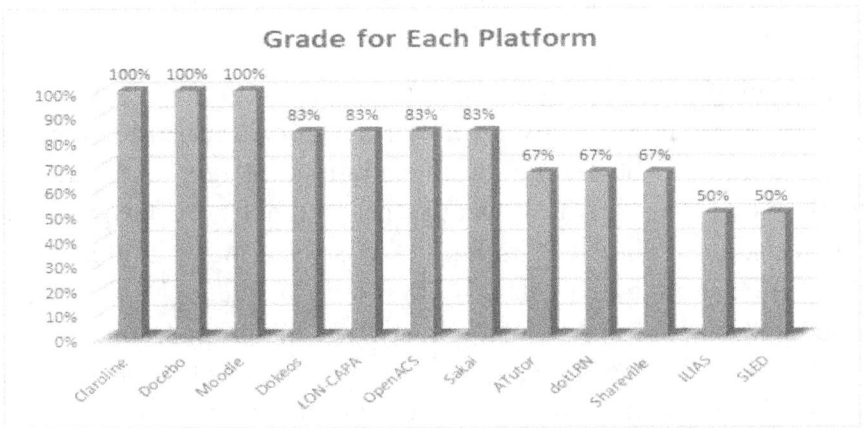

Figure 2: Indicative grading of the reviewed platforms based on the proportion of essential features provided.

Figure 1 indicates that Claronine, Docebo and Moodle can support all the essential features needed for case based teaching. Furthermore two out of the three best platforms Claronine and Moodle are free to use under the General Public License (GPL) license; the Docebo platform is offered as a paid service.

Case Based Learning in Computer Science Teaching

Computer science teaching poses a challenge to case based teaching and learning pedagogies because, unlike the other sciences, computer science deals with problems from a wide spectrum of unrelated disciplines. However, we observe that teaching in computer science is generally still based on traditional teaching approaches. Below, we propose how case based teaching principles could be used to design and conduct two undergraduate computer science courses, namely; Introduction to Programming and Software Engineering.

Example 1: a Procedural Programming Language Course

The learning of code programming is central in computer science and it requires a range of activities to be developed: learn the language features and attributes, outline the program design, and build and comprehend a program. Typically the textbooks for programming courses suggest similar learning methods – starting with declarative knowledge about a particular programming language. However, case based teaching is suitable for application in any programming course. For example, Esteves *et al.* (2010) report a recent attempt where the Second Life environment has been used to teach Programming

Course Description. The course considered here is Introduction to Programming. The course is run during the first year of a four year undergraduate program leading to a Bachelor degree in Computer Engineering at the Technological Educational Institute of Epirus, Greece. The course is taught over a period of 13 weeks; every week involves two hours for theory, two hours for tutoring and two hours of practice in the computer laboratory.

The course covers the basic programming principles and techniques for the C programming language. Procedural programming languages are based on the concept of the unit and scope (the data viewing range of an executable code statement). A procedural program is composed of one or more units or modules, which are either user coded or provided in a code library. Each module is composed of one or more procedures, also called a function, routine, subroutine, or method, depending on the language.

The main topics include Variables, Loops, Conditions, Functions and Files. This course aims to provide students with the necessary knowledge and ability to write their own very basic C applications (Robins *et al.*, 2003).

Teaching Strategy through Cases. Our literature review revealed two quite different proposed structures for a course on Programming;

one by Lin *et al.* (1992), the other by Spooner *et al.* (1997). These differences can be seen in Table 4.

Structure A (Lin *et al.*, 1992)	Structure B (Spooner *et al.*, 1997)
1. Programming Problem statement 2. Solution process description 3. Code listing 4. Study questions 5. Test questions	1. Motivation 2. Background 3. Algorithm development 4. New Programming concepts 5. Solution program 6. Discussion 7. Further study

Table 4: Two structures for a Programming course

In our view structure B is the most suitable for case based teaching and learning for the following reasons.

1. Motivation. This section defines the problem and aims to attract the student's interest by providing a simple motivation

2. Background. Several details and necessary information are provided to assist the student to solve the problem. For example, pointers highlight to the student other types of information such as web links and books.

3. Algorithm Designing. A stepwise approach is suggested to encourage good software engineering practices such as functional programming. The user is asked to outline the program that he has designed.

4. New Programming Concepts. This section addresses the question of what new programming concepts are needed to implement the algorithm designed in step 3.

5. Solution Program. An indicative complete program which solves the problem is set out.
6. Discussion. Here a discussion is inaugurated to enable all the students on the course to discuss the provided solution program and the meaning of the results.
7. Further Study. Students are provided with pointers to external links that could help them to explore alternative programming solutions.

Example 2: a Software Engineering Course

Our Software Engineering course is usually taught during the 6th or 7th semester; it aims to teach students to develop integrated IT systems. We find that a case based learning approach in most suitable for this course because it is ideal for use by small groups of technologically mature and motivated students. A dedicated faculty tutor will teach them basic software engineering concepts in the context of real software engineering cases. The proposed process follows the following basic steps:

- A real application software engineering problem is presented to the students who are arranged into small groups. They organise their ideas to deal with the given problem by using their existing knowledge and then attempt to define the broad nature of the problem.

- Through discussion, students pose questions to each other in order to delineate aspects of the problem that they do not understand. The answers to the questions are organised to create a Software Requirement Analysis. This analysis is evaluated by the tutor who poses new questions to the team and continually encourages the students to define what they know about the problem and, more importantly, what they don't know. The finalised requirements analysis exposes the analysis of the real problem.

- Then the students work in groups to update the software requirement analysis and to describe the final functional and non-functional requirements of the system. In each stage of the analysis the students develop a corresponding study (such as a feasibility study and a study of anticipated costs, etc.) that the tutor has to evaluate. This is done not by error correction but by posing relevant questions or dilemmas so that students will update their reports and minimise the gap with the real case scenario.

- The next stage of the case based learning approach requires the group to start the modular software design and software architecture. Each member initiates a detailed analysis of a system module and tests all the modules of the other group members. In this phase, students work on their own but they also have to collaborate with the other team members. The modular approach helps students to improve their skills in interfacing, reusability, cost evaluation, implementation cost, and effort estimation. At this stage we do not focus the students on the software implementation of the project but on creating a proper full software design report. This will use software illustration procedures such as use cases diagrams, activity and state diagrams, collaboration diagrams and etc. These diagrams would be used by any qualified software developer in order to create the integrated software which solves the real problem.

- Finally, the students compare their outputs with the indicated real problem output and reflect on what they have learned, integrating their new knowledge in to the context of the problem. Students are also encouraged to summarise their knowledge and connect new software engineering problems to old ones. They continue to define new learning approaches as they progress through the problem. By now students will understand that Software Engineering is an ongoing process with new methodologies and techniques even though the principles regarding the system requirement description remain the same.

In the Computer Engineering department of the Technological Educational Institute of Epirus, Greece, the Software Engineering course incorporates the case based learning process described above. An e-learning approach based on the Moodle platform is now being developed to coordinate the weekly assignments, resources and case based learning material. Moreover, we are introducing the use of the kaltura add-on (kaltura.org) as a video library of useful in class recordings and the bigbluebutton (bigbluebutton.org) add-on for group and tutor sessions to evaluate the progress on the real software engineering case.

Conclusions

This chapter has described a representative sample of available e-learning platforms and set out the features each has that would make them suitable for developing case based teaching. These analyses indicate that the Moodle platform is the most suitable one because it offers all the features needed. Furthermore, it is a free platform that is actively supported by a world-wide community of user/developers and provides a large number of features. However, no single platform can be the perfect one for case based teaching and learning. Designers and developers should realise that a new case based teaching platform will not always stand alone; it has to be able to work in conjunction with other ICT platforms such as kaltura for on line video storage and big blue button for webinars.

Most importantly, tutors have to realise that case based teaching platforms require their support during the design and development stage so they will be able to build efficient databases of case examples. In addition they will need ICT tools which incorporate mechanisms to produce efficiency metrics at the end of each case based learning session. This will enable the tutor and developer to evaluate and update the session.

The improved functionality offered by available case based teaching approaches is leading to increasing take up by educators. Furthermore, almost every significant platform provides regular updates and new useful features.

We recommend that the designers of such systems should enable more and more cross-platform operations and inter-operability. This could be achieved either with an external add-on or with an embedded module. In our view this would significantly increase the value and effectiveness of case based learning.

The user interfaces for all the tools we have examined in this chapter are well designed web platforms providing the user with excellent browsing via a personal computer. However the same cannot be said for portable devices such as the tablets and smartphones that are becoming increasingly popular. We exhort interface designers to focus on creating modern, responsive web interfaces and bespoke applications for iOS or Android-based devices. This is because a major success factor of e-platforms is the ability to learn wherever and whenever you want – including the comfort of the TV room. Accordingly tutors should press the platform designers to create intuitive interfaces for their platforms which are aligned with WebTV and Smart TV protocols. Such features would also prove extremely useful in the classroom because the tutor, using an installed Smart TV could navigates to a movie or video or web source, discuss this with his class, and then encourage the students to use their smart phones to search for relevant information that will strengthen their knowledge. The addition of linkages to a cloud computing shared disc space could further interest and engage students.

Case based teaching and learning platforms need to be capable of inter-operating with third party platforms. In our observation existing virtual worlds and educational tools for simulation lack the support of add-ons for creating easy and fast new scenarios. The solution will be for developers to create a universal prototyping and modelling language for creating real case scenarios in a formal and machine readable format. Such a protocol, when accompanied by the necessary ICT tools, will promote the reusability and modular construction of case based learning materials and provide a better quality of features and services to the students and tutors.

About the Authors

Stefanos Petsios is a Researcher at the Laboratory of Knowledge & Intelligent Computing of the Department of Computer Engineering at the Technological Educational Institute of Epirus, Greece. He can be contacted at this email: stefanos@kic.teiep.gr

Petros Karvelis is a Postdoctoral Researcher at the Laboratory of Knowledge & Intelligent Computing of the Department of Computer Engineering at the Technological Educational Institute of Epirus, Greece. He can be contacted at this email: pkarvelis@gmail.com

Chrysostomos Stylios is Associate Professor in the Department of Computer Engineering at the Technological Educational Institute of Epirus, Greece. He can be contacted at this email: stylios@teiep.gr

Chapter fourteen

The Use of Fuzzy Cognitive Maps for Learning and Development of Medical Case Learning Scenarios

Voula Georgopoulos and Chrysostomos Stylios

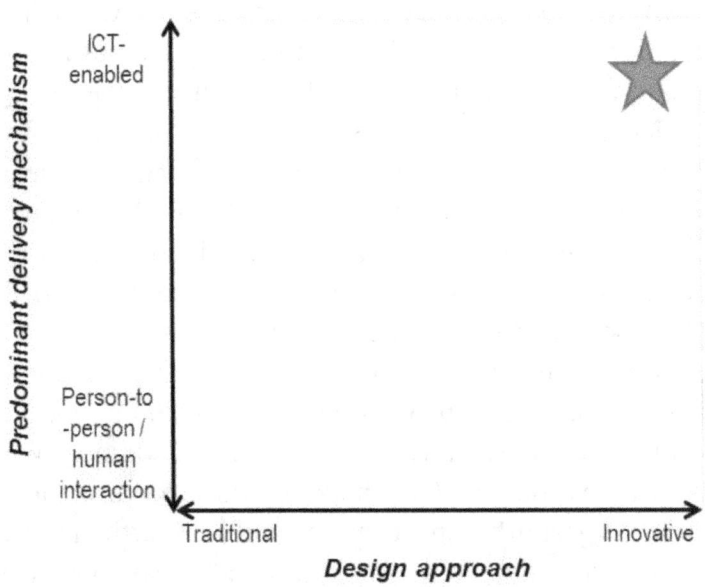

Introduction

Case studies are widely used in medical education to teach reasoning and decision-making skills and to prepare medical students and young professionals to move on to clinical practice. With case studies, students can see how they can transfer their knowledge and skills to the actual clinical setting without the pressure, constraints, and stress of being actually involved with a patient in a critical situation.

Scenario-based learning (SBL) refers to any educational approach that involves the intentional use of, or dependence upon, scenarios to bring about desired learning outcomes. Scenarios within this context may be a given set of circumstances that can potentially occur in a particular case, such as a description of human behaviour, trigger events, critical incidents or even a human dilemma, (Errington, 2003; Tripp, 1993; Wilkie, 2000).

Fuzzy Cognitive Map (FCM) development is a soft computing approach based on exploiting human knowledge and experience through an interactive procedure where a group of subject matter experts is assembled to provide their experience and to design the FCM. Then, by way of aggregation, an integrated FCM is produced. In a similar way, a group of learners can collaborate and co-work to study and understand a problem. Based on this they suggest and create a mental model and represent it in the form of a FCM. The abstract model produced by every group of students is compared with an established model put forward by the teacher. The students are then able to change and update their proposed model and to examine different scenarios so that at the end they have acquired thorough knowledge and experience of the problem.

Case studies and scenarios are particularly useful for the area of medical decisions and problem-solving; typically, these are complex and potential outcomes have a degree of uncertainty. Within the context of this work, FCM methodology is used to create abstract models and suggest different scenarios within a particular case study that impose various inputs, events, facts and behaviours which may lead to different outcomes.

This chapter introduces Fuzzy Cognitive Maps as a methodology for case based learning. It briefly describes Fuzzy Cognitive Maps, how they could be used as a teaching tool using case learning scenarios and specifically explores Medical Decision Case Scenarios.

About Fuzzy Cognitive Maps

Concept mapping is an established technique for representing knowledge in graphs. It was developed by Novak in the 1960s, applied over a 12 year period and reported much later (Novak, 1998). In essence, it is an individual's diagrammatic interpretation of ideas, since it connects two or more concepts by words and expressions that describe their relationship. It has been used in education for more than 25 years to promote learning and understanding of difficult concepts. According to a recent systematic review (Daley & Torre, 2010) concept maps foster in the learner the development of meaningful learning, critical thinking and problem solving. They reported that in medical education, through concept maps, students are able to integrate basic and clinical science information as well as demonstrate more integrated holistic thinking patterns. This is an essential element in medical decision making.

On the other hand, a *cognitive map* is a graphical representation that specifically indicates causal relationships between concepts. It is a directed graph of nodes (concepts) that are connected by edges (directional lines) that represent positive or negative causal relationships. For example, concept A has a positive causal relationship to concept B when an increase in Concept A causes an increase in Concept B. Alternately, when concept A has a negative causal relationship to concept B then an increase in Concept A will cause an decrease in Concept B. Cognitive maps were developed by political scientist Robert Axelrod (1976). In his design the edge values between concepts were +1 (positive causality), -1 (negative causality), or 0 (no causality). This implies that cognitive maps represent formal, bivalent, true or false logical relationships. In many sciences where there is a great degree of uncertainty in the knowledge base (for example, in social sciences, medical sciences, and business), concepts are, for the most part, not related by such crisp (0,1) relationships. There is a degree of causality in relationships between concepts that experts can best describe in linguistic terms. Such terms are: "sometimes", "not likely", "very likely", "always", "never" etc. These linguistic terms may correspond to fuzzy values *between* 0 and 1 (as opposed to crisp) through membership functions. Additionally, in these sciences experts do not always agree on the degree of causality; so, for example, one expert may consider the causal relationship between two concepts as "very likely", a second expert as "likely", while a third one "very likely". The mathematical field of Fuzzy Logic allows mathematical operations between membership functions so that this collective knowledge is represented in a more complex concept mapping tool, the Fuzzy Cognitive Map.

A Fuzzy Cognitive Map (FCM) is a flexible soft computing tool that is based on a synergistic cooperation of Fuzzy Logic and Neural Network methodologies and it has been successfully applied in a large variety of disciplines. FCMs model the world as a collection of concepts and causal relations between concepts that are created exploiting the experience and knowledge of experts. In a graphical illustration, an FCM appears as a signed, weighted graph with feedback that consists of nodes and weighted arcs (Kosko, 1986), as shown in Figure 1.

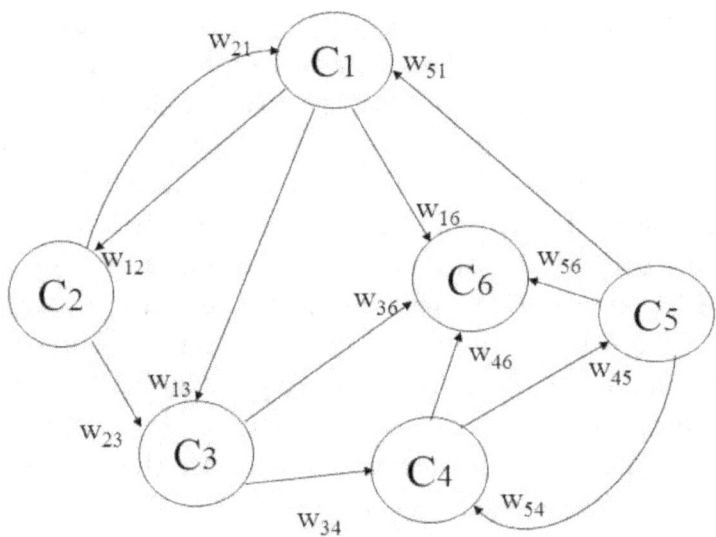

Figure 1. A Fuzzy Cognitive Map comprised of nodes (C_i) and weights (W_{ij})

Nodes are concepts that are key elements used to describe the behaviour of the system being modelled. The concepts can be events, actions, goals, values, or trends of the system being modelled by the FCM. FCMs are considered as fuzzy feedback models of causality, where the weighted interconnections between concepts represent the existing causality between the corresponding entities, thus creating an interconnected network of interrelated concepts, like an abstract mental model. A weighted arc value W_{ij} from causal concept C_i to affected concept C_j describes the degree by which the first concept influences the latter, either positively or negatively. Feedback interconnections are permitted along with 'if-then' inferencing. This allows FCMs to model complex, nonlinear, dynamic systems such as medical and patient systems.

Medical decisions can be complex because they may involve a number of possible diagnoses and/or management options, a large amount of data to be handled, determination if the existing data and information is sufficient or if further testing is required and, finally, consideration of the risk of complications. Therefore, approaches that model medical decisions are complex ones which frequently involve a significant number of variable factors including changing characteristics, unexpected events, new facts, and combinations of alarm situations.

Medical Decision Support Systems (MDSS) have been introduced to provide consultation and support to medical professionals automatically. Typically they are developed by using methodologies that resemble human-like decision-making procedures. FCMs have been used successfully to design and implement Medical Decision Support Systems because these use a human-like reasoning approach and can handle information which is vague, incomplete, complementary and/or conflicting.

Due to the way in which an FCM MDSS is constructed, it is a suitable tool for formalising understandings of conceptual and causal relationships (Kosko, 1993). Such a FCM MDSS can be used to teach reasoning and decision-making skills and to prepare students to become problem-solving clinicians. This can be achieved by two separate tasks.

In the first task, the students themselves are the 'experts' and draw their own fuzzy cognitive map of the decision process after reading up/learning all relative theoretical material. Linguistic Causal relationships between concepts are established by each student. Comparisons of maps and discussion lead to a 'group of experts' version of the map. The aggregated FCM designed by the group of students is then compared to an actual FCM MDSS designed, approved and used in everyday practice by clinicians.

In the second task, medical learning scenarios are established using the dynamic nature of FCMs inherently in the structure and operation of the MDSS. We will explain and illustrate these in the next section.

Learning Based on Fuzzy Cognitive Maps

Fuzzy Cognitive Mapping can be used as a teaching tool because it is an illustrative approach that enables learners to enhance their comprehension of a field being studied. FCMs are suitable for illustrating cases because of the way they are developed – that is, the concept-nodes and the interrelations between them (weights) are determined by subject matter experts using their background knowledge and experience. An FCM represents the key concepts, the causal directions among them and their relationship using linguistic variables.

A learning procedure using FCMs starts with the learner studying the relevant subject matter and then understanding the causal relationships between key concepts by drawing cognitive maps with linguistic connections between concepts chosen by the learner. Each learner creates his/her map based on their comprehension of the subject matter. Learners in groups discuss, argue and finally aggregate their opinions and maps into a final concluded map with linguistic connections. The teacher provides an FCM that has been designed by field experts and has proved its merit in practice. Then learners, in consultation with the teacher, are able to compare the learner map and the subject matter experts' maps concerning concepts included and interconnections between concepts. This procedure is shown in Figure 2, where the feedback discussion and comparison approach has great importance for enhancing learners' knowledge and understanding.

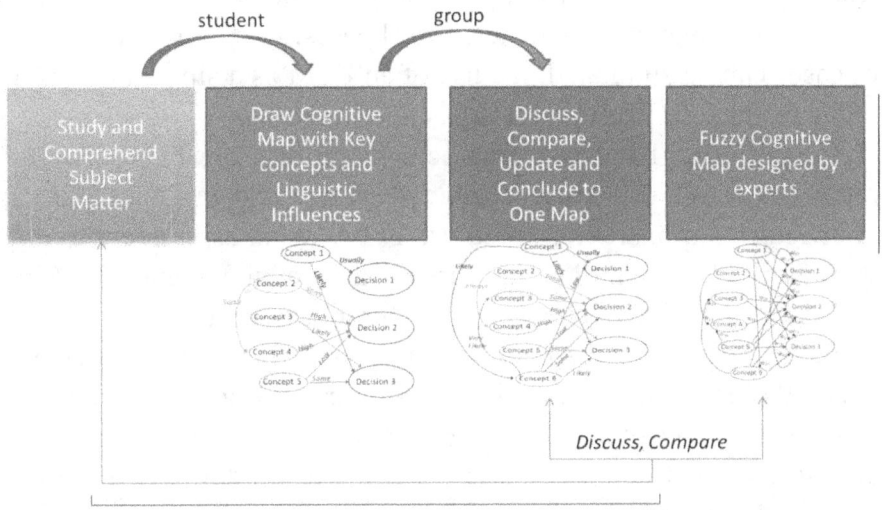

Figure 2. Learning through case problem understanding and solving

For every case, the FCM designed by experts is a reference one which allows comparison and manipulation by the learners. Therefore, a learner who is using the FCM-based teaching tool has already studied the corresponding field and is able to increase his/her comprehension by testing it with the FCM tool. The learner is able to understand the problem and 'decipher' the relative concepts/variables of the FCM tool by activating/deactivating them (following the procedure shown in Figure 3). The learner is able to choose different initialisation values for the concepts and in this way to test and run different scenarios. When a case problem is given to the learner s/he should activate the appropriate concepts by applying their existing knowledge to the specific case and following the influence that this has on the output concepts (outcomes) of FCM. Then, s/he may make one or more modifications to the initial values of the input concepts or alter the activation level among the concepts and this may lead to different outcomes. In this way, the learner can implement various scenarios based on real or hypothetical suggestions and can perceive the behaviour and notice any differences resulting from a change.

From a pedagogical viewpoint, this complementary method of learning offers the opportunity to apply the theoretical knowledge in virtual situations that characterise real cases. And, because a variety of cases can be simulated, the use of an FCM as a simulation/testing tool can enhance learning through experiment.

On the other hand, any instructor could use the FCM tool as a means to check or create didactic scenarios and evaluate learners' knowledge. An instructor could use FCMs as an assessment tool for various didactic scenarios (i.e. cases with varying parameters). Since FCMs are sensitive to changes – they produce different outcomes for slight changes – the instructor could use an FCM tool to assess or to check the correctness of a didactic scenario, to quantify the degree of interaction between the concepts/variables with each other, and to choose the most appropriate scenario for using during the learning process. More specifically, an instructor is able to evaluate possible cases that illustrate different circumstances by activating different concepts.

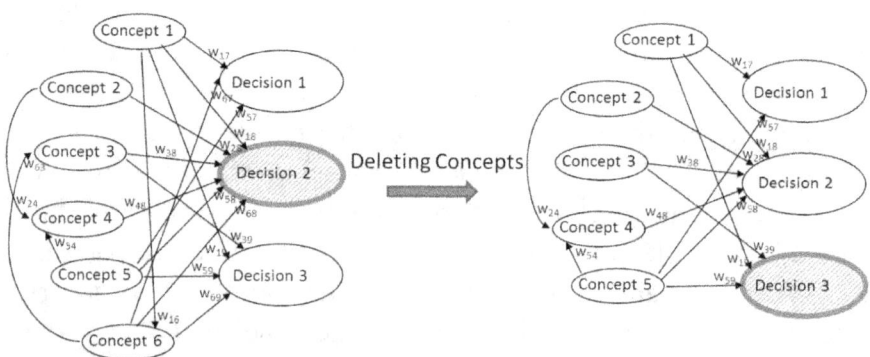

Figure 3. Illustrative scenario testing by deactivating concept 6 and observing that the decision is changed from 'Decision 2' to 'Decision 3'

Another pedagogical aspect of the FCM tool is that it can support instructors in evaluating learners. As a learner evaluation tool the proposed method accords with modern strategies of teaching and training that require the learner to be active and able to discover knowledge through practice and experiential learning methods.

FCMs have been implemented for a wide variety of fields and they are highly applicable to the domain of medicine. Many FCM models have been developed for medical decision support in a variety of situations, namely; making a decision, concluding to a diagnosis, characterising tumours or providing a clinical guideline. Fuzzy Cognitive Map Medical Decision Support Systems (FCM MDSSs) have been successfully used for differential diagnosis in speech and language pathology (Georgopoulos, Malandraki, & Stylios, 2003), making decisions during labour (Stylios, Georgopoulos, Malandraki, & Chouliara, 2008; Stylios & Georgopoulos, 2010), decision-making choices in external beam radiation therapy (Georgopoulos & Stylios, 2008), emergency room triage (Georgopoulos & Stylios, 2013a) and post-triage decisions (Georgopoulos & Stylios, 2013b), and many other medical applications.

The above mentioned FCM MDSSs have been developed to assist medical professionals' decisions. However, due to their design, they could also be applied to the education process in order to allow further and deeper understanding of the specific medical decision process. Therefore, for an inexperienced clinician or learner, this tool can be valuable as it can assist him/her, as well as enhancing the learning experience.

Case Learning Scenarios Based on FCM Models

In case based teaching and learning scenarios, each case represents a particular problem/situation that may lead to specific decision or set of possible decisions made by medical personnel (e.g. doctors, nurses, speech and language pathologists, etc.). The FCM MDSSs are initiated by subject matter experts that determine the main concepts and the weighted interrelation among concepts through a reasoning process similar to the one that they would normally use to reach a decision.

Scenarios within these cases are built by manipulating various parameters of the FCM MDSS model to reflect changes by adding, deleting and altering concepts and/or by updating the interconnections among them. The results of each change are revealed by new values of the outcome concepts as well as by any nodes that are directly or indirectly affected by the change introduced by the scenario.

This type of learning model allows integration of theoretical knowledge with in-depth exploration of the decision-making process as well as critical analysis of 'what-if' situations. These speculation-based scenarios prepare medical professionals for clinical practice by allowing them to experience a much wider range of potentially critical situations than is possible within a more traditional education setting. At the same time this particular kind of case-based process allows medical professionals to follow the impact various changes can have both on the final outcome and on the intermediate values of components of the model.

The use of FCMs for case learning scenarios has important characteristics:

- They are easy to understand, develop and apply since they are designed in a highly intuitive manner.
- FCMs have a high level of information integration allowing a wide variety of types of information to be represented using discrete and continuous scales.
- They can easily be adjusted for new information and new situations.
- The availability of feedback and non-linearities within the system model uncovers potentially critical situations that may arise.

How FCM MDSS Learning is Applied to Obstetrics

The rich scenario building capabilities of FCM MDSSs are particularly well suited to use in the field of medicine. In the section we will discuss in detail how it is applied in the area of Obstetrics and specifically during the delivery.

The target audience is young doctors during their specialisation training to become obstetricians. These obstetrics learners are able to manipulate parameters that are measurements or events and follow them through to the output decision (outcome). They can then compare their own decision with that advocated by the MDSS and, at the same time, explore 'what-if' scenarios.

The FCM MDSS case model is run using a series of pre-set sets of parameter values representing the various cases initially set up by the instructors and aiming to mirror the authentic clinical reasoning process; these can easily be expanded with scenarios simulating evolving patient situations. The scenarios are defined by the instructors to ensure specific learning outcomes, as well as by learners to explore their own 'what-if' questions.

During the crucial stage of labour, obstetricians continuously evaluate the entire health situation of the mother and the child. As time progresses, or with the appearance of an event, they take into consideration a wide variety of factors in order to make a decision. Their decisions may be related to the well-being of the infant who is close to full-term delivery or to the risk to the maternal health when continuing with the pregnancy would outweigh the risk to the infant being delivered.

Therefore, is it vital that an obstetrician is able to decide on the basis of physical measurements whether to continue with a natural delivery or to proceed with a Caesarean section. These measurements will include fetal heart rate (FHR), the interpretation of the cardiotocograph (CTG) that monitors the fetal heart rate and the mother's contractions, and other essential indicators and metrics. In essence, any decision is based on 'weighing' the risks of maternal and/or fetal health complications.

One particular case study is concerned with the decision to carry out an emergency Caesarean section when there is a fetal distress – that is, there are vital signs that the fetus is not well, either before or during childbirth. Factors to be taken into consideration include abnormal CTG and/or acidosis and/or cord prolapse and/or abruption, obstructed labour, prolonged labour, or delivery at maternal risk compared with that from a routine, elective Caesarean section. In most real situations these factors are intrinsically fuzzy. Accordingly obstetricians use linguistic terms to characterise them – terms such as "stable", "moderate", "intense", "increased" etc.

Obstetricians consider a variety of maternal indications and fetal indications. The labour surveillance monitoring has three main components: fetal condition, progress of labour, and maternal conditions. Fetal health condition is mainly reflected in the interpretation of the Fetal Heart Rate (FHR) signal and some other physiological measurements or observations such as the colour of liquor (meconium) and vaginal examinations. Progress of labour is based on physiological examinations (descent of head, dilation of the cervix), measurement of the strength and frequency of uterine contractions, quantity and kind of drugs given to augment/induce the labour, and the elapsed time. Maternal conditions measured include pulse rate and blood pressure.

Medical Decision Support Systems – and particularly those based on Fuzzy Cognitive Maps – are well suited for labour modelling because clinicians are not always in agreement on the importance of each individual parameter, especially in situations involving induction or augmentation of labour. Clinical disagreements can also exist about what constitutes excessive FHR because of uterine activity and what management strategies to undertake when it occurs (Simpson & Miller, 2011). As a result, FCM scenario-based MDSS are particularly well-suited for training medical clinicians.

So the specific FCM MDSS case study for obstetrics has been developed to model the way in which the obstetrician decides between a normal delivery or a Caesarean section. It is a dynamic procedure where the obstetrician evaluates whether either the mother or the fetus is at serious risk and, therefore, if s/he must intervene by stopping the physiological delivery and performing an emergency Caesarean section instead of continuing with natural delivery. According to evidence-based practice, labour abnormalities and unnecessary Caesarean birth are associated with risks to the mother and baby. On the other hand, excessive uterine activity may have a negative effect on fetal oxygenation during labour and fetal acid-base status at birth (Simpson & Miller, 2011). A similar decision support system developed by Warrick *et al.* (2010) focuses on hypoxia detection based on recordings of the uterine pressure and fetal heart rate, both of which are routinely monitored during labour. The variability of these factors makes it essential to reach the best decision for both mother and baby.

The FCM MDSS takes into consideration factors based on the main parameters that an obstetrician evaluates. These parameters constitute the 13 concepts of the FCM case study model for obstetrics, which are:

- Concept 1: Decision for Normal Delivery
- Concept 2: Decision for Emergency Caesarean section
- Concept 3: Fetal Heart Rate (FHR) evaluation
- Concept 4: Meconium (Colour of liquor: from clear, to mild blood staining, to heavier bleeding)
- Concept 5: Time duration of labour in comparison to progress of the delivery
- Concept 6: Contractions of the uterus (strength and frequency)
- Concept 7: Medication (quantity of oxytocin given to mother)
- Concept 8: Diastole of Cervix (measurement)
- Concept 9: Evaluation of Cervix commendation (4 linguistic values)
- Concept 10: Position of placenta (3 linguistic values)

- Concept 11: Position of fetus (5 linguistic values)
- Concept 12: Contra-indication
- Concept 13: Fetal weight estimation (3 linguistic values)

These concepts are depicted in Figure 4. It is important to note that concepts are interrelated and these interrelationships have been included in the FCM-MDSS model according to clinical evidence-based best practice.

Given the different values that concepts 3-13 may take and the interrelationships among concepts, scenarios are built on cases by varying the parameters appropriately to reflect changes. In Figure 4 yellow squares are used to indicate that Concepts 3, 4, 7 and 8 are susceptible to change. The values of these concepts are manipulated by the learner to match the case scenario and then the FCM MDSS for labour is allowed to run step by step. The changes to the various concepts are observed as the FCM algorithm evolves. The final outcome is either Caesarean section or Normal delivery.

As well as these critical parameters, the learner has the ability to review or obtain additional information by accessing relevant material stored in the system. For example by selecting the small square on the concept 'Medication', recent literature on oxytocin dosage (Clark *et al.*, 2009) can be accessed directly from the publisher's website, as shown in Figure 5. This or other selections would have been added by the teacher as reference materials. Similarly, for fetal heart rate evaluation the latest literature on classification categories of FHR can be reviewed (Coletta *et al.*, 2010).

Due to the fact that in complex systems, such as medical systems, there can be unexpected events, the FCM scenario-based MDSS allows the possibility of trigger/alarm events that may alter the outcome unexpectedly. Such an event is, for example, Concept 3(Fetal Heart Rate (FHR) evaluation) as indicated by the red triangle in Figure 4. These trigger events occur while the user is running the FCM scenario-based MDSS and as a result may affect a number of concept values, as well as the outcome. This provides the learner with the opportunity to observe how dynamic, high-risk and unusual case scenarios evolve, allowing learning in a safe environment without placing actual patients at risk.

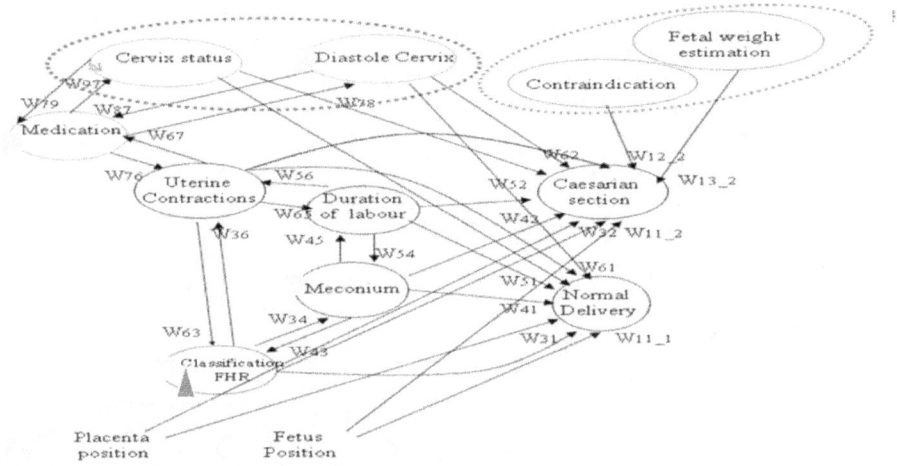

Figure 4. FCM Scenario-Based MDSS with alarm triggers for Labour Decision Support

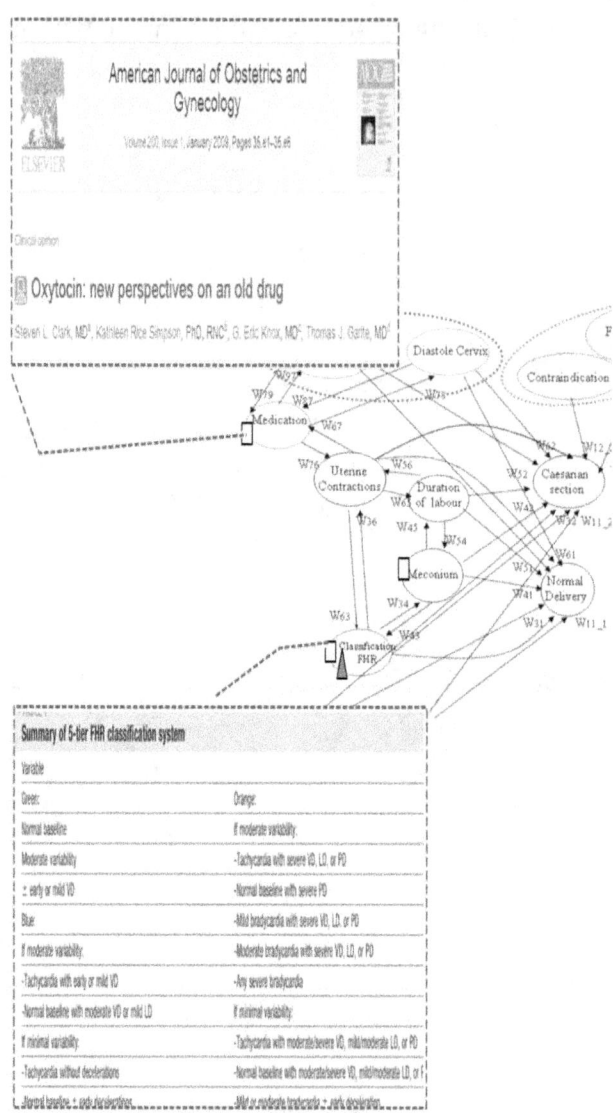

Figure 5. Access to relevant resource material (Clark et al., 2009; Coletta et al., 2010) during scenario learning in FCM MDSS for Labour Decision Support

Illustration of the Impact of Changes in Measurements

An example learning scenario is presented here for a particular patient, a pregnant woman where complications occur during labour:

- A 32 year old patient at 40 weeks gestation period in the first stages of labour is observed with temperature 36.7°C, blood pressure 120/80 mm Hg, pulse rate of 110 beats/min and has clear liquor draining. The fetal heart rate according to the monitor is 155 beats per minute. The estimated birth weight is 3 kg.
- All these indications would lead to a normal delivery and thus, the FCM MDSS for labour is run and concludes to the decision of Normal labour.
- But according to the scenario, during the labour procedure the liquor becomes meconium stained while the other parameters would initially remain the same; at this point a careful examination of factors that are influenced by this change would be required. Presence of meconium is an indication of fetal distress.
- Within the FCM Scenario-based MDSS this can be used as a trigger event altering the FHR to 114 beats/min that implies that the fetus is in distress; thus, the FCM MDSS would now advocate an emergency Caesarean delivery.

Therefore, for the learner, running such a scenario reinforces the connection between meconium staining and fetal heart rate and the possibility of an adverse outcome for the baby by proceeding with normal delivery.

Conclusions and Pedagogical Goals

Fuzzy Cognitive Mapping is an essential tool that could be used for case based and scenario learning and could be established as a complementary tool during any learning procedure. It is a versatile tool that could be useful for the learner as a way to represent and evaluate his/her knowledge by simulating cases. For the instructor it is a means to check or create didactic scenarios based on real cases. In addition, the FCM tool can be used for testing of learners because it allows the instructor to monitor students/learners and evaluate their understanding by simulating cases that are based on real events using their knowledge and principles.

A Medical Decision Support System combines the human clinical experience acquired through practice with widely-accepted, systematic, analytic approaches. Here, previously designed Fuzzy Cognitive Map Medical Decision Support System (FCM MDSS) reflecting the medical decision making process are enhanced by variety of scenarios by using a '"what-if' approach and/or trigger events to understand how a decision is made and what conditions need to be addressed in order to avoid adverse patient events.

This type of learning model allows integration of theoretical knowledge with in-depth exploration of the decision making process as well as critical analysis of 'what-if' situations. In medical education Fuzzy Cognitive Map learning tools contribute to learners being able to:

- recognise symptoms and factors correlated with the problem,
- make critical judgment and identify the importance and impact of each factor on how changes of a factor impact an end result as well as intermediate values of components in the model,
- practise and test their skills under unusual or adverse conditions without putting patients at risk due to the ability to dynamically present trigger events,
- set up their own scenarios.

Although this chapter describes the application of FCM as a case scenario based learning tool in the medical field, it is important to note that the methodology is general and can easily be adapted appropriately to other disciplines. These include business and social sciences where FCMs have also been used extensively for solving a variety of critical problems.

About the Authors:

Voula Georgopoulos is Professor in the School of Health and Welfare Professions, Technological Educational Institute of Western Greece. She can be contacted at this email: voula@teipat.gr

Chrysostomos Stylios is Associate Professor in the Department of Computer Engineering at the Technological Educational Institute of Epirus, Greece. He can be contacted at this email: stylios@teiep.gr

Collected Bibliography

AACSB (Association to Advance Collegiate Schools of Business) (2002). Management Education at Risk: Report of the Management Education. *Task Force to the AACSB International Board of Directors*. Available online: http://www.aacsb.edu/~/media/AACSB/Publications/research-reports/management-education-at-risk.ashx [Accessed 10 April, 2014].

Adler, N.J. (2006). The arts and leadership: Now that we can do anything, what will we do? *Academy of Management Learning & Education*, Vol. 5, pp. 486-499.

Adriansen, H.K. (2010). "How Criticality Affects Students' Creativity". In C. Nygaard; N. Courtney & C Holtham (Eds.) (2010). *Teaching creativity: Creativity in Teaching*, pp. 65-84. Faringdon, Oxfordshire: Libri Publishing.

Advocacy Training Council (2013). Available at http://www.advocacytrainingcouncil.org [Accessed 31 January 2014].

Alexander, R. (2008). Education for All, the quality imperative and the problem of pedagogy. *CREATE Research Monograph*, No 20. Brighton, UK: University of Sussex.

Allan, J.; K. Clarke & M. Jopling (2009). Effective Teaching in Higher Education: Perceptions of First Year Undergraduate Students. *International Journal of Teaching and learning in Higher Education*, Vol. 21, No. 3, pp. 362-372.

Allchin, D. (2013). Problem– and Case–Based Learning in Science: An Introduction to Distinctions, Values and Outcomes. *CBE–Life Science Education* Vol. 12, No. 3, pp. 364-372

Allen, J (2009). Valuing practice over theory: How beginning teachers re-orient their practice in the transition from the university to the workplace. *Teaching and Teacher Education*, Vol. 25, No. 5, pp. 647-654

Amabile, T.M. (1998). How to kill creativity. *Harvard Business Review*, Vol. 76, No. 5, September-October, pp. 77-87.

Ashfield, M.; D. Harte & V. Jackson (2013). "Social Media and Employability – Creating New Resources with Students." In C. Nygaard, S. Brand, P. Bartholomew & L. Millard (Eds.) *Student Engagement, Identity, Motivation and Community.* Farringdon, Oxfordshire: Libri Publishing.

Athavale, M. (2008). The Integrated Business Curriculum: An Examination of Perceptions and Practices. *Journal of Education for Business,* Vol. 83, No. 5, pp. 295-301.

Auster, E.R. & K.K. Wylie (2006). Creating Active Learning in the Classroom: A Systematic Approach. *Journal of Management Education*, Vol. 30, No. 2, pp. 333-353.

Austin, R.D.; R.L. Nolan, & S. O'Donnell (2009). The technology manager's journey: An extended narrative approach to educating technical leaders", *Academy of Management Learning & Education*, Vol. 8, No. 3, pp. 337-355.

Australian Institute for Teaching and School Leadership [AITSL] (2014). Accredited programs list. Available at: http://www.aitsl.edu.au/initial-teacher-education/accredited-programs-list.html [Accessed 9 January 2014].

Ausubel, D.P. & F.G. Robinson (1969). *School Learning: An introduction to educational psychology.* New York: Holt, Rinehart & Winston.

Ausubel, D.P. (1968). *Educational Psychology: A Cognitive View.* New York: Holt, Rinehart and Winston.

Axelrod, R. (1976) "The Analysis of Cognitive Maps," in R. Axelrod (Ed.), *Structure of Decision: The Cognitive Maps of Political Elites.* Princeton, NJ: Princeton University Press, pp. 55-73.

Bailey, J. & C. Ford (1996). Management as science versus management as practice in postgraduate business education. *Business Strategy Review*, Vol. 7, No. 4, pp. 7-12.

Banning, J. (2003). The Effect of the Case Method on Tolerance for Ambiguity, *Journal of Management Education,* Vol. 27, pp. 556–67.

Bar Standards Board (2013). Bar Professional Training Course: Course Specification Requirements and Guidance. Available at https://www.barstandardsboard.org.uk/media/1542061/bptc_handbook_2013-14.pdf [Accessed 31 January 2014].

Baran, E. (2006). *The effects of video-case based instruction on preservice teachers' achievement of course content*, Masters thesis, Department of Educational Sciences, The Middle East Technical University

Barnes, L.B.; C.B. Christensen & A.J. Hansen (1994). *Teaching and the case method: text, cases and readings*, 3rd ed., Boston, Mass.: Harvard Business School Press

Barnett, R. (2004). Learning for an Unknown Future. *Higher Education Research & Development*, Vol. 23, No. 3, pp. 247-260.

Barrows, H.S. (1998). The Essentials of Problem-Based Learning. *Journal of Dental Education*, Vol. 63, pp. 630-632.

Barton, K.; P. McKellar & P. Maharg. (2007). Authentic Fictions: Simulation, Professionalism and Legal Learning. *Clinical Law Review*, Vol. 14, No. 1, pp. 143-93

Baumgartner, P. (2010). "Von didaktischen Erfahrungen lernen - aber wie? Zur Systematik von Gestaltungsebenen bei Blended Learning Szenarien." In: E.S. Schiedt (Ed.). *Digitale Medien für Lehre und Forschung.* Muenster: Waxmann, pp. 188-198

Baumgartner, P. (2011). *Taxonomie von Unterrichtsmethoden.* Muenster: Waxmann.

Baumgartner, P. (2013). Educational Dimensions of MicroLearning - Towards a Taxonomy for MicroLearning. Available at http://peter.baumgartner.name/ wp-content/uploads/2013/04/Baumgartner_2013_Educational-Dimensions-for-MicroLearning.pdf [Accessed 25 March 2014]

Beck, R.J.; A. King & S.K. Marshall (2002). Video Case Construction and Preservice Teachers' Observations, *Journal of Experimental Education*, Vol. 70, No. 4, pp. 345-362.

Beckman H.B. & R.M. Frankel (1994). The use of Videotape in Internal Medicine Training, *Journal of General Internal Medicine*, September; Vol. 9, No. 9, pp. 517-21.

Bell, F. (2011). Connectivism: Its place in theory-informed research and innovation in technology-enhanced learning. *International Review of Research in Open and Distance Learning*, Special Issue – Connectivism: Design and Delivery of Social Networked Learning, Vol. 12, No. 3. Available at: http://www.irrodl.org/index.php/irrodl/article/view/902/1664 [Accessed 9 January 2014].

Bengtsson, L. (1999). *Att arbeta med case*. Malmö: Liber Ekonomi.

Bennett, S.; B. Harper & J. Hedberg (2002). Designing real life cases to support authentic design activities. *Australian Journal of Educational Technology*, Vol. 18, No. 1, pp. 1-12.

Bergmann, J. & A. Sams (2012). *How the Flipped Classroom Is Radically Transforming Learning*. Available online at http://www.thedailyriff.com/articles/how-the-flipped-classroom-is-radically-transforming-learning-536.php [Accessed March 24 2014].

Berragan, L. (2011). Simulation: An effective pedagogical approach for nursing? *Nurse Education Today*, Vol. 31, pp. 660 – 663

Biesta, G. (2009). Witnessing Deconstruction in Education: Why quasi-transcendentalism matters. *Journal of Philosophy of Education*, Vol. 43, No. 3, pp. 391-404.

Biggs, J. & C. Tang (2007). *Teaching for Quality Learning at University*. Maidenhead: Open University Press.

Biggs, J. (2003). *Teaching for Quality Learning at University*. (2nd ed.). Maidenhead: Open University Press, McGraw-Hill Education.

BIM (British Institute of Management) (1960). *Case Study Practice*. Bedford: The Sidney Press.

Blake, M. (1987). Role-play. An inset in the *Journal of Higher Education*, Vol. 11, No.3, Autumn

Bland, A.; A. Topping & B. Wood (2011). A concept analysis of simulation as a learning strategy in the education of undergraduate nursing students. *Nurse Education Today*, Vol. 31, pp. 664 – 670

Bligh, J. & A. Bleakley (2006). Distributing Menus to Hungry Learners: can learning by simulation become simulation of learning? *Medical Teacher*, Vol. 28, No. 7, pp. 606 – 613

Bloom, B.S. (1964). *Stability and Change in Human Characteristics.* New York: Wiley.

Bolt, B. (1998). Encouraging cognitive Growth through Case Discussions. *Journal of Teaching in Physical Education.* Vol. 18, No. 1, pp. 90-102

Booth, C.; S. Bowie; J. Jordan & A. Rippin (2000). The Use of the Case Method in Large and Diverse Undergraduate Business Programmes: problems and issues. *The International Journal of Management Education*, Vol. 1, No. 1, pp. 62-75.

Boud, D.; R. Cohen & D. Walker (Eds.) (1997). *Using Experience for Learning.* London, UK: Open University Press

Bovill, C., A. Cook-Sather & P. Felten (2011). "Students as co-creators of teaching approaches, course design, and curricula: implications for academic developers." In D. Green *et al.* (Eds.) *International Journal for Academic Development*, Vol. 16, Iss. 2, pp. 133-145.

Boyatzis, R. (1998). *Transforming Qualitative Information: Thematic Analysis and Code Development.* London: SAGE Publications.

Boyce, B.A. (1993). The Case Study Approach for Pedagogists. Paper presented at the Annual Meeting of *the American Alliance for Health, Physical Education, Recreation and Dance*. Washington, DC, 24–28 March.

Boyd, F.A. (1991). Business English and the Case Method: a reassessment. *TESOL Quarterly*, Vol. 25, No. 4, pp. 729–734.

Bradley, K. & B. Smyth (2004). An Architecture for Case-Based Personalized Search, In proceedings of *ECCBR 2004*, Madrid, Spain, August 30-September 2, pp. 518-532.

Branch, J.; P. Bartholomew & C. Nygaard. (Eds.) (2014). Case-based Learning in Higher Education, Faringdon, Oxfordshire: Libri Publishing

Brandes, D. & H. Phillips (1977). *Gamesters' Handbook*, Cheltenham: Stanley Thornes

Brayne, H., N. Duncan & R. Grimes (1998). *Clinical Legal Education, Active Learning in your Law School*, London: Blackstone Press.

Broder, J.; H. Klein; R. Martin; A. Rosenbloom & P. Zufan (2003). "An International Survey of Case Use in Higher Education: Report of the WACRA case standard setting committee". In H. Klein (Ed.), *Case method research and application: Interactive, innovative teaching and training, including distance and continuing education, case method, and other techniques* (pp. 3–12). Madison, WI: The World Association for Case Method Research and Application.

Brown, G.A.; J. Bull & M. Pendlebury (1997). Assessing oral communication. Chapter 10 in *Assessing Student Learning in Higher Education*, London: Routledge.

Brubaker, J. (2011). Undergraduate Political Communication in Action: volunteer experiences in a situated learning course, *Innovations in Educating and Teaching International*, Vol. 48, No. 1, pp. 3-12.

Bruner, J (1960). *The Process of Education*, Boston: Harvard College.

Brunvand, S. (2010), Best Practices for Producing Video Content for Teacher Education, *Contemporary Issues in Technology and Teacher Education*, Vol. 10, No. 2, pp. 247-256.

Burgoyne, J. & A. Mumford (2001). *Learning from the Case Method*. Cranfield: The European Case Clearing House.

Burrell, G. & G. Morgan (1979). *Sociological Paradigm and Organizational Analysis*. London, UK: Heinemann.

Burridge, R. (1998). "Role-play and Simulation in the Clinic", in H. Brayne, N. Duncan & R. Grimes (Eds.) *Clinical Legal Education, active learning in your law school*, London: Blackstone Press, pp. 173-208.

Bussière, D. (2005). Forensic Marketing: The Use of the Historical Method in a Capstone Marketing Course, *Journal of Marketing Education*, Vol. 27, pp. 61–7.

Campbell Stephens, L. (2004). "Designing and developing a video-case based interactive program for English language arts teacher preparation", in J. Brophy (Ed.) Using video in teacher education, *Advances in Research on Teaching*, Vol. 10, pp. 73-101.

Carroll, J.M. & M. Borge (2007). Articulating Case-Based Learning Outcomes and Assessment. *International Journal Teaching and Case Studies*. Vol. 1, No. 1/2, pp. 33-49

Carroll, J.M. & M.B. Rosson (2005). Towards Even More Authentic Case-Based Learning. *Educational Technology*, Vol. 45, No. 6, pp. 5-11

Çevik, Y. & T. Andre (2013). Examining Preservice Teachers' Decision Behaviors and Individual Differences in three Online Case-Based Approaches, *International Journal of Educational Research*. Vol. 58, pp. 1-14

Challenge Based Learning Organization. Available at: http://www.challengebasedlearning.org/ [Accessed 6 May 2024]

Christensen C.R.; D.A Garvin & A. Sweet (1991). *Education for Judgement*. Boston, MA: Harvard Business School Press.

Christensen, C.R. (nd). The Case method at HBS. The C. Roland Christensen Center for Teaching and Learning, Harvard Business School. Available at http://www.hbs.edu/teaching/inside-hbs/ [Accessed 25 June 2014]

Christensen, C.R. (1987). *Teaching and the case method*. Boston, Mass: Harvard Business School Press.

Cinneide, B.O. (2006). Developing and Testing Student Oriented Case Studies: The production process and classroom/examination experiences with "entertaining" topics. *Journal of European Industrial Training*, Vol. 30, No. 5, pp. 349 – 364.

Clark, S.L., K.R. Simpson, G.E. Knox, & T.J. Garite (2009). Oxytocin: new perspectives on an old drug. *American journal of obstetrics and gynecology*, Vol. 200, No.1, pp. 35.e1-6.

Clerke, T. (2013) Unpublished research paper, UTS.

Colby, A.; T. Ehrlich; B. Sullivan & J. Dolle (2011). *Rethinking Undergraduate Business Education: Liberal Learning for the Profession*. San Francisco: Jossey-Bass.

Coletta J., E. Murphy, Z. Rubeo, & C. Gyamfi-Bannerman (2012). The 5-tier System of Assessing Fetal Heart Rate Tracings Is Superior to the 3-Tier System in Identifying Fetal Academia. *American journal of obstetrics and gynecology*, Vol. 206, pp. 226.e1-5.

Collier, K. (2005). Spotlight on Role Play: interrogating the theory and practice of role play in adult education from a theatre arts perspective. Doctoral Thesis, University of Technology, Sydney

Copeland, W.D. & D.L. Decker (1996). Video Cases and the Development of Meaning Making in Pre-Service Teachers. *Teaching and Teacher Education*, Vol. 12, No. 5, pp. 467-481.

Copley, J. (2007). Audio and video Podcasts of Lectures for Campus-Based Students: production and evaluation of student use, *Innovations in Education and Teaching International*, Vol. 44, No. 4, November, pp. 387-399.

Cownie, F. (2011). Exploring values in legal education. *Web Journal of Current Legal Issues*. Available at: http://www.bailii.org/uk/other/journals/WebJCLI/2011/issue2/cownie2.html [Accessed 19 March 2014]

Cox, S. (2009) *Case Studies for Active Learning*, Higher Education Academy Network for Hospitality, Leisure, Sport and Tourism

Crawa, S.; N. Wiratungaa & R. Roweb (2006). Learning Adaptation Knowledge to Improve Case-Based Reasoning, *Artificial Intelligence*, Vol. 170, No. 16–17, pp. 1175–1192.

Cruikshank, D & F. Broadbent (1968). *The Simulation and Analysis of Problems of Beginning Teachers.* Project 5-0798, Office of Education, U.S. Department of Health, Education and Welfare

Cruikshank, D (1971). "Teacher Education Looks at Simulation: a review of selected uses and research results". In P. Tansey (Ed.) (1971). *Educational aspects of simulation*. Maidenhead, McGraw-Hill Publishing.

Daley, B.J. & D.M. Torre (2010). Concept Maps in Medical Education: an analytical literature review. *Medical education*, Vol. 44, No.5, pp. 440-448.

Dalziel, J. (2011). Visualising Learning Design in LAMS: A historical view. *Teaching English with Technology*, Special Edition on LAMS and Learning Design, Vol. 11, No. 1, pp. 19-34.

Darso, L. (2004). *Artful Creation*. Frederiksberg: Samfundslitteratur.

Datar, S.; D.A. Garvin & P.G. Cullen (2010). *Re-thinking the MBA*. Cambridge, MA.: Harvard Business School Publishing.

David, F. (2003). Strategic Management Case Writing: Suggestions after 20 Years of Experience. *S.A.M. Advanced Management Journal,* Vol. 68, pp. 36–43.

Davies, C. & E. Wilcock (2003). *Learning Materials Using Case Studies.* Liverpool, UK: The Higher Education Academy/UK Centre for Materials Education/Guides, University of Liverpool. Available at: www.materials.ac.uk/guides/casestudies.asp [Accessed 9 January 2014]

Deci, E., R. Koestner & R. Ryan (2001). Extrinsic Rewards and intrinsic Motivation in Education: Reconsidered once again. *Review of Educational Research,* Vol. 71, No. 1, pp. 1-27.

Dede, C. (2009). Technologies that facilitate Generating Knowledge and Possibly Wisdom, *Educational Researcher,* Vol. 38, No. 4, pp.260-263.

Dewing, A. (1931). "An Introduction to the Use of Cases", in C. Fraser (Ed.) (1931). *A Case Method of Instruction.* New York: McGraw-Hill.

Dobozy, E. (2007). *The Learning of Democratic Values: How four 'out-of-the-ordinary' schools do it.* French Forest, NSW, Australia: Pearson.

Dobozy, E. (2011). "Resisting Student consumers and Assisting Student Producers", in C. Nygaard; N. Courtney & C. Holtham (Eds.) *Beyond Transmission - Innovations in University Teaching,* pp. 11-25. Faringdon, Oxfordshire: Libri Publishing

Dobozy, E. (2012). The deBono LAMS Sequence Series: Template designs as knowledge-mobilising strategy for 21st Century Higher Education. *Teaching English with Technology,* Special Issue on LAMS and Learning Design, Vol. 12, No. 2, pp. 88-102.

Dobozy, E. (forthcoming). "The Pre-designed Lesson: Teaching with transdisciplinary pedagogical templates (TPTs)". Invited paper presentation. 12th International Innovations in Education Colloquium: *Leadership in Learning,* 8–11 May 2014, Brescia, Italy.

Dobozy, E. (2014). "Situating Case-Based Teaching among other Learning-Centric Pedagogies". Branch, J.; P. Bartholomew & C.

Nygaard. (Eds.) (2014). *Case-based Learning in Higher Education*, Faringdon, Oxfordshire: Libri Publishing

Dobozy, E.; J. Dalziel & B. Dalziel (2013). "Learning Design and Transdisciplinary Pedagogical Templates (TPTs)". In C. Nygaard; J. Branch & C. Holtham (Eds.) *Learning in university education – Contemporary standpoints.* Faringdon, Oxfordshire: Libri Publishing.

Dörnyei, Z. & P. Skehan (2003). "Individual differences in Second Language Learning." In C.L. Doughty and M.H. Long (Eds.) *The Handbook of Second Language Acquisition.* Malden, Oxford and Melbourne and Berlin: Blackwell, pp. 589-630.

Dörnyei, Z. (1998). Motivation in Second and Foreign Language Learning. *Language Teaching*, Vol. 31, Iss. 3, pp. 117-135. London: Thames Valley University

Dörnyei, Z. (2005). *The Psychology of the Language Learner. Individual Differences in Second Language Acquisition.* Mahwah, New Jersey and London: Laurence Erlbaum Associates, Publishers

Duch, B.J.; S.E. Groh & D.E. Allen (Eds.) (2001). *The Power of Problem-Based Learning: a practical "how to" for teaching undergraduate courses in any discipline.* Sterling VA.: Stylus Publishing, LLC

Duda, R. (2005). "Assumptions and Hidden Agendas in ICT Materials: How does autonomization come in?" In J-M. Debaisieux & A. Boulton (Eds.) TIC et Autonomie dans l'Apprentissage des Langues *Mélanges CRAPEL*, Vol. 28, pp. 67-75). Nancy: CRAPEL.

Duncan, N, & A. Wolfgarten (Eds) (2012). *Opinion Writing and Case Preparation.* 2nd ed. Oxford: Oxford University Press.

Duncan, N, (2007). 'Feed-Forward': Improving students' use of tutors' comments, *Assessment & Evaluation in Higher Education*, Vol 32, Iss 3, pp 271-283.

Duncan, N, (2011). "Addressing Emotions in Preparing Ethical Lawyers", in P. Maharg & C. Maughan, (Eds.) *Affect and Legal Education: Emotion in Learning and Teaching the Law*, Farnham: Ashgate, pp257-282.

Edge, A. & D. Coleman (1986). *The Guide to Case Analysis and Reporting*, Hawaii: System Logistics Inc.

EHEA (European Higher Education Area) (2012). *Bucharest Communiqué*. Available at http://www.ehea.info/Uploads/%281%29/Bucharest%20 Communique%20 2012%282%29.pdf [Accessed 25 January 2014]

Ellington, H. (1999). Games and Simulations - Media for the New Millenium. In proceedings of the *1999 SAGSET Conference*, SAGSET.

Ellington, H. (2002). *Using Games, Simulations, Case Studies and Role-Play to Stimulate Students' Creativity.* York: Higher Education Academy Imaginative Curriculum Guide

Ellington, H.; E. Addinall & F. Percival (unpublished). *The Different Types of Game.*

Ellington, H.; J. Fowlie & M. Gordon (1998). *Using Games and Simulations in the Classroom: A Practical Guide for Teachers.* London: Routledge

Elliot, G. (1986). Video Production in Education and Training, *New Patterns of Learning Series*, Law Book Co of Australasia.

Emmet, D. (Ed.) (2012). *Drafting,* 16th ed., Oxford: Oxford University Press.

Erpenbeck, J. & W. Sauter (2007). *Kompetenzentwicklung im Netz: New Blended Learning mit Web.* Berlin/Ulm: Luchterhand.

Errington, E. (2011) "As close as it gets: developing professional identity through the potential of scenario-based learning". In: *Learning to Be Professional through a Higher Education,* a wiki by Surrey Centre for Excellence in Professional Training and Education (SCEPTrE), Surrey, UK, pp. 1-15.

Erskine, J.A.; M.R. Leenders & L.A Maufette-Leenders (1981, reprinted 1998 & 2003). *Teaching with cases*, third edition. Waterloo, Ontario, Canada: Ivey Publishing

Esteban, A. & M. Canado (2004). Making the Case Method Work in Teaching Business English: a case study. *English for Specific Purposes,* Vol. 23, pp. 137–161.

Esteves, M.; B. Fonseca; L. Morgado & P. Martins (2010). Improving Teaching and Learning of Computer Programming through the Use of the Second Life Virtual World, *British Journal of Educational Technology*, Vol. 42, No. 4, pp. 624–637

Feagin, J., Orum, A., & Sjoberg, G. (Eds.). (1991). *A Case for the Case Study*. Chapel Hill, NC: The University of North Carolina Press.

Fedorowicz, J. (2004). Twelve Tips for Successfully Integrating Enterprise Systems across the Curriculum. *Journal of Information Systems Education*, Vol. 15, No. 3, pp. 235-244.

Flechsig, K.-H. (1996). *Kleines Handbuch didaktischer Modelle*. Eichenzell, Germany: Neuland Flechsig, K.-H.

Flynn, A & J. Klein (2001). The Influence of Discussion Groups in a Case-Based Learning Environment. *Educational Technology Research & Development* Vol. 49, No. 3, pp. 71-86

Flyvbjerg, B. (2006). Five Misunderstandings about Case-Study Research. *Qualitative Inquiry*, Vol. 12, No. 2, pp. 219-245

Forrester, J. (1994). System Dynamics, Systems Thinking, and Soft OR. *System Dynamics Review*, Summer, Vol. 10, No. 2. Available at http://www.clexchange.org/ftp/documents/Roadmaps/RM7/D-4405-1.pdf [Accessed 20 June 2014]

Fortin, J.C. (2012). Role-Playing and Simulation Based Learning in Higher Education: Case study in model United Nations. *Honors Projects in History and Social Sciences. Paper 15*. Available at http://digitalcommons.bryant.edu/honors_history/15. [Accessed 20 May 2014]

Frank, C. (2003). *Conceptual Design of Web-Based Case Method - A Pedagogical Perspective*. Unpublished doctoral dissertation, University of Paderborn. Available at http://digital.ub.uni-paderborn.de/ubpb/urn/urn:nbn:de:hbz:466-20030101113 [Accessed 25 January 2014]

Franke, G. (2005). *Facetten der Kompetenzentwicklung*. Bielefeld, Germany: Bertelsmann.

Freire, P. (1970). *Pedagogy of the Oppressed*. Harmondsworth, UK: Penguin.

Gao F.; J.J. Noh & M.J. Koehler (2009). Comparing Role-playing Activities in Second Life and Face-to-face Environments. *Journal of Interactive Learning Research* Vol. 20, No 4, pp. 423-443

Garrett, B.; M. MacPhee & C. Jackson (2011). Implementing High-Fidelity Simulation in Canada: Reflections on 3 years of practice. *Nurse Education Today*, Vol. 31, pp. 671 – 676

Garrison, J & B. Kersh (1969). The comparison of Two Forms of a Classroom Simulation Test Designed to Enhance Future Teachers' Self-Definition and Teaching Style. Final report of Project 9-1-033, Oregon College of Education, Monmouth, Oregon, USA. Available at: http://www.eric.ed.gov/ERICWebPortal/contentdelivery/servlet/ERICServlet?accno=ED038364 [accessed 20/10/09]

Gartner IT Glossary (2012). http://www.gartner.com/it-glossary/immersive-learning-environments-iles [Accessed 26 January 2014]

Garvin D.A. (2003). Making the Case: Professional education for world practice. *Harvard Magazine,* September-October, Vol. 106, No. 1, pp. 56-65.

Garvin, D. (2007). Teaching Executives and Teaching MBAs: Reflections on the Case Method. *Academy of Management Learning and Education*, Vol. 6, pp. 364–74.

Georgopoulos, V.C. & C.D. Stylios (2008). Complementary Case-Based Reasoning and Competitive Fuzzy Cognitive Maps for Advanced Medical Decisions. *Soft Computing*, Vol. 12, pp 191-199.

Georgopoulos, V.C. & C.D. Stylios (2012). Introducing Fuzzy Cognitive Maps for Developing Decision Support System for Triage at Emergency Room Admissions for the Elderly. *Proceedings of the 8th IFAC Symposium on Biological and Medical Systems*, 29-31 August, Budapest, Hungary.

Georgopoulos, V.C. & C.D. Stylios (2013a). "Fuzzy Cognitive Map Decision Support System for Successful Triage to Reduce Unnecessary Emergency Room Admissions for the Elderly". In R. Seising & M. Tabacchi (Eds.) *Fuzziness and Medicine: Philosophical Reflections and Application Systems in Health Care*, pp. 415-436, Berlin Heidelberg: Springer

Georgopoulos, V.C. & C.D. Stylios (2013b). Fuzzy Cognitive Map Hierarchical Triage Decision Support for the Elderly. *Proceedings of the SIMULTECH 2013 - 3rd International Conference on Simulation and Modeling Methodologies, Technologies and Applications*, Reykjavik, Iceland, July 29–31.

Georgopoulos, V.C., G.A. Malandraki, & C.D. Stylios (2003). A Fuzzy Cognitive Map Approach To Differential Diagnosis of Specific Language Impairment, *Journal of Artificial Intelligence in Medicine*, Vol. 29, No. 3, pp. 261-278.

Geyer, W.; R.S. Silva Filho; B. Brownholtz & D.F. Redmiles (2008). The Trade-offs of Blending Synchronous and Asynchronous Communication Services to Support Contextual Collaboration. *Journal of Universal Computer Science*, Vol. 14, pp. 4-26.

Ghasemi, B. & M. Hashemi (2011). ICT: New wave in English language learning/teaching. *Procedia - Social and Behavioral Sciences* Vol. 15, pp. 3098–3102. Elsevier Ltd.

Gilligan, C. (1982). *In a Different Voice: Psychological theory and women's development*. Cambridge, MA: Harvard University Press.

Giroux, H. (1994). "Toward a Pedagogy of Critical Thinking". In K. Walters (Ed.) *Re-Thinking Reason: New Perspectives in Critical Thinking*. Albany, NY: State University of New York Press.

Giroux, H. (2010). Bare Pedagogy and the Scourge of Neoliberalism: Rethinking higher education as a democratic public sphere. *The Educational Forum*. Vol.74, No. 3, pp. 184–196.

Gloeckler, G. (2008). The Case against Case Studies, *BusinessWeek*, February 4, pp. 66-67

Gnahs, D. (2010). *Kompetenzen - Erwerb, Erfassung, Instrumente: Studientexte für Erwachsenenbildung*. Bielefeld, Germany: Bertelsmann.

Goodhew, P.J. (2011). Teaching Materials Engineering: an Updated Guide, 2nd edition. Available at: http://www.materials.ac.uk/resources/Teaching-Materials-Engineering.pdf [Accessed 20th March 2014].

Goodschild, S. & B. Sriraman (2012). Revisiting the Didactic Triangle: from the particular to the general. *ZDM Mathematics Education.* Vol. 44, No. 5, pp. 581-585

Grabinger, R.S. & J.C. Dunlap (1995). Rich Environments for Active Learning: a definition. *Association for Learning Technology Journal,* Vol. 3, No. 2, pp. 5-34.

Grant, R. (1997). A Claim for the Case Method in the Teaching of Geography. *Journal of Geography in Higher Education,* Vol. 21, No. 2, pp. 171-185

Green, J.C. (2004). Student Reactions to the Use of a Computer-Based Simulation as an Integrating Mechanism for a MBA Curriculum. *Developments in Business Simulation and Experiential Learning,* Vol. 31, pp. 286-289.

Greiner, L.E.; A. Bhambri & T.G. Cummings (2003). Searching for a Strategy to Teach Strategy. *Academy of Management Learning and Education,* Vol. 2, pp. 402–20.

Griffin, M. (2009). The Narrative Case Study Meets Hypertext: case studies in the Digital Age, MERLOT Journal of Online Learning and Teaching. Vol. 5, No. 4, December, pp. 703-708

Grosse, C.U. (1988). The Case Study Approach to Teaching Business English. *English for Specific Purposes*, Vol. 7, No. 2, pp. 131–136.

Grupe, F.H. & J.K. Jay (2000). Incremental Cases: Real-Life, Real-Time Problem Solving, *College Teaching*, Vol 48, Iss 4, pp 123-128.

Gudjons, H. & R. Winkel (Eds.) (2002). *Didaktische Theorien.* Hamburg, Germany: Bergmann.

Gunz, H. (1988). Information Technology in Management Education: Myths and Potentialities, *Personnel Review*, Vol. 17, Iss. 5, pp. 3-11

Hafer, J. *et al.* (2010). "Fallstudien in Medialen Räumen." In: Engbring, Dieter *et al.* (Eds.) *HDI2010 - Proceedings of the 4th conference on Hochschuldidaktik Informatik,* pp. 93-98, Paderborn, Germany: University Press

Häferle, H. & K. Maier-Häferle (2010). *101 e-Le@rning Seminarmethoden.* Bonn, Germany: managerSeminare

Hakkarainen, P. & T. Saarelainen (2005). "Towards Meaningful Learning through Designing, Producing and Solving Digital Video-Supported Cases with Students". In G. Richards (Ed.) Electronic versions (CD) of papers presented at *E-Learn 2005 Conference*, pp. 2081-2088

Hakkarainen, P.; T. Saarelainen & H. Ruokamo (2007). Towards Meaningful Learning through Digital Video Supported, Case Based Teaching, *Australasian Journal of Educational Technology*, Vol. 23, No. 1, pp. 87-109.

Han, I.; M. Eom & W.S. Shin (2013). Multimedia Case-Based Learning to Enhance Pre-Service Teachers' Knowledge Integration for Teaching with Technologies, *Teaching and Teacher Education*, Vol. 34, pp. 122-129.

Hannam, P. & E. Echeverria (2009). *Philosophy with Teenagers: Nurturing a moral imagination for the 21st century.* New York, N.Y.: Continuum.

Harrington, H.L. (1995). Fostering Reasoned Decisions: case-based pedagogy and the professional development of teachers. *Teaching and Teacher Education*, Vol. 11, No. 3, pp. 203-214.

Hartman, E. M. (2006). Can We Teach Character? An Aristotelian Answer, *Academy of Management Learning and Education*, Vol. 5, pp. 68–81.

Harvard Business School, (2014). The HBS Case Method. Available online: http://www.hbs.edu/mba/academic-experience/Pages/the-hbs-case-method.aspx [Accessed 10th February 2014].

Hatlevik, I. (2012). The Theory/Practice Relationship: reflective skills and theoretical knowledge as key factors in bridging the gap between theory and practice in initial nursing education. *Journal of Advanced Nursing*, Vol. 68, No. 4, pp. 868–877

Hattie, J. (2008). *Visible Learning: a synthesis of over 800 meta-analyses relating to achievement.* Oxford: Routledge.

Hattie, J. (2012). *Visible Learning for Teachers. Maximizing Impact on Learning.* London: Routledge.

HBS (2013). Leading in the Classroom. Christensen Center for Teaching & Learning. Available at http://www.hbs.edu/teaching/

case-method-in-practice/leading-in-the-classroom/ (Accessed 19 February 2014)

Healy, M.E. (1947). Le Play's Contribution to Sociology: his method. *The American Catholic Sociological Review,* Vol. 8, No. 2, pp. 97–110

Heath, J. (2002). *Teaching and Writing Case Studies: a practical guide.* Cranfield: ecch UK Registered Office Publications.

Hermansen, M. (2005). *Relearning.* Copenhagen: Danish University of Education Press/CBS Press.

Herreid, C.F. (1994). Case study in Science - A Novel Method of Science Education. *Journal of College Science Teaching,* Vol. 23, No. 4, pp. 221–229

Herreid, C.F. (2005). Using Case Studies to Teach Science. *American Institute for Biological Sciences.* Available online at: http://www.actionbioscience.org/education/herreid.html [Accessed 25 January 2014]

Herreid, C.F. (2012). My Favorite Case and what Makes it so, *Journal of College Science Teaching,* Vol. 42, No. 2, pp. 70–5

Heskett, J. (2008). Is Case Method Instruction Due for an Overhaul? *HBR Network.* Available at: http://www.businessweek.com/stories/2008-01-23/the-case-against-case-studies [Accessed 10th February 2014].

Hirschel, R.; C. Yamamoto & P. Lee (2012). Video Self-Assessment for Language Learners, *Studies in Self-Access Learning Journal,* Vol. 3, No. 3, pp. 291-309.

Holden, R.; S. Jameson & A. Walmsley (2007). New Graduate Employment within SMEs: still in the dark? *Journal of Small Business and Enterprise Development,* Vol. 14, No. 2, pp. 211-227.

Hollyhead, A. (2010). A Case Study Approach to Evaluate a Vocationally Focused Virtual Environment. *The Online Educational Research Journal* (OERJ)

Hope, A.; J. Garside & S. Prescott (2011). Rethinking Theory and Practice: pre-registration student nurses experiences of simulation teaching and learning in the acquisition of clinical skills in preparation for practice. *Nurse Education Today*, Vol. 31, pp. 711-715

Howard, N.; P. Bennett; J. Bryant & M. Bradley (1993). Manifesto for a Theory of Drama and Irrational Choice, *Journal of Operational Research Society*, Vol. 44, No. 1, pp. 99-103

Hudson, B. & A.M. Meyer (2011). "Introduction: finding common ground beyond fragmentation." In. B. Hudson & A.M. Meyer (Eds.) *Beyond Fragmentation: Didactics, Learning and Teaching in Europe*. Opladen and Farmington Hills: Barbara Budrich.

Iacono C.; Brown A. & C. Holtham, (2011). The Use of the Case Study Method in Theory Testing: The Example of Steel eMarketplaces, *Electronic Journal of Business Research Methods*, Vol. 9, No. 1, pp. 57-65.

Iqbal S. & K. Harsh (2013). A Self Review and External Review Model for Teaching and Assessing Novice Programmers, *International Journal of Information and Education Technology*, Vol. 3, No. 2, pp. 120-123.

Jackson L.J. (Ed.) (2013). *Civil Procedure (the White Book)*, London: Sweet & Maxwell.

Jackson, D. (2009). An International Profile of Industry-Relevant Competencies and Skill-Gaps in Modern Graduates. *International Journal of Management Education,* Vol. 8, No. 1, pp. 85-98.

Jackson, J. (1998). Reality-based Decision Cases in ESP Teacher Education: windows on practice. *English for Specific Purposes*, Vol. 17 No. 2, pp. 151–167.

Jennings, D. (1997). Researching and Writing Strategic Management Cases: a systems view. *Management Decision*, Vol. 35, pp. 100–5.

Johnson, D. & R. Johnson (1988). Critical Thinking through Structured Controversy. *Educational Leadership*, Vol. 45, No. 8, pp. 58-64.

Johnson, T. (2004). A Customized ERP/SAP Model for Business Curriculum Integration. *Journal of Information Systems Education,* Vol. 15, No. 3, pp. 245-253.

Johnston, V. & J. Shapland (1990). *Developing Vocational Legal Training for the Bar*, Sheffield: Institute for the study of the legal profession.

Johnstone, R (2011). "Whole-of-Curriculum Design in Law" in S. Kift; M. Sanson; J. Cowley & P. Watson (Eds.) *Excellence and Innovation in Legal Education*, Sydney: Lexis Nexis,

Jonassen, D.H. (1997). Instructional design models of well-structured and ill-structured problem-solving. *Educational Technology Research and Development*, Vol. 45, pp. 65-94.

Jones, K. (1997). "Damage Caused by Simulation and Games" in D. Saunders & B. Cox (Eds.) *The International Simulation and Gaming Yearbook, Volume 5*. London: Kogan Page

Jordan, L. (2009). Using Online Role-Play to Assess Distance Learning Students in Construction Law. CEBE Case Study. Available at http://www.cebe.heacademy.ac.uk/learning/casestudies/case_pdf/LindsayJordan09.pdf [Accessed 10th February 2014].

Kay, R.H. (2012). Exploring the Use of Video Podcasts in Education: a comprehensive review of the literature, *Computers in Human Behaviour*, Vol. 28, pp. 820-831.

Keeffe, M. & L. Austin (2012). "Reciprocity, the Rascal of Resolution - Collaborative Problem Solving in an Online Role Play". In M. Helfert; M.J. Martins & J. Cordeiro (Eds.) *Proceedings of the CSEDU 2012*, SciTePress, pp. 252-257

Kerres, M. (2012). *Mediendidaktik. Konzeption und Entwicklung mediengestützter Lernangebote.* Munich: Oldenbourg.

Kieser, A. (1994). Why Organization Theory Needs Historical Analyses – and How this Should be Performed? *Organization Science*, Vol. 5, pp. 608–20.

Kift, S.; M. Sanson; J. Cowley & P. Watson (Eds.) (2011). *Excellence and Innovation in Legal Education*, Sydney: Lexis Nexis.

Kintner, P.; Merrick, T.; Morrison, P. & P. Voss (Eds.). (1994). *Demographics: a casebook for business and government*. Santa Monica, CA: RAND.

Kleinfeld, J. (1990). *The Case Method in Teacher Education*. Alaskan Models.

Koc, Y.; D. Peker & A. Osmanoglu (2009). Supporting Teacher Professional Development through Online Video Case Study Discussions: an assemblage of pre-service and in-service teachers and the case teacher, *Teaching and Teacher Education*, Vol. 25, pp. 1158-1168.

Koestler, A. (1964). *The Act of Creation*. London: Hutchinson.

Kolb D.A. (1984). *Experiential Learning Experience as a Source of Learning and Development*. New Jersey: Prentice Hall.

Kolb, D.A. (1976). On Management and the Learning Process, *California Management Review*, Vol. 18, Iss. 3, pp. 21-31.

Kolodner, J.L. (1997). Educational Implications of Analogy: a view from case-based reasoning. *American Psychologist*, Vol. 52, No. 1, pp. 57–66.

Kolodner, J.L.; P.J. Camp; D. Crismond; B. Fasse; J. Gray; J. Holbrook; S. Puntambekar & M. Ryan (2003). Problem-based Learning Meets Case-Based Reasoning in the Middle-school Science Classroom: putting Learning by Design™ into practice. *Journal of the Learning Sciences*. Vol. 12, No. 4, pp. 495–547.

Kolodner, J.L.; C.E. Hmelo & N.H. Narayanan (1996). "Problem-based Learning Meets Case-Based Reasoning". In D.C. Edelson & E.A. Domeshek (Eds.) *Proceedings of ICLS '96*, pp. 188–195, Charlottesville, VA: AACE.

Kosko, B. (1986). Fuzzy Cognitive Maps. *International journal of man-machine studies*, Vol. 24, No. 1, pp. 65-75.

Kosko, B. (1993). *Fuzzy Thinking: the new science of fuzzy logic*. New York: Hyperion.

Kozma, R.B. & R.E. Anderson (2002). Qualitative Case Studies of Innovative Pedagogical Practices Using ICT. *Journal of Computer Assisted Learning*, Vol. 18, Iss. 4, pp. 387–394, December

Krathwohl, D.R. (2002). A Revision of Bloom's taxonomy: an overview. *Theory Into Practice*, Vol. 41, No. 4, pp. 212-218.

Kunselman, J.C. & K.A. Johnson (2004). Using the Case Method to Facilitate Learning, *College Teaching*, Vol 52, Iss 3, pp 87-92.

Ladkin, D. & S. Taylor (2010). Leadership as Art: variations on a theme. *Leadership*, Vol. 6, No. 3, pp. 235-241.

Lawrence, P. (1953). "The Preparation of Case Material", in K. Andrews (Ed.) *The Case Method of Teaching Human Relations and Administrations*. Cambridge, MA.: Harvard University Press.

LeBlanc, D. (2011). Jared Spool on Creating Intuitive Designs #drupalcon. Available at http://www.cmswire.com/cms/enterprise-20/jared-spool-on-creating-intuitive-designs-drupalcon-010477.php [Accessed 13 Jan 2014].

Lee, S-H.; J. Lee; X. Liu; C.J. Bonk & R.J. Magjuka (2009). A Review of Case-Based Learning Practices in an Online MBA Program: a program-level case study. *Educational Technology & Society*, Vol. 12, No.3, pp. 178-190.

Lee, Y.S. (1983). Public Management and Case Study Methods. *Teaching Political Science*, Vol. 11, No. 1, pp. 6–14.

Leenders, M.R. & J.A. Erskine (1989). *Case research, the case writing process,* 3rd ed., London, Canada: School of Business Administration, The University of Western Ontario Research and Publications Division School of Business Administration

Leenders, M.R., Maufette-Leenders, L.A and Erskine, J. A. (1973; reprinted 2010). *Writing Cases*, fourth edition, Ivey, Canada.

Lefebvre, H. (1991). *The Production of Space.* London: Blackwell

Leigh, E. (2003) *A Practitioner Researcher Perspective on Facilitating an Open, Infinite, Chaordic Simulation.* Doctoral Thesis, University of Technology, Sydney, Available at http://epress.lib.uts.edu.au/research/handle/2100/308 [Accessed 26 January, 2014]

Lenstrup, C. (2013). "Social-media Learning Environments." In C. Nygaard, J. Branch & C. Holtham (Eds.) *Learning in Higher Education - Contemporary Standpoints*. Farringdon, Oxfordshire: Libri Publishing.

Leung, Y. & T. Yuen (2009). Participatory Citizenship and Student Empowerment: case study of a Hong Kong school. *International Journal of Citizenship Teaching and Learning*, Vol. 5, No. 1, pp. 18-34.

Levin, B.B. (1995). Using the Case Method in Teacher Education: the role of discussion and experience in teachers' thinking about cases, *Teaching and Teacher Education*, Vol. 11, pp 63-79.

Liang, N. & J. Wang (2004). Implicit Mental Models in Teaching Cases: an empirical study of popular MBA cases in the United

States and China. *Academy of Management Learning & Education.* Vol. 3, No. 4, pp. 397-413.

Linn, M. & M. Clancy (1992). The Case for Case Studies of Programming Problems. *Communications of the ACM,* Vol. 35, No. 3, pp. 121-132

Liu, M. (2012). Discussing Videocases Online: perspectives of preservice and inservice EFL teachers in Taiwan, *Computers and Education,* Vol. 59, pp. 120-133.

Llinares, S. & J. Valls (2009). The Building of Pre-Service Primary Teachers' Knowledge of Mathematics Teaching: interaction and online video case studies, *Instructional Science,* Vol. 37, No. 3, pp. 247-271.

Löfvall, S. & C. Nygaard (2013). "Interrelationships between Student Culture, Teaching and Learning in Higher Education." In C. Nygaard, J. Branch & C. Holtham (Eds.) *Learning in Higher Education - Contemporary Standpoints.* Farringdon, Oxfordshire: Libri Publishing.

Lombardi, M.M. (2007). Authentic Learning for the 21st century: an overview, *Educause learning initiative,* edited by D.G. Oblinger. Available at http://www.educause.edu/ir/library/pdf/ELI3009.pdf. [Accessed 6 May 2014]

Love, T. (2013). Design Practice Research PhD Case Studies, Listserv, PhD-design@jiscmail.ac.uk.

Lowe, G. (2011). Computer Simulation in Initial Teacher Education: a bridge across the faculty/practice divide or simply a better viewing platform? EdD thesis, University of Nottingham.

Lyford, C.; J. Beierlein & K. Harling (2000). Scholarship and Decision Cases: pedagogy and standards for publication. *International Food and Agribusiness Management Review,* Vol. 3, pp. 369–79.

Lynn, L.E. (1999). *Teaching & Learning with Cases – a guidebook.* New York: Chatham House Publishers.

Maharg, P, & C. Maughan (Eds.). (2011). *Affect and Legal Education: emotion in learning and teaching the Law*, Farnham: Ashgate.

Maharg, P. (2003). *Curriculum Models for the Diploma in Legal Practice*, Glasgow: Law Society of Scotland

Maharg, P. (2007). *Transforming Legal Education: learning and teaching the law in the early twenty-first century*, Farnham: Ashgate.

Mannix, E.; M. Neale & J. Goncalo (2009). (Eds.). *Creativity in groups*. Bingley, UK: Emerald Group Publishing.

Marchussen, A. (2013). llan, IKT-initiativet – Videooptagelser på CBS, *Copenhagen Business School internal report*

Martin, P. & D. Chapman (2006). An Exploration of Factors that Contribute to the Reluctance of SME Owner-managers to Employ First Destination Marketing Graduates. *Marketing Intelligence & Planning*, Vol. 24, No. 2, pp. 158-173.

Marton, F. & S. Booth (1997/2009). *Learning and Awareness*. New York: Routledge.

Marton, F.; P. Fensham & S. Chaiklin (1994). A Nobel's Eye View of Scientific Intuition: discussions with the Nobel prize-winners in physics, chemistry, and medicine (1970-1986). *International Journal of Science Education*, Vol.16, pp. 457-473.

Mascolini, M.V. & C.P. Freeman (1982). Focusing on Information: using the case method in introductory business writing. Paper presented at the *Midwest Regional Meeting of the American Business Communication Association*, Indianapolis, IN, 23–24 April.

Mathiasen, H. (2008). "Is There a Nexus Between Learning and Teaching? Communication as a Facilitator of Students' Knowledge Construction." In C. Nygaard & C. Holtham (Eds.). *Understanding Learning-Centred Higher Education*, Copenhagen: Copenhagen Business School Press, pp. 131-144.

Mattisson, O. & U. Ramberg (2013). The LUSEM Case Method – an Alternative Approach? Reflections on Hands-On Learning and Abstract Thinking, *International journal of case method research & application.* Vol. XXV, No 2, pp. 93-99.

Maufette-Leenders, L.A.; J.A. Erskine & M.R. Leenders (1997; 4th edition 2007). *Learning with cases*, Waterloo, Ontario, Canada: Ivey Publishing

Maughan, C. & J. Webb (2005). *Lawyering Skills and the Legal Process*, 2nd ed,, Cambridge: Cambridge University Press.

McGarrity, M. (2011). quoted in Leigh, E (2013) "Simulations for Project Management Research", in N, Drouin; R. Müller & S. Sankaran (Eds.) (2013). *Novel Approaches to Organizational Project Management Research: translational and transformational.* Copenhagen: Copenhagen Business School Press

McNair, M. (1954). *The Case Method at the Harvard Business School*, New York, NY: McGraw-Hill.

McPeake, R, (Ed.) (2013). *Advocacy,* 25th ed., Oxford: Oxford University Press.

McShane, S.L. & M.A. Von Glinow (2009) (2007). *Organizational Behaviour [Essentials].* New York, NY: McGraw-Hill/Irwin

Merseth, K. (1991). The Early History of Case-Based Instruction: insights for teacher education today. *Journal of Teacher Education,* Vol. 42, No. 4, pp. 243-149.

Miles, M.B. (1987). Innovative Methods for Collecting and Analyzing Qualitative Data: vignettes and pre-structured cases. Paper presented at the Annual Meeting of the *American Educational Research Association*, Washington, DC, 20–24 April, 1987.

Miles, M.B. & A.M. Huberman (1994). *Qualitative Data Analysis,* 2nd ed., Newbury Park, CA: Sage.

Milheim, W.D. (1996). Utilizing Case Studies for Teaching Effective Instructional Design Principles. *International Journal of Instructional Media*, Vol. 23, No. 1, pp. 23–30.

Miller, D. & P. Friesen (1977). Strategy-Making in Context: ten empirical archetypes. *Journal of Management Studies*, Vol. 14, pp. 253–80.

Mingers, J. (2000). What Is it to Be Critical? *Management Learning*, Vol. 31, No. 2, pp. 219-237.

Ministry of Justice (2013). *Civil Procedure Rules and Practice Directions.* Available at http://www.justice.gov.uk/courts/procedure-rules/civil/rules. [Accessed 31 January 2014]

Mintzberg, H. (1990) The Design School: reconsidering the basic premises of strategic management. *Strategic Management Journal*, Vol. 11, No. 3, pp. 171-195

Mintzberg, H. (2004). *Managers Not MBAs: a hard look at the soft practice of managing and management development.* London: Pearson Education

Mondahl, M.S.; L.P. Svendsen; C. Lenstrup & A.Z. Faizi (2013). Sprogkernen II - Global Citizenship through Language and Culture - a report on the practical implementation of the recommendations from Sprogkernen I - the interpersonal challenge and facilitation of action competence. *Copenhagen Business School Research report.* Available at http://eduglo.dk/media/34636/sprogkernen_ii-2_-_globalt_medborgerskab.pdf [Accessed 8 January 2014].

Monk, N.; C. Chillington Rutter; J. Neelands & L. Heron (2011). *Open-Space Learning: a study in trans-disciplinary pedagogy*, London: Bloomsbury

Mostert, M.P. & M.R. Sudzina (1996). Undergraduate Case Method Teaching: pedagogical assumptions vs. the real world. Paper presented at the *Annual Meeting of the Association of Teacher Educators*, St. Louis, MO, February, 1996.

Mustoe, L.R. & A.C. Croft (1999). Motivating Engineering Students by Using Modern Case Studies. *European Journal of Engineering Education*, Vol. 15, No. 6, pp. 469-476

Nagel, G.K. (1991). Case Method: its potential for training administrators. *NASSP-Bulletin*, Vol.75, No. 539, pp. 37–43.

Naumes, W. & M. Naumes (1999). *The Art and Craft of Case Writing.* London: Sage.

Navarro, P. (2008). The MBA Core Curricula of Top-Ranked U.S. Business Schools: a study in failure? *Academy of Management Learning & Education,* Vol. 7, No. 1, pp. 108-123.

Neelands, J. (1991). *Structuring Drama Work.* Cambridge, U.K.: Cambridge University Press

Neelands, J. (2009). Acting Together: ensemble as a democratic process in art and life, research in drama education. *The Journal of Applied Theatre and Performance*, Vol. 14, No. 2, pp. 173-189.

Nelson, M. (1997). The Art of Case Teaching: a literature review of instructional methods. *Fourteenth International Conference on Case Method Research and Application*. World Association for Case Method Research & Application, Boston, Massachusetts. Available at http://www.healthsci.utas.edu.au/faculty/cases/refs.html. [Accessed 19 February 2014]

Nemirovsky, R. & A. Galvis (2004). Facilitating Grounded Online Interactions in Video-Case-Based Teacher Professional Development, *Journal of Science Education and Technology*, March, Vol. 13, No. 1, pp. 67-79

Nilsen, S. & A. Baerheim (2005). Feedback on Video Recorded Consultations in Medical Teaching: why students loathe and love it – a focus-group based qualitative study, *BMC Medical Education*, Vol. 5, No. 28

Nisula, K. (2012). ERP-based Business Learning Environment. *The 4th International conference on computer supported education*, Porto, Portugal. 16–18 April

Novak, J.D. (1998). *Learning, Creating, and Using Knowledge: concept maps as facilitative tools in schools and corporations*, Mahwah, NJ: Lawrence Erlbaum Associates.

Nygaard, C. & P. Bramming (2008). Learning-centred Public Management Education. *International Journal of Public Sector Management*, Vol. 21, No. 4, pp. 400-416.

OECD (2005). The Definition and Selection of Key Competencies: executive summary. Available online: http://www.oecd.org/pisa/35070367.pdf [Accessed 9 January 2014].

Ören, T. (2011). The Many Facets of Simulation through a Collection of about 100 Definitions, *SCS M&S Magazine*. 2011/2, April

Paget, N. (1988). Using Case Methods Effectively, *Journal of Education for Business*, Vol. 63, No. 4, pp. 175–180.

Palmer, G.C.A. & A.K. Leonard (2012). Critical Thinking: making room for emotion in classroom Spaces, *19th International Conference on Learning*, London.

Palmer, G.C.A. (2005). Marketing and Strategy Faculty's Use of Case Studies in Teaching Strategy at a Business School. Unpublished MA thesis.

Palmer, G.C.A. (2006). Moving Outside the Box? A conceptual and practical review of teaching reflective and critical thinking with undergraduates. *LILI, UK Centre for Legal Education (UKCLE)*. Available at www.ukcle.ac.uk/interact/lili/2006/papers/palmer.html [Accessed 14 January 2014]

Palmer, G.C.A. (2013). Below the Surface, Behind the Headlines, Beyond Cognition? A Case of Creating Cases. *World Association for Case Method Research and Application, 30th Conference*, Berlin.

Palmer, G.C.A.; C. Lambert & L.J. Heron (2009). Helping Law Students Via Spaces and Performance. *LILAC, UK Centre for Legal Education (UKCLE)*. Available at www.ukcle.ac.uk/resources/teaching-and-learning-practices/palmer/ [Accessed 14 January 2014]

Pansiri, J. (2005). Pragmatism: a methodological approach to researching strategic alliances in tourism. *Tourism and Hospitality Planning & Development,* Vol. 2, No. 3, pp. 191-206.

Parker, P. & P. Baughan (2009). Providing Written Assessment Feedback that Students will Value and Read, *The International Journal of Learning*, Vol 16, pp 5-18.

Paroutis, S. & G.C.A. Palmer (2007). Developing Capabilities for Practice: do we really teach MBAs how to be effective strategists? *3rd Organization Studies Summer Workshop*, Crete.

Passig, D. & R. Moshe (2008). Enhancing Pre-Service Teachers' Awareness to Pupils' Test-Anxiety with 3D Immersive Simulation. *Journal of Educational Computing Research*, Vol. 38, No. 3, pp. 255–278

Patten, R. & D. Swanson (2003). Using Cases in the Teaching of Statistics. In H. E. Klein (Ed.), *Interactive Innovative Teaching and training: case method and other techniques* (pp. 21–30). Needham, MA: World Association for Case Method Research & Applications.

Patterson, C. (1994). Portraits of Teaching: using work-based vignettes. Paper presented at the *Annual Meeting of the Australian Teacher Education Association*, Brisbane, Queensland, Australia, 3–6 July

Perkins, D. (1999). The Many Faces of Constructivism, *Educational Leadership*. Vol 57, Iss 3

Perry G. & S. Talley (2001) Online Video Case Studies and Teacher Education: a new tool for pre-service teacher education, *Journal of Computing in Teacher Education*, Vol. 17, Iss 4, pp.6–31

Peterßen, W.H. (1999). *Kleines Methoden-Lexikon.* Munich: Oldenbourg.

Pfeffer, J. & C.T. Fong (2002). The End of Business Schools? Less Success than Meets the Eye. *Academy of Management Learning and Education*, Vol. 1, pp. 78–95

Philips, D.C. (1995). The Good, the Bad and the Ugly: the many faces of constructivism, *Educational Researcher*, Vol 24, Iss 7, pp 5-12.

Pike, T. & V. O'Donnell (2010). The Impact of Clinical Simulation on Learner Self-Efficacy in Pre-Registration Nursing Education. *Nurse Education Today*, Vol. 30, pp. 405 – 410

Piotrowski, M.U. (1982). Business as Usual: using the case method to teach ESL to executives. *TESOL Quarterly*, Vol. 16, pp. 229–238.

Podio website: www.podio.com [Accessed 10 January 2014].

Postman, N. (1995). *The End of Education.* New York: Random House.

Poulsen, C. & S. Löfvall (2014). "Video-Supported Case-Based Teaching", in J. Branch; P. Bartholomew & C. Nygaard (Eds.) *Case-based Learning in Higher Education*, Faringdon, Oxfordshire: Libri Publishing Ltd pp. 161-176

Powell, R. (2000). Case-based Teaching in Homogeneous Teacher Education Contexts: a study of pre-service teachers' situative cognition, *Teaching and Teacher Education*, Vol. 16, pp. 389.

Pursel, B. & H.-N. Fang (2012). Lecture Capture: current research and future directions, *The Schreyer Institute for teaching excellence*. Available at http://www.psu.edu/dept/site/pursel_lecture_capture_2012v1.pdf, (Accessed on 19 December 2013).

Race, P. (2003). "Why Assess Innovatively?" in S. Brown & A. Glasner (Eds.) *Assessment Matters in Higher Education, Choosing and Using Diverse Approaches,* pp. 56-70. Celtic Court 22 Ballmoor, Buckingham: The Society for Research into Higher Education & Open University Press.

Raju, P.K. & C.S. Sanker (1999). Teaching Real-World Issues through Case Studies. *Journal of Engineering Education,* Vol. 88, No. 4, pp. 501-508

Reddy, I.K. (2000). Implementation of a Pharmaceutics Course in a Large Class through Active Learning Using Quick-Thinks and Case-Based Learning, *American. Journal of Pharmaceutical Education,* Vol. 64, pp. 348.

Reynolds, J. (2006). Learning-Centred Learning: a mindset shift for educators. *Inquiry,* Vol. 11, No. 1, pp. 55-64.

Ricketts, B. (2011). The Role of Simulation for Learning within Pre-Registration Nursing Education — a Literature Review. *Nurse Education Today,* Vol. 31, pp. 650 – 654

Roberts, K. (2002). Ironies of Effective Teaching: deep structure learning and constructions of the classroom. *Teaching Sociology,* Vol. 30, January, pp. 1–25.

Robins, A; J. Rountree & N. Rountree (2003). Learning and Teaching Programming: a review and discussion, *Computer Science Education,* Vol. 13, No. 2, pp.137-172

Robinson, K. (2001). *Out of Our Minds: learning to be creative.* Oxford: Capstone.

Rogers, C. (1982). *Freedom to Learn for the 80s,* Ohio: Charles E. Merrill Publishing Company

Rutten, N.; W. van Joolingen & J. van der Veen (2012). The Learning Effects of Computer Simulations in Science education. *Computers & Science Education,* Vol. 58, pp. 136 -153

Ryberg, T.; L. Buus & M. Georgsen (2012). "Differences in Understandings of Networked Learning Theory: connectivity or collaboration?" in L. Dirckinck-Holmfeld, V. Hodgson, & D. McConnell (Eds.) *Exploring the Theory, Pedagogy and*

Practice of Networked Learning. Chapter 3, pp. 43-58. Springer Science+Business Media B.V.

Ryberg, T.; L. Dirckinck-Holmfeld & C. Jones (2011). "Catering to the Needs of the "Digital Natives" or Educating the "Net Generation"?" in M.J.W. Lee & C. McLoughlin (Eds.) *Web 2.0-Based E-Learning: applying social informatics for tertiary teaching,* pp. 301-318. Hershey, New York: Information Science Reference

Savery, J.R. & T.M. Duffy (1995). Problem Based Learning: an instructional model and its constructivist framework, *Educational technology,* Vol. 35, No. 5, pp. 31-38.

Scalise K. & B. Gifford (2010). Computer-Based Assessment in E-Learning: a framework for constructing intermediate constraint questions and tasks for technology platforms, *The Journal of Technology, Learning, and Assessment,* Vol. 4, No. 6.

Schoenfeld, A.H. (2012). Problematizing the Didactic Triangle. *ZDM Mathematics Education.* Vol. 44, No. 5, pp. 587-599

Schön, D.A. (1983). *The Reflective Practitioner.* Cambridge, Mass.: Basic Books

Schön, D.A. (1987). *Educating the Reflective Practitioner.* San Francisco: Jossey Bass.

Schrader, P.; D. Leu Jr.; C. Kinzer; R. Ataya; W. Teale; L. Labbo et al. (2003). Using Internet Delivered Video Cases to Support Pre-Service Teachers' Understanding of Effective Early Literacy Instruction: an exploratory study. *Instructional Science,* Vol. 31, pp. 317-340.

Schreiber, B.E.; J. Fukuta & F. Gordon (2010). Live Lecture Versus Video Podcast in Undergraduate Medical Education: a randomized controlled trial, *BMC Medical Education,* Vol. 10, No. 68

Schröder, H. (2001). *Didaktisches Wörterbuch.* Munich: Oldenbourg.

Schulman, L. (2005). Signature Pedagogies in the Professions, *Daedalus,* Summer, Vol. 134, No. 3, pp 52-59

Shulman, L. (1992) "Toward a pedagogy of cases", in J. Shulman (Ed.) *Case method in teacher education.* New York: Teachers College Press, pp. 1-30.

Siemens, G. & P. Long (2011). Penetrating the Fog: analytics in learning and education. *EDUCAUSE Review.* Vol. 46, No. 5, pp. 31-40

Simpson, K.R. & L. Miller (2011). Assessment and Optimization of Uterine Activity During Labor. *Clinical Obstetrics and Gynecology,* Vol. 54, No. 1, pp. 40–49

Smith, G. (1987). The Use and Effectiveness of the Case Study Method in Management Education - a Critical Review. *Management Education and Development,* Vol. 18, No. 1, pp. 51–61.

Smith, J.; P. Flowers & M. Larkin (2012). *Phenomenological Analysis: theory, method and research,* 2nd Ed. London, UK: Sage.

Smithenry, D.W.; J. Prouty & B.M. Capobianco (2013). Collaborative Exploring the Use of a Video Case-Based Book as a Professional Development Tool, *Journal of Scientific Educational Technology,* Vol. 22, pp. 735-750.

Sobchack, V. (1992). *The Address of the Eye: a phenomenology of film experience.* Princeton NJ.: Princeton University Press

Solicitors' Regulation Authority (2001). *Joint Statement.* Available at: http://www.sra.org.uk/documents/students/academic-stage/academicjointstate.pdf (Accessed 31/01/2014).

Soroka, V. & S. Safaeli (2006). Invisible Participants: how cultural capital relates to lurking behaviour. In proceedings of the *15th International Conference on the World Wide Web,* Edinburgh, Scotland: ACM Press

Soy, S.K. (1997). *The Case Study as a Research Method.* Unpublished paper, University of Texas at Austin.

Spool, J.M.; C. Snyder; T. Scanlon & T. DeAngelo (1999). *Web Site Usability: a designer's guide.* San Francisco, CA: Morgan Kaufmann Publishers

Spool, J.M.; R.J. Wolfe & D.M. McCracken (2004). *User-Centered Web Site Development: a human-computer interaction approach.* London: Pearson Education.

Spooner, D. & M. Skolnick (1997). Science and Engineering Case Studies in Introductory Computing Course for Non-Majors. *SIGCSE CA,* pp. 154-158.

Srinivasan M.; M. Wilkes; F. Stevenson; T. Nguyen & S. Slavin (2007). Comparing Problem-Based Learning with Case-Based Learning: effects of a major curricular shift at two institutions, *Academic Medicine*, Vol. 82, No. 1, pp. 74-82.

St John, M.J. (1996). Business is Booming: Business English in the 1990s. *English for Specific Purposes*, Vol. 15, No. 1, pp. 3–18.

Stähli, A. (2001). *Management-Andragogik 1: Harvard Anti Case*, Berlin Heidelberg: Springer

Stähli, A. (2006). *Management Andragogics 2: Zurich Living Case*, Berlin Heidelberg: Springer

Staley, A. & D. Faniglione, (2010). Shareville's Map – SHAREVILLE v.2.0, Available at http://shareville.bcu.ac.uk [Accessed 15 January 2014]

Staley, A.; N. Mackenzie; M. Hetherington & D. Faniglione (2009). Ready for Action: how Shareville can prepare students for the workplace. *JISC* (formerly the UK's Joint Information Systems Committee). Available at http://www.jisc.ac.uk/whatwedo/programmes/elearningpedagogy/elpconference09/programme/ [Accessed 15 January 2014]

Stokoe, E.H. (2000). Constructing Topicality in University Students' Small-Group Discussion: a conversation analytic approach, *Language and Education*, Vol. 14, Iss. 3, pp 184-203.

Stone, J. (2011). Questioning Education: a critique of philosophy for children. Masters thesis. Available at: http://www.jsafire.co.uk/jsafire/blog/10-11/MA-Dissertation-IOE-Sep-2011.pdf [Accessed 13 January 2014].

Strauss, A.L. & J.M. Corbin (1998). *Basics of Qualitative Research: techniques and procedures for developing grounded theory*. Thousand Oaks, CA: Sage.

Strayer, J. (2007). The Effects of the Classroom Flip on the Learning Environment: a comparison of learning activity in a traditional classroom and a flip classroom that used an intelligent tutoring. Doctor of Philosophy thesis, Ohio State University, Educational Theory and Practice. Available online: http://rave.ohiolink.edu/

etdc/view?acc_num=osu1189523914 [Accessed, March 24, 2014].

Stumpf, S.A. & M.D. Nevins (1999). "Redefining Management Education: Developing Professionals to Meet 21st Century Leadership Challenges", in R. Berndt (Ed.) *Management Strategien 2000*, Berlin: Springer Verlag

Stylios, C.D. & V.C. Georgopoulos (2010). Fuzzy Cognitive Maps for Medical Decision Support - a Paradigm from Obstetrics. In proceedings of *International Conference of the IEEE Engineering in Medicine and Biology Society (EMBC)*, pp. 1174-1177.

Stylios, C.D., V.C. Georgopoulos, G.A. Malandraki, & S. Chouliara (2008). Fuzzy Cognitive Map Architectures for Medical Decision Support Systems. *Applied Soft Computing*, Vol. 8, No. 3, pp. 1243-1251.

Suddaby, R. (2006). From the Editors: what grounded theory is not. *Academy of Management Journal*, Vol. 49, pp. 633-642.

Sung, E. & R.E. Mayer (2013). Online Multimedia Learning with Mobile Devices and Desktop Computers: an experimental test of Clark's methods-not-media hypothesis, *Computers in Human Behaviour*, Vol. 29, pp. 639-647.

Svendsen, L.P. & M.S. Mondahl (2013). "How Social-Media Enhanced Learning Platforms Support Students in Taking Responsibility for their Own Learning." In D. Stockley, P. Blessinger & C. Wankel (Eds.) Exploring socially mediated spaces for learning. *Journal of Applied Research in Higher Education*, Vol. 5, No. 2, pp. 261-272.

Svendsen, L.P. (2012). "How Social Media Enhanced Learning Platforms Challenge and Motivate Students to Take Charge of their Own Learning Processes." In L.A. Wankel & P. Blessinger (Eds.) *Increasing Student Engagement and Retention Using Social Techniques - Facebook, E-portfolios and Other Social Networking Services.* pp. 57-88. Cutting-Edge Technology in Higher Education Series. Bingley, UK: Routledge

Swanson D.A. & P.A. Morrison (2010). Teaching Business Demography Using Case Studies, *Population Research and Policy Review*, Vol. 29, pp. 93 – 104.

Swanson, D. (2005). Deep Structure Learning and Statistical Literacy. *Delta Education Journal*, Vol. 3, No. 1, pp. 41–52.

Swanson, D., & J. McKibben (1999). "Teaching Statistics to Non-Specialists: a course aimed at increasing both learning and retention" In L. Pereira-Mendoza, L. Kea, T. Kee, & W. Wong (Eds.) Statistical education - expanding the network: *Proceedings of the fifth international conference on teaching statistics, International Association for Statistical Education*, pp. 159–166. Voorburg, Netherlands: International Statistical Institute

Swiercz, P. & K. Ross (2003). Rational, Human, Political, and Symbolic Text in Harvard Business School Cases: a study of structure and content, *Journal of Management Education*, Vol. 27, pp. 407–30.

Tang, C.; P. Lai ; W. Tang; H. Davies; S. Frankland; K. Oldfield; M. Walters; N. Mei Leung; G. Taylor; A. Tiwai; M. Yim & E. Yuen (1997). Developing a Context Based PBL Model. *Research and Development in Problem Based Learning*, Vol. 4, Newcastle, NSW: Australian Problem Based Learning Network (pp. 579–595).

Tansey, P.J. (1970). Simulation Techniques in the Training of Teachers. *Simulation and Games*, Vol. 1, No. 3, pp. 281–303

Taousanidis, N.I. & M.A Antoniadou (2008). The Greek Challenge in Work-Based Learning. *Industry and Higher Education*, Vol. 22, No. 3, pp. 177 – 182.

Taylor, J. (1977). "Instructional gaming procedures in planning education", in J. Megarry (Ed.) *Aspects of Simulation and Gaming*. London: Kogan Page. pp. 103 - 115.

The Case Centre (2014). University Challenge - Using Cases with Undergraduates. Available at http://www.thecasecentre.org/educators/casemethod/resources/features/universitychallenge. [Accessed 24 June 2014]

Thomson, N. & C. Baden-Fuller (2010). *Basic Strategy in Context: European text and cases*, London: Wiley-Blackwell

Todd, S. & C. Säfström (2008). Democracy, Education and Conflict: rethinking respect and the place of the ethical. *Journal of Educational Controversy*, Vol. 3, No. 1. Available at: www.

wce.wwu.edu/Resources/CEP/eJournal/v003n001/a012.shtml [Accessed 9 January 2014].

Tripp, D. (1993). *Critical Incidents in Teaching*, London: Routledge.

University of Michigan. http://www.crlt.umich.edu/tstrategies/tsal [Accessed 12 January, 2014]

University of Minnesota. http://www1.umn.edu/ohr/teachlearn/tutorials [Accessed 12 January 2014]

University of Sydney. http://sydney.edu.au/staff/fye/during_semester/active_learning.shtml [Accessed 12 January 2014]

University of Texas (1997) Case Study as a Research Method, LIS 391D.1 Available at https://www.ischool.utexas.edu/~ssoy/useusers/l39dlb.htm (1997) [Accessed 23 March, 2014]

Van Ments, M. (1983). *The Effective Use of Role-Play*, London: Kogan-Page

Vintimilla, M. (2012). Aporetic Openings in Living Well with Others: the teacher as a thinking subject. PhD Thesis. Available from: https://circle.ubc.ca/bitstream/handle/2429/42557/ubc_2012_fall_delgadovintimilla_mariacristina.pdf?sequence=5 [Accessed 9 January 2014].

Wahlgren, M. & A. Ahlberg (2013). Monitoring and Stimulating Development of Integrated Professional Skills in University Study Programmes. *European Journal of Higher Education*. Vol. 3, No. 1, pp. 62-73.

Walls, S.M.; J.V. Kucsera; J.D. Walker; T.W. Acee; W. Taylor; N.K. McVaugh & D.H. Robinson (2010). Podcasting in Education: "Are students as ready and eager as we think they are?" *Computers & Education*, Vol. 54, No. 2, pp.371-378.

Warrick, P.A.; E.F. Hamilton; D. Precup & R.E. Kearney (2010). Classification of Normal and Hypoxic Fetuses from Systems Modeling of Intrapartum Cardiotocography, *IEEE Transactions on Biomedical Engineering*, Vol. 57, No. 4, pp. 771-779.

Wassermann, S. (1994). *Introduction to Case Method Teaching - a Guide to the Galaxy*. New York, NY.: Teachers College Press

Webb, J. (1995). Where the Action Is: developing artistry in legal education, *International Journal of the Legal Profession,* Vol 2, p. 187.

Weber, J.W. (2011). Enhancing Business Education through Integrated Curriculum Delivery. *Journal of Management Development,* Vol. 30, No. 6, pp. 558-568

Weber, M. (2003 in translation) *Udvalgte tekster,* København: Hans Reitzels Forlag

Welty, W. (1989). Discussion Method Teaching: how to make it work. *Change: The Magazine of Higher Learning,* July/August, pp. 40–49.

Westerfield, K. (1989). Improved Linguistic Fluency with Case Studies and a Video Method. *English for Specific Purposes,* Vol. 8, pp. 75–83.

Whitehouse, P. (2011). Networked Teacher Professional Development: the case of Globaloria. *Journal of Interactive Learning Research,* Vol. 22, No. 1, pp. 139-165.

Whitley-Grassi, N. & J.S. Baizer (2010). Video Lecture Capture in Physiology Courses: student attendance, video viewing and correlations to course performance, *International Journal of Instructional Technology and Distance Learning,* Vol. 7, No. 10.

Wilkie, K. (2000). "The nature of PBL" in S. Glen & K. Wilkie (Eds.) *PBL in Nursing: a new model for a new context.* London: Macmillan Press.

Willey, D. & J. Hilton III (2009). Openness, Dynamic Specialisation, and the Disaggregated Future of Higher Education, *The International Review of Research in Open and Distance Learning,* Vol. 10, No. 5.

Witherell, C. & N. Noddings (1991). "An invitation to our readers" in C. Witherell & N. Noddings (Eds.) (1991) *Stories Lives Tell: narrative and dialogue in education,* pp. 1-12. New York, NY: Teachers College Press

Wittgenstein, L. (1953) "Philosophical Investigations (PI)", in G.E.M. Anscombe and R. Rhees (Eds.) (translation by G.E.M. Anscombe), Oxford: Blackwell

Wittgenstein, L. http://plato.stanford.edu/entries/wittgenstein/ [Accessed 26 January 2014]

Woods, A. & C. Dennis (2009). What Do UK Small and Medium Sized Enterprises Think about Employing Graduates? *Journal of Small Business and Enterprise Development,* Vol. 16, No. 4, pp. 642-659

Woolfolk, A. & K. Margetts (2013). *Educational Psychology,* 3rd ed. Frenchs Forest, NSW Australia: Pearson.

Wright, A.E. & C. Heeran (2002). Utilizing Case Studies: connecting the family, school, and community. *School Community Journal,* Vol. 12, Iss. 2, pp. 103-115.

Yadav, A.; M. Lundeberg; M. DeSchryver; K. Dirkin; N. Schiller; K. Maier & C. Herreid (2007). Teaching Science with Case Studies: a national survey of faculty perceptions of the benefits and challenges of using cases. *Journal of College Science Teaching.* Vol. 37, No. 1, pp. 34-38.

Yeh, Y. (2004). Nurturing Reflective Teaching during Critical-Thinking Instruction in a Computer Simulation Program. *Computers & Education,* Vol. 42, pp. 181–194

Yeh, Y. (2007). Aptitude-Treatment Interactions in Pre-Service Teachers' Behavior Change During Computer-Simulated Teaching. *Computers & Education,* Vol. 48, pp. 495 – 507

Yilmaz, S. & C. Seiffert (2011). Creativity through Design Heuristics: a case study of expert product design. *Design Studies,* Vol. 32, No. 4, pp. 384-415.

Zbylut, M.L. (2007). *Case Method Instruction: 25 minutes of discussion can make a difference.* Alexandria, Va.: U.S. Army Research Institute for the Behavioral and Social Sciences

Zoll, A.A. (1966). Dynamic Management Education: an introduction to the selection, creation and use of cases, in-basket exercises, the action maze, business games and other dynamic techniques. Seattle: Management Education Associates.

The Casemaker Platform

User Manual

The Casemaker platform for teaching and learning with case studies is available for free access at http://www.casemaker.dk

About Casemaker

Casemaker's origins

Casemaker is a 3-year transversal research and development initiative 75% funded by the EU via Project # 531169-LLP-1-2012-1-DK-KA3-KA3MP for the EU Lifelong Learning Programme, Key Action 3 (ICT), Multilateral Projects.

Casemaker promotes new learning and teaching practices in higher education and secondary vocational education by creating an innovative open source web-based ICT-platform specifically designed to enhance case-based teaching and learning. The overall rationale for initiating the Casemaker project is to further integrate academia and practice in order to enhance student learning, to help students develop transferable skills, to improve students' employability, and at the same time provide advanced, sophisticated tools to teachers.

The Project Partners and 25% co-funders are Copenhagen Business School Denmark [CBS], Lund University Sweden [LU], Birmingham City University UK [BCU], Cass Business School UK [Cass], Lübeck Fachhockschule Germany [LUAS], Technological Educational Institute of Epirus Greece [TEIEP], and the Danish software house Phases. The Case Centre (formerly the European Case Clearing House) is an Associate Partner.

The Developers

The following have collaborated in the creation and development of the Casemaker platform:
  Andreas Dorich (LUAS)
  Dr Christian Poulsen (CBS)
  Prof. Chrysostomos Stylios (TEIEP)
  Prof. Clive Holtham (Cass)
  Daniel Horn (Phases)
  Dario Faniglione (BCU)
  Jis Jose (Phases)
  Prof. Lisbet Pals Svendsen (CBS)
  Prof. Margrethe Mondahl (CBS)
  Mark Hetherington (BCU)
  Muhammad Ansar Majeed (Phases)
  Dr. Nigel Courtney (Cass)
  Dr. Petros Karvelis (TEIEP)
  Prof. Ola Mattisson (LU)
  Stefanos Petsios (TEIEP)
  Dr Steffen Löfvall
  Thomas Muschal (LUAS)
  Prof. Ulf Ramberg (LU)
  Prof. Voula Georgoploulos (TEIEP)
  Yaron Schwartz (CBS)

The purpose of Casemaker

Casemaker is a freely available service which aims to facilitate and enhance case-based teaching by enabling three participant communities – case writers, teachers and students – to develop and work with case studies, to review progress of study (of individuals or groups), and to give feedback. In short, to foster and gauge the learning taking place.

The three participant communities are not mutually exclusive; teachers can be case authors and vice versa, students can be co-creators of cases. However, for the sake of clarity this User Manual is arranged to highlight sections which illustrate and explain the 'dashboard' designed and provided specifically for the case author, the teacher and the student.

The Casemaker platform

The Casemaker platform can be used for the benefit of teachers and learners at secondary and tertiary education level in any culture and learning environment. It achieves this by:

- facilitating collaborative work between teachers and researchers to create online multimedia cases,
- enabling groups of students to collaborate in analysing complex case material,
- allowing teachers, researchers and students to get detailed information about the learning being developed.

In technical terms the platform is an online app which is accessed via a browser. It is designed around three integrated software components:

a) CaseDeveloper. This facilitates the collaborative development of multimedia-cases

b) CaseTeacher. This support teachers to plan their case-based teaching by formulating case-based assignments, competence profiles, and learning objectives for students

c) CaseAnalyser. This allows students to analyse and solve cases, and teachers to be able to view and assess the learning being achieved by individual students.

The Casemaker platform is designed to simplify the introduction and application of case based teaching and learning in a wide range of learner communities including doctors, engineers, lawyers, managers, nurses, teachers and many other vocations and professions.

Contents

About Casemaker

The purpose of Casemaker

The Casemaker platform

1. General data flow

2. Common user operations

2.1. Signup

2.2. Login – First Page

2.2.1. Forgot Password

2.3. Profile Editing

2.4. Invite New Members to the Casemaker Platform

3. The Author's Dashboard

3.1. Flow chart of operations available to authors

3.2. Create a new case

3.2.1. Preparing a case

3.2.2. Add Co-Author

3.2.3. Import Resources from other cases

3.2.4. Attach case files

3.2.5. Managing a case in progress

3.3. An author's case list

4. The Teacher's Dashboard

4.1. Selecting a case for teaching

4.2. Preparation for teaching a case

4.2.1. Splitting a case into parts

4.2.2. Assign titles, files and tasks for each split

4.2.3. Sending assignments to students

4.3. Surveying and annotating the teaching cases

4.3.1. Overview of a teaching case

4.3.2. Viewing reports

5. The Student's Dashboard

5.1. Operation flow

5.2. My student cases

5.3. Search my student cases

5.3.1. Working on case splits

5.3.2. Annotating and reporting

5.4. Case Analtytics

5.5. Student as co-author (in the CaseDeveloper area)

1. General data flow

Figure 1 describes the basic steps for achieving case based teaching within the Casemaker platform. The three main steps cover:

- the creation of a multimedia case from one or more authors. This is described in detail in section 3.
- the preparation of a completed multimedia case for teaching by a teacher. This is described in detail in section 4.
- the analysis of the case by the participating students, as described in detail in section 5.

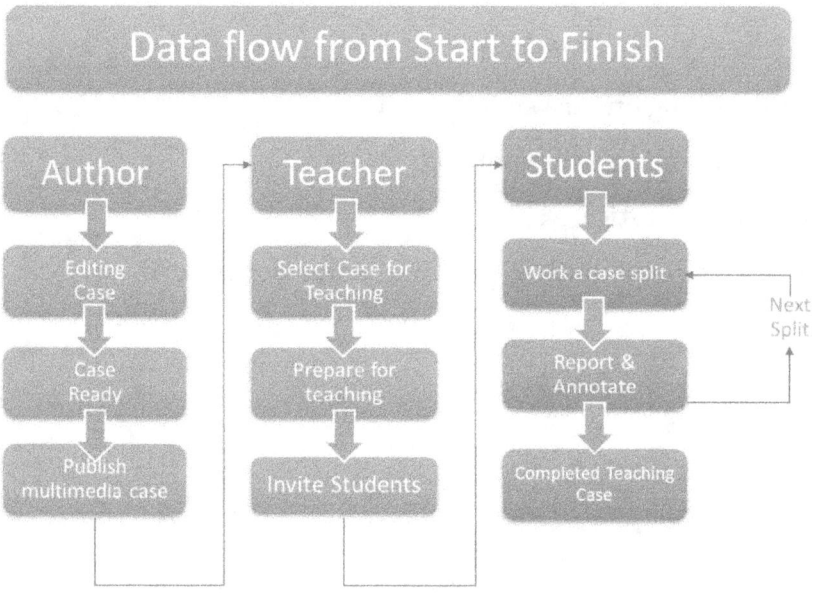

Figure 1: Walkthrough for Case Based Teaching based on Casemaker platform. In green (left column), the steps performed in CaseDeveloper; in orange (centre column), the steps performed in CaseTeacher; and in blue (right column), the steps performed in CaseAnalyser.

2. Common user operations

2.1. Signup

First, the user (teacher or student) has to apply for an account at the Casemaker platform, after approving the General Terms and Data Use Policy. The flow of the operations that the user follows is described in the diagram below.

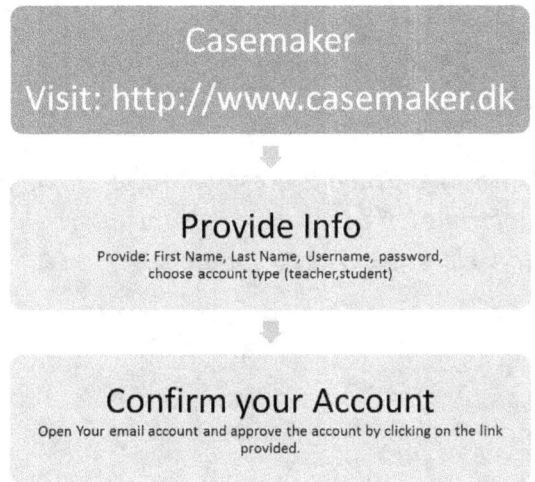

Figure 2: *The operation flow followed by a user for the Sign Up procedure.*

The screenshots of the procedure followed by a user for signing up for the Casemaker platform are displayed in a sequential way in Figure 3, below.

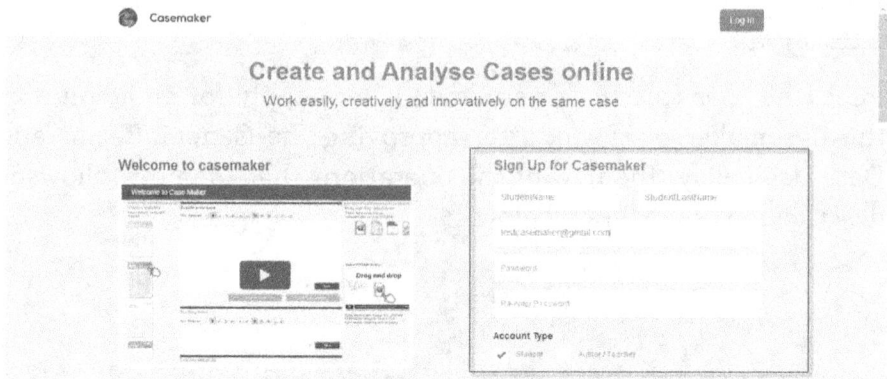

Figure 3: The user is applying for a Student account to the Casemaker platform providing all the information needed (First Name, Last Name, e-mail, Username, password, Select account type Student).

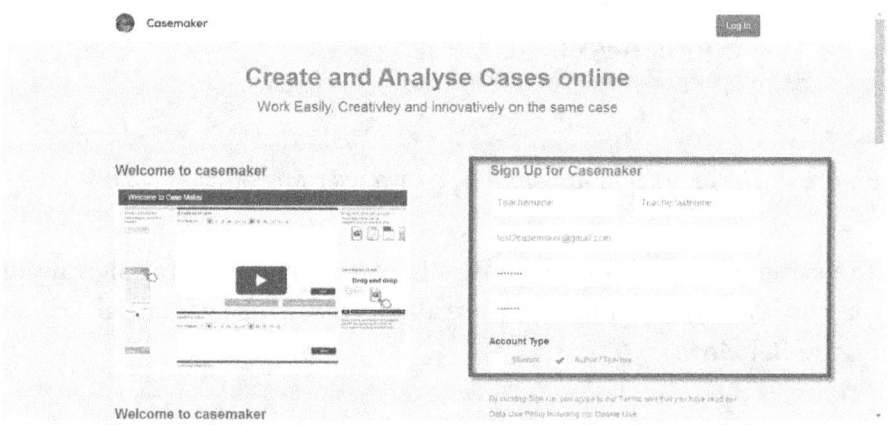

Figure 4: The user is applying for a Teacher account to the Casemaker platform providing all the information needed (First Name, Last Name, e-mail, Username, password, Select account type Author/Teacher).

2.2. Login – first page

The user follows the Login procedure in order to enter into the Casemaker platform – as described in Figure 5 below.

Figure 5: The Login procedure.

Figure 6 shows what the login page looks like.

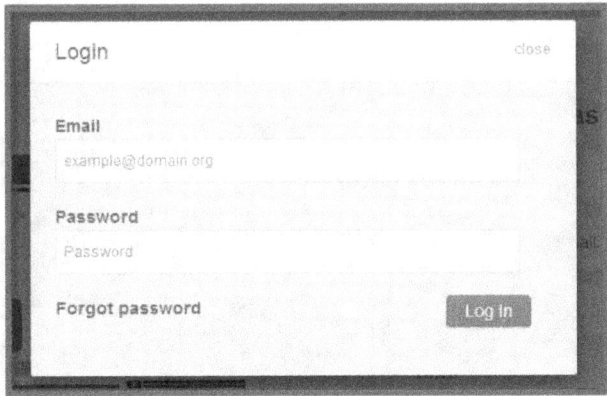

Figure 6: The Login page where the user must provide his/her username and password.

2.2.1. Forgot Password

The user can always retrieve the **Password** of the username used in the Casemaker platform by requesting it from the **Login** page. The user enters his/her email and clicks **Submit**. A password is then sent by email:

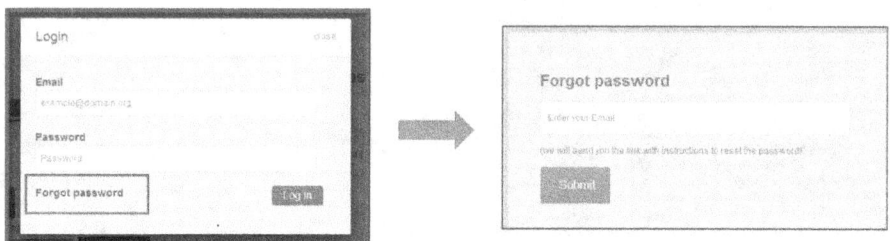

Figure 7: A user requesting his/her password from the Login page.

2.3. Profile editing

After the user has entered the Casemaker platform he/she is able to edit the profile settings (First Name, Last Name, Time Zone, Date Format):

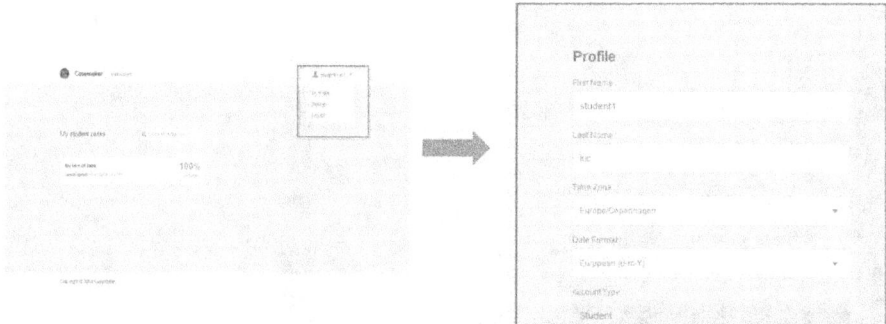

*Figure 8: The user can edit his profile by clicking on the **My Profile** button.*

2.4. Invite new members to the Casemaker platform

Any user of the Casemaker platform can invite someone to the platform by providing the person's email address and composing a message of invitation.

Figure 9 below illustrates this with an example in which the user 'teacher1 kic' invites someone with the email Claus@fictitious.email.com and adds a short message of invitation.

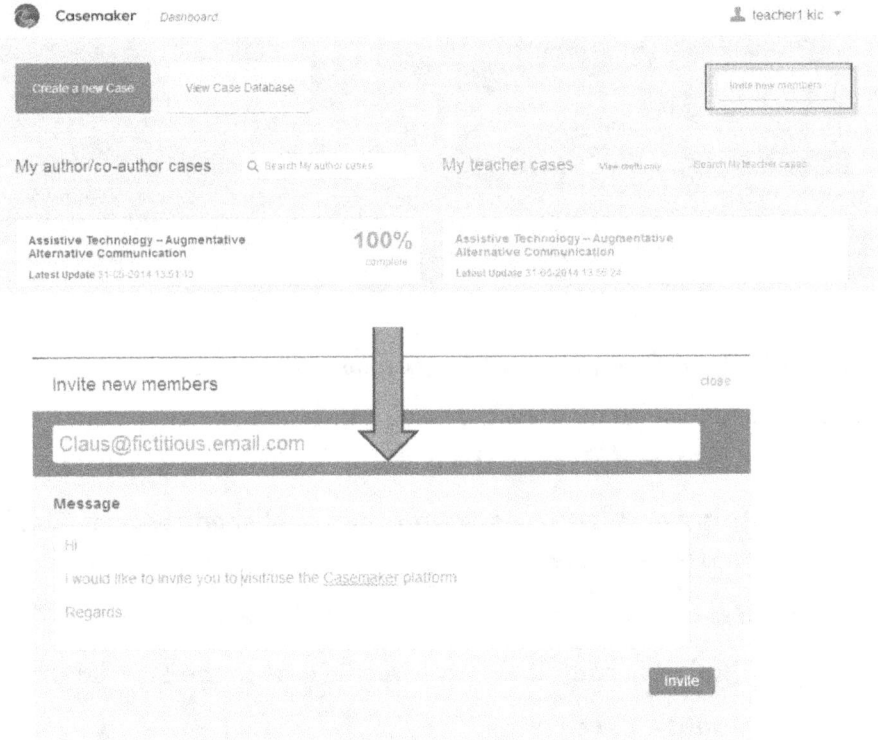

Figure 9: Any user of the Casemaker platform can invite someone by providing the email and a short message.

3. The Author's Dashboard

3.1. Flow chart of operations available to authors

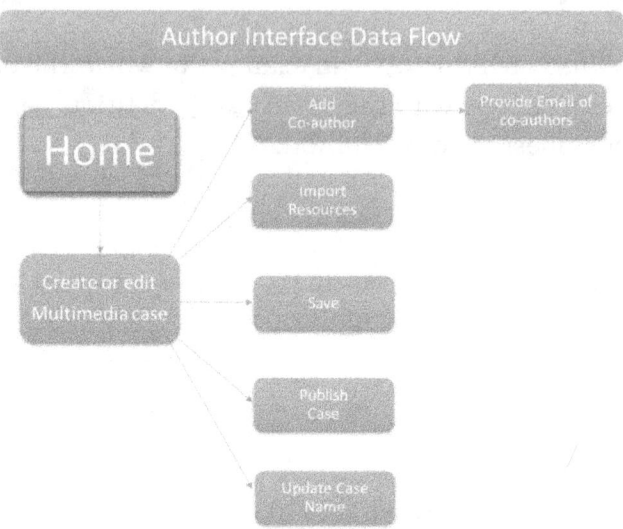

Figure 10: The author interface process flow.

The Author's dashboard offers the following options:

- **Add Co-author** to the working multimedia case.
- **Import Resources** from other published cases available in the database.
- **Save** a draft work on progress of a case
- **Publish** a completed multimedia case to the case database.
- **Update Case Name**.

3.2. Create a new case

Clicking on the **Create a new Case** button takes you to a page which allows you to input your case-specific data. The page is divided into a number of sections allowing you to be modular with the inputting of your data.

The first section requires you to input a case title and add specific case study text. You are also able to add additional coauthors to the case you have created.

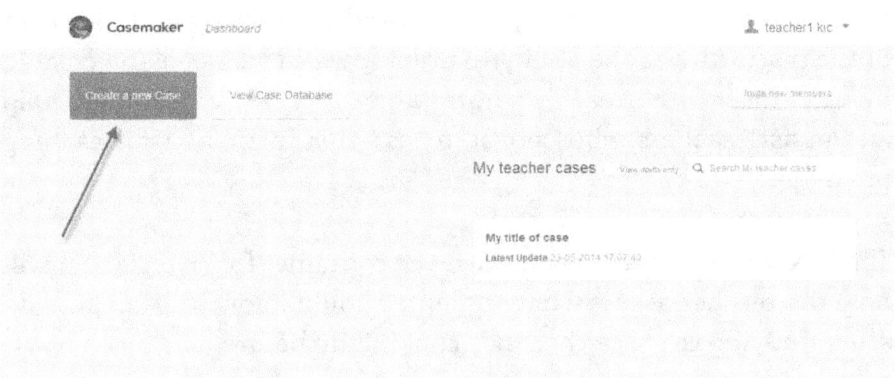

3.2.1. Preparing a case

The author of the case is offered the following options:
- Give a title of the case
- Add information about the case
- Import case files
- write the abstract
- write teaching notes
- write the learning objectives
- set the case progress
- add co-authors
- import resources from other cases

The **Abstract** space (which offers an 'edit box' into which text can be uploaded) gives you the opportunity to outline in one paragraph what your case study is about. Here you have the option of posing a question that underpins determines the entire case and possibly any findings relating to the case study.

The **Teaching Notes** space allows you to add specific teaching details to the designed case. The Casemaker platform is a repository of uploaded cases from many authors and/or teachers and each user of the platform has the ability to utilise cases developed and created by other users. The teaching notes associated with a case will help and assist teachers who choose to use this in their own teaching provision.

The **Learning Objectives** space is the container for criteria that will help the teacher assess what students should know or be able to do after studying the case that they couldn't do before.

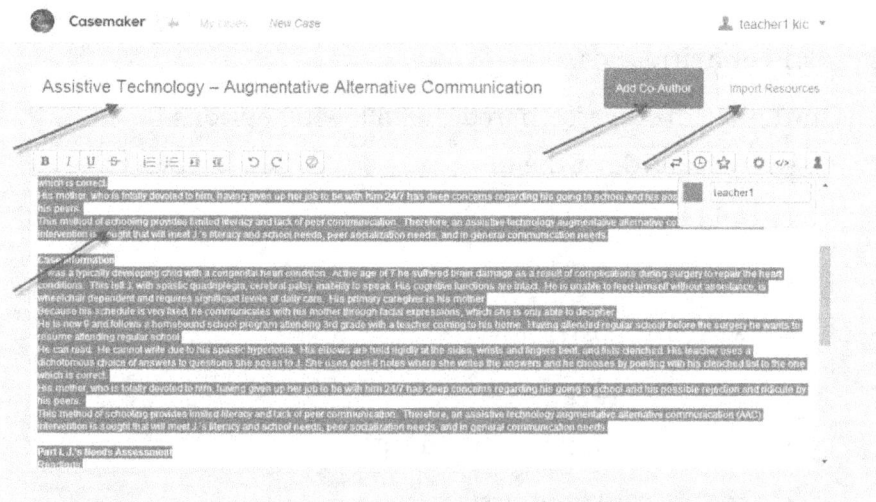

Figure 12: Available options for an author when creates a new case.

Figure 12 highlights the title of the example case is displayed, the case information that has been inserted, and the buttons of **Add Co-Author** and **Import Resources**. After this stage has been completed the author continues with the operations depicted in Figure 13.

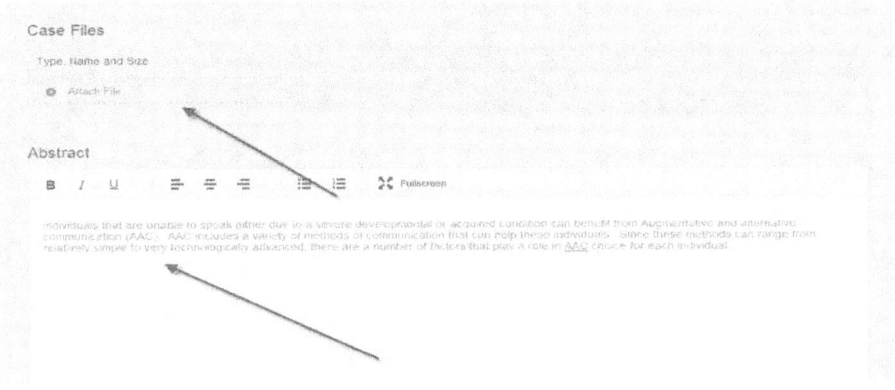

Figure 13: The author can attach a file to his/her case.

Once the desired files have been uploaded they will be listed in the **Case Files** section. The author has the ability to continue to add more files if required, or to delete files if they are no longer needed. Each file will bear the title given from the file uploader and have a unique icon representing its designation.

Figure 13 illustrates the **Attach File** process and shows some descriptive text that has been uploaded into the **Abstract** edit box. The user is able to attach any type of file to the case. For example:

- Images (*.png, *.jpg, *.tif),
- Powerpoint presentations (*.ppt, *.pptx),
- Excel files (*.xls, *.xlsx),
- Text Files (*.doc, *.txt, *.docx),
- PDF files (*.pdf).

Once the author completes these steps, s/he can add **Teaching Notes** and **Learning Objectives** as depicted in Figure 14.

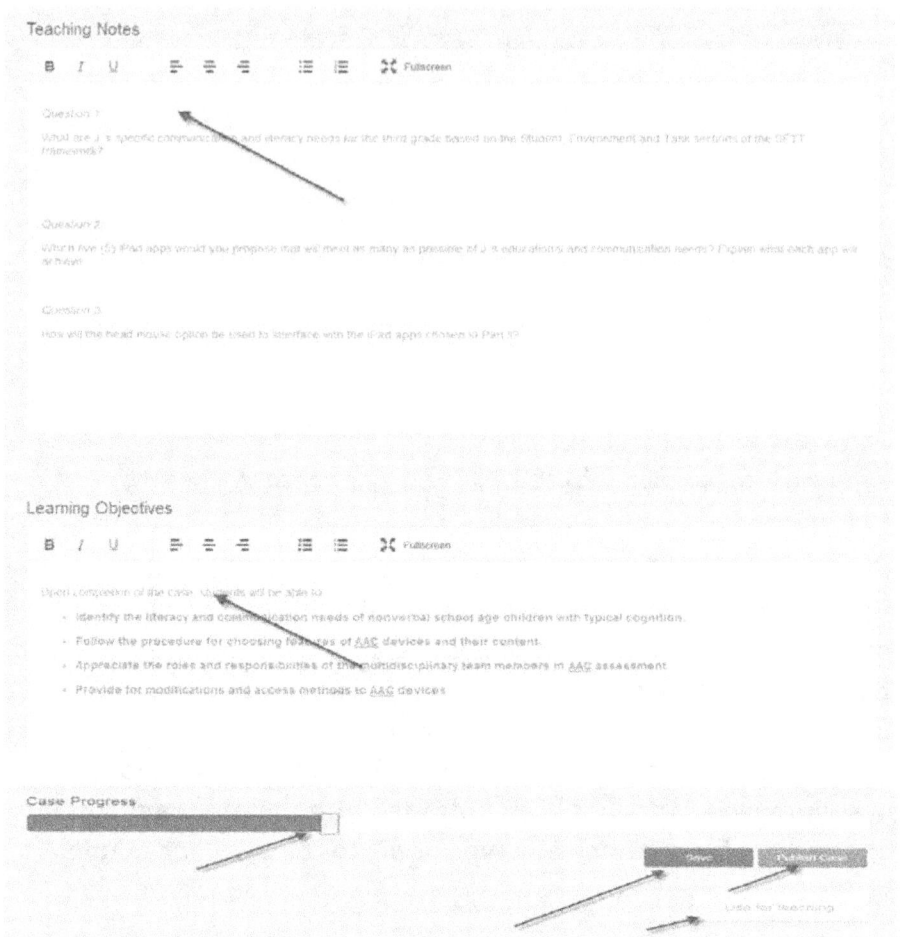

*Figure 14: The Teaching Notes and Learning Objectives spaces; the Case Progress bar and the **Save** and **Publish Case** buttons.*

In the example depicted in Figure 14 the author has filled in the Teaching Notes and Learning Objectives of the case. Below these fields is the Case Progress indicator bar (adjusted by the author) and the **Save**, **Publish Case** and **Use for teaching** buttons.

Note: the **Use for teaching** button is available only when the case progress reaches 100%.

3.2.2. Add Co-Author

Figure 15 shows the place where an author may add or remove co-authors. In order to add a co-author the author has to know the invitee's e-mail address in order for an invitation to be sent.

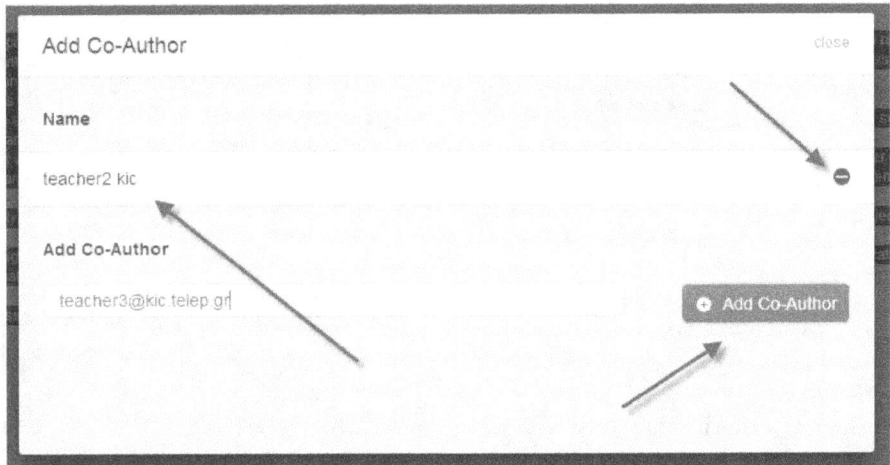

Figure 15: Any author can add co-authors to the case he/she has published.

3.2.3. Import Resources from other cases

Figure 16 illustrates how an author can import other the resources (pdf, images, etc) from any published case which is already contained in the Casemaker platform case database. A multiple tick box is available in order to import resources from multiple available cases.

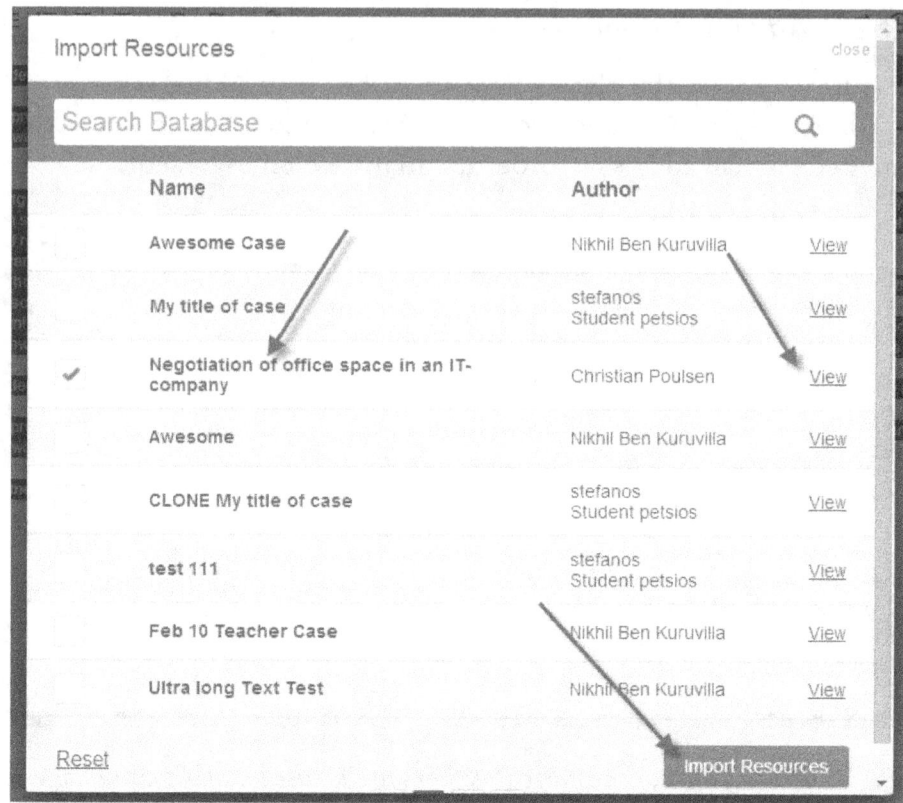

*Figure 16: The author can **Import Resources** from other cases.*

Figure 17 shows the files that have been attached to the author's case by importing them from the 'Negotiation of office space in an IT company' case that was selected (by tick box) in Figure 16.

Figure 17: The author can choose which resources to add to the case he/she has published.

3.2.4. Attach case files

The author can also add a file by clicking the **Attach file** button, as highlighted in Figure 18.

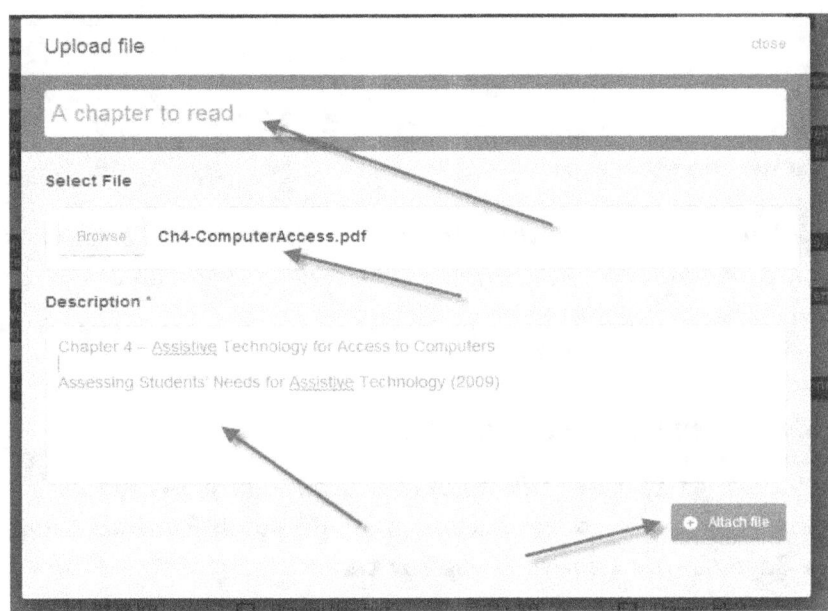

Figure 18: A file added to a case.

In Figure 18 the author has added and described a new file named "A chapter to read". The new file then appears in the **Case Files** list shown in Figure 19.

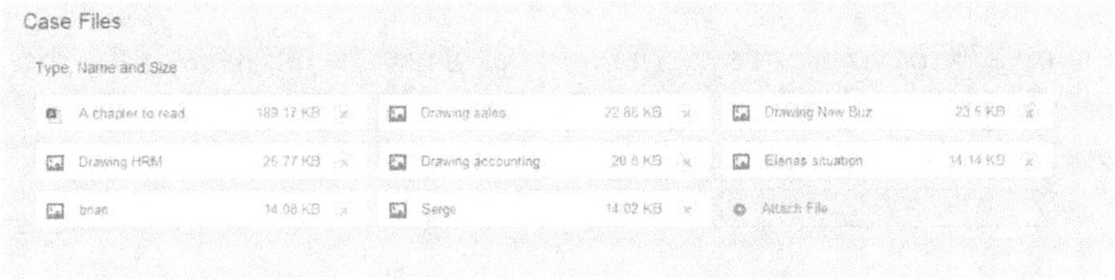

*Figure 19: The attached file is shown in the **Case Files**.*

An author can remove one or more files by clicking on the "X" box (as shown in Figure 19). Before the system carries out the instruction it displays a confirmation question at the top of the screen. The author must click on **OK** for the action to proceed - or Cancel.

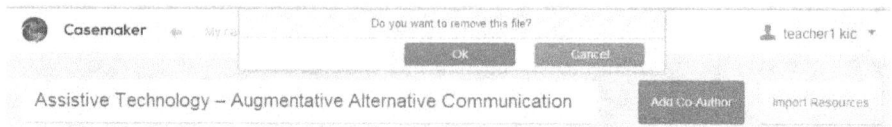

Figure 20: when an author wants to delete a file from the case there is a 'fail safe' mechanism: a confirmation message appears and must be actioned.

3.2.5. Managing a case in progress

Figure 21 (an extract of the screen shown in Figure 14) highlights the options available to the author, namely; **Save**, **Publish Case**, **Delete Case**, **Clone Case** and **Use for teaching**.

Figure 21: The user can save the case being worked on, publish the case, delete the case, or clone the case. The 'Use for teaching' button becomes available when the case is 100% complete.

3.3. An author's case list

When an author logs on to the Casemaker platform a list of his/her available cases is displayed. This also shows the stage of completion of cases still being authored (see Figure 22).

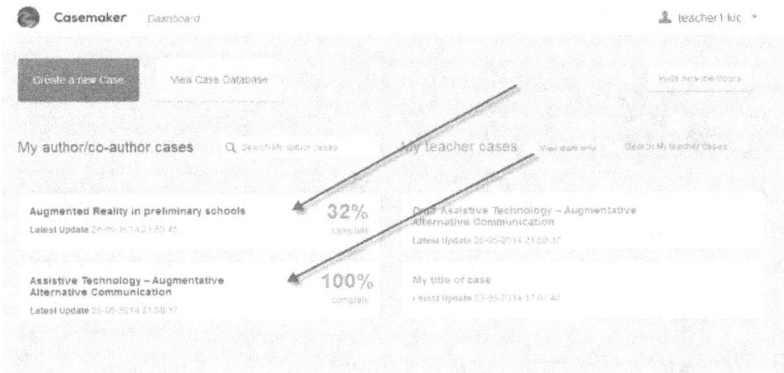

Figure 22: the list and progress of cases available to teacher (the fictitious) teacher1kic.

4. The Teacher's Dashboard

The flow chart of processes available to a teacher is shown in Figure 23.

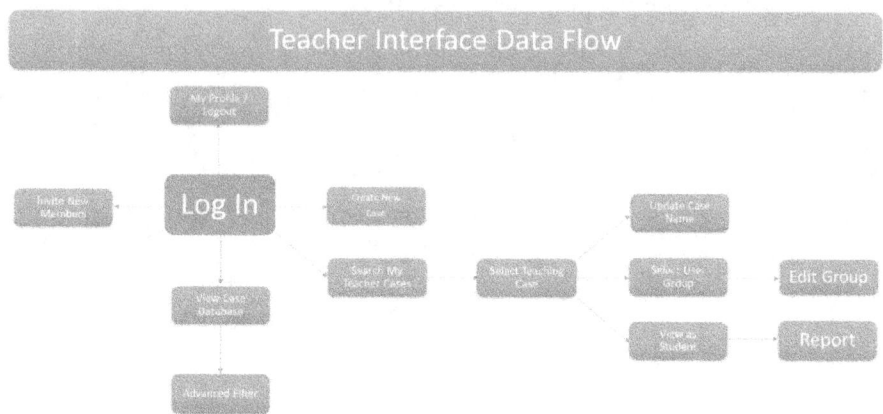

Figure 23: The teacher interface process flow.

A Casemaker user logging on as a teacher has the following options:
- **View** the entire case database and use advanced filters
- **Search** the user's teaching cases
- **Select** a particular case for teaching
- Prepare a case for teaching
- Send students a case for them to work on
- View reporting and annotations of a teaching case.

4.1. Selecting a case for teaching

The user can either use a case of which s/he is an author or can search the entire Casemaker case database by clicking on **View Case Database**.

Figure 24 shows the cases available to 'teacher1kic', and the status of those cases.

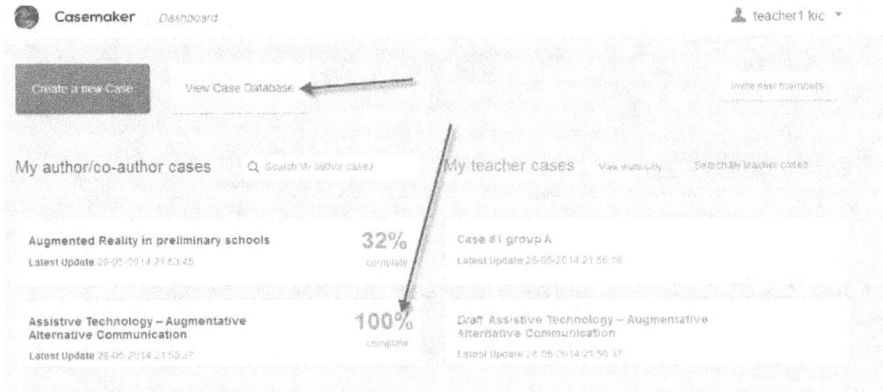

Figure 24: The View Case Database button.

After clicking on **View Case Database** the teacher can use the **Advanced Filter** to search for a case that suits their current teaching requirements.

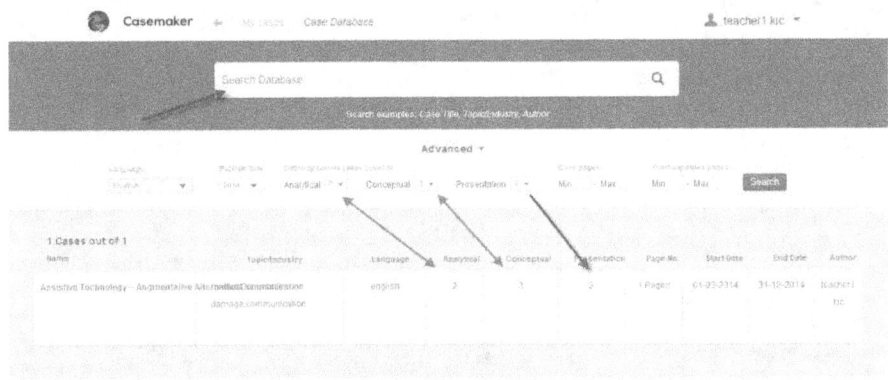

Figure 25: The advanced search filter options.

Once a case is selected, the teacher clicks the **Use for teaching** button. This is situated at the bottom of the case editing page, as mentioned above in section 3.2.5.

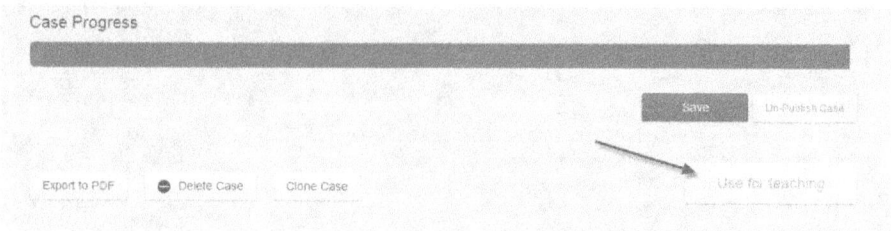

*Figure 26: By clicking **Use for teaching** the case can be used.*

4.2. Preparation for teaching a case

Here a case about Assistive Technology is used as an illustration. In this example the case is amenable to being split into parts that can be released to the students in a planned sequence.

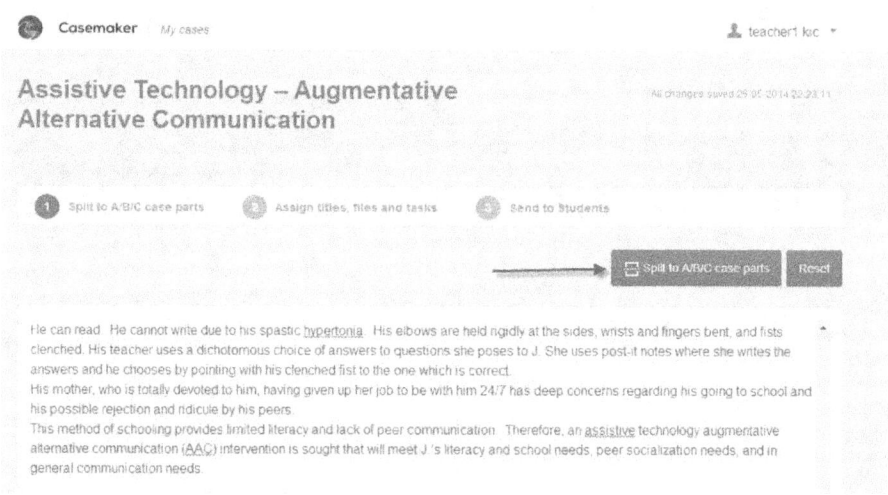

*Figure 27: The **Split to A/B/C case parts** button enables the case to be split into two or more parts.*

4.2.1. Splitting a case into parts

The teacher has the option to split a case into two or more parts that will be worked on by the students in successive stages. For example, each part may have a different learning objective.

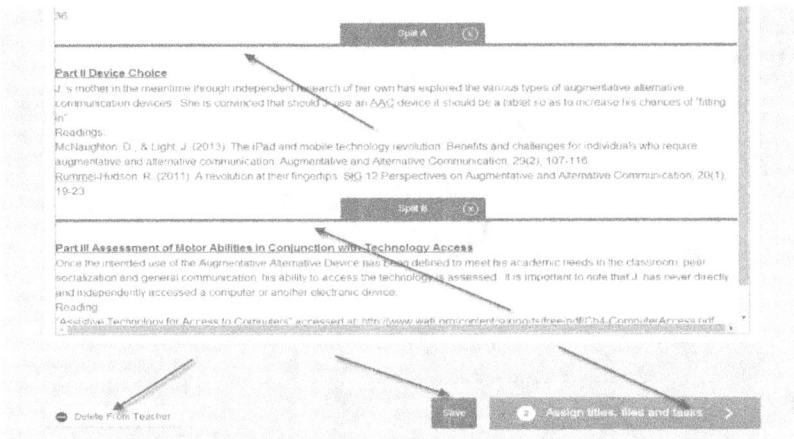

Figure 28: Illustration showing Splits A and B of the 'Assistive Technology' case.

Figure 28 depicts the case splitting process. The teacher must point the cursor to the exact position in the text where the split is required and clicking the button **Split to A/B/C parts** (as highlighted in Figure 27). The teacher then has the option to **Delete** or **Save** the split.

Once the teacher has finalised the splitting of the case s/he has to click on the **Assign titles, files and tasks** button.

4.2.2. Assign titles, files and tasks for each split

In Figure 29, the available teaching options for each split are displayed. The teacher can edit the title of this split and select the related resources – files which will be available to the students – and use the **Assignments and Tasks** edit box to place instructions for the students.

Once the teacher has finished all the editing, s/he is ready to send the case to the students by clicking the appropriate button to the bottom of the page.

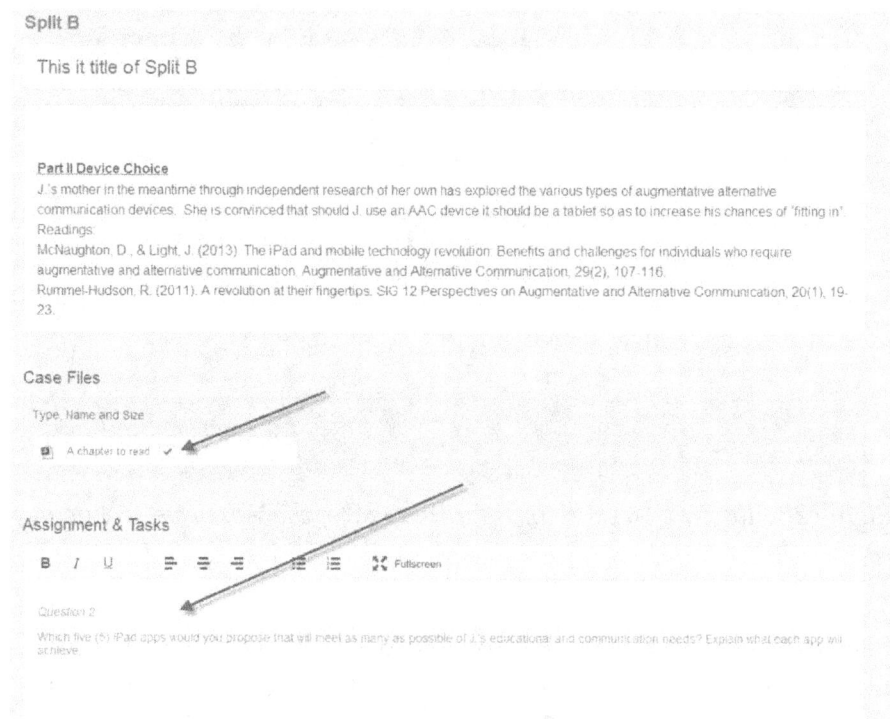

Figure 29: Giving each part a title, associating relevant files and assigning tasks that students are required to carry out for that part of the case.

4.2.3. Sending assignments to students

Figure 30 shows the steps for a teacher to create a named group of students by entering their email addresses. The group can be created either by using the on-screen editor or by using a comma separated value (CSV) formatted file.

THE CASEMAKER PLATFORM

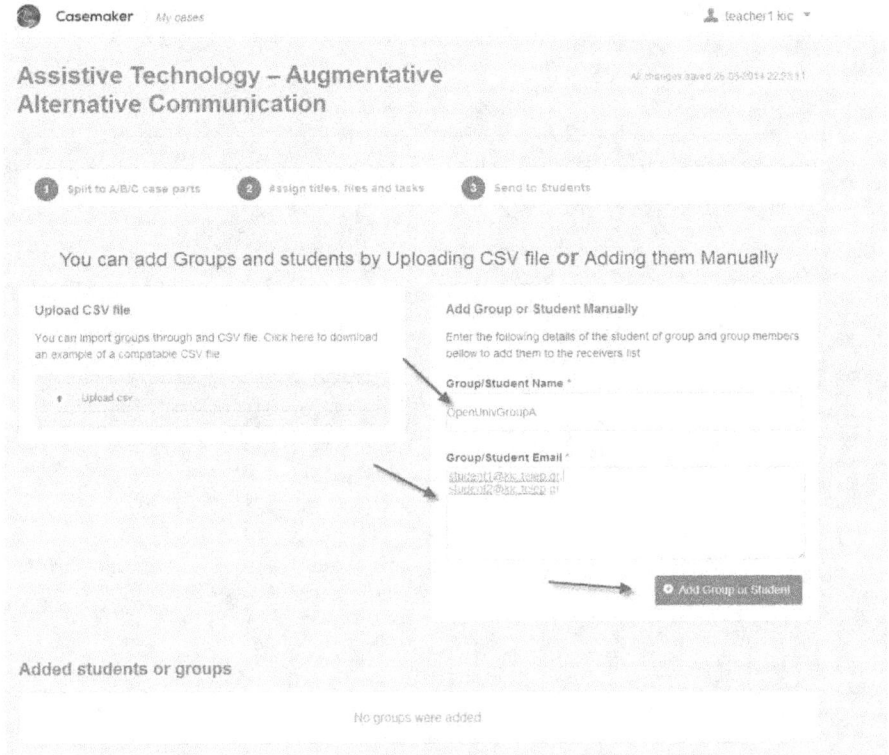

Figure 30: Sending the case to a student or a group of students by entering their email address(es).

The added group of students then appears the Added students or groups screen (see Figure 31) where there is also an extra option to **Edit** or **Delete** the email addresses. Then, the teacher has the option to specify a **Release date** and **End date** for each part of the split case.

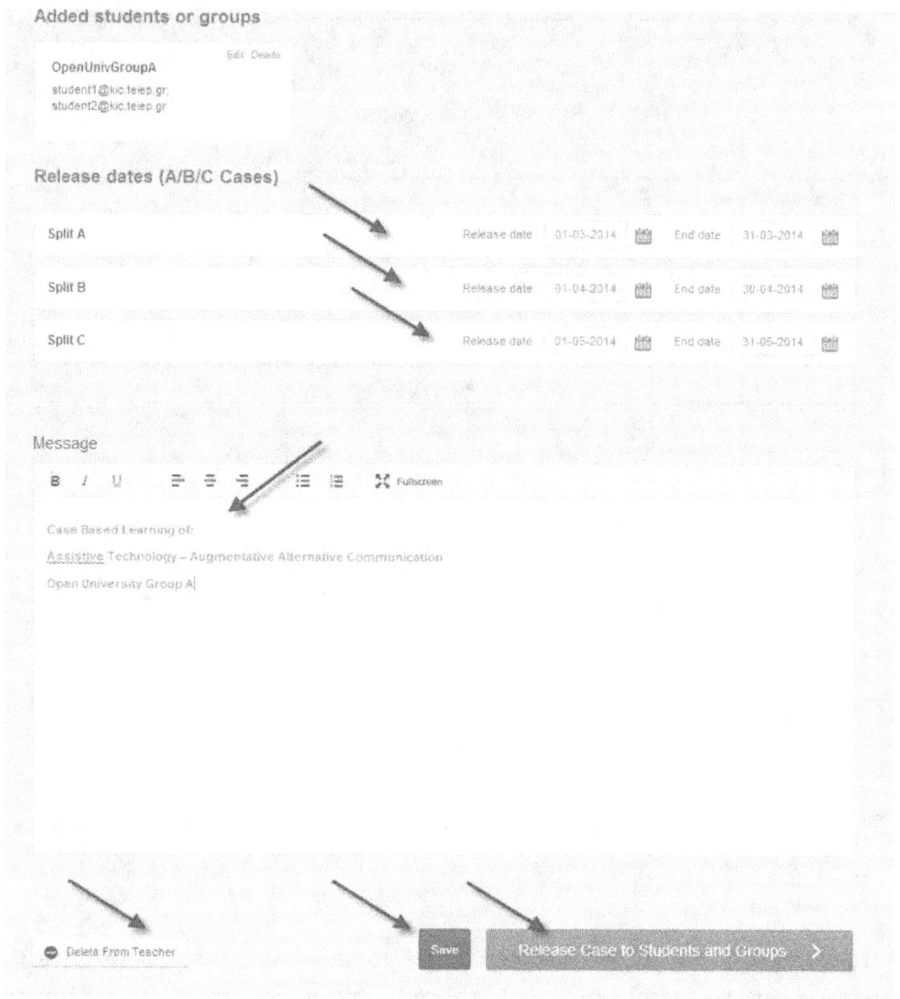

Figure 31: The teacher chooses the release date and end date of each part of the split case.

At this stage the teacher can simply save his/her editing work or save and release the case to the students – with or without an accompanying message. A confirmation screen is then visible to the teacher (see Figure 32).

THE CASEMAKER PLATFORM A29

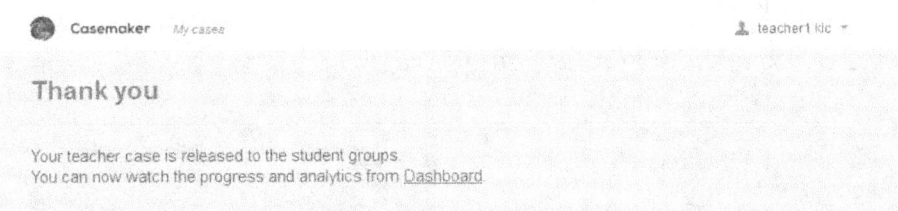

Figure 32: the screen the teacher sees after releasing the teaching case to the students

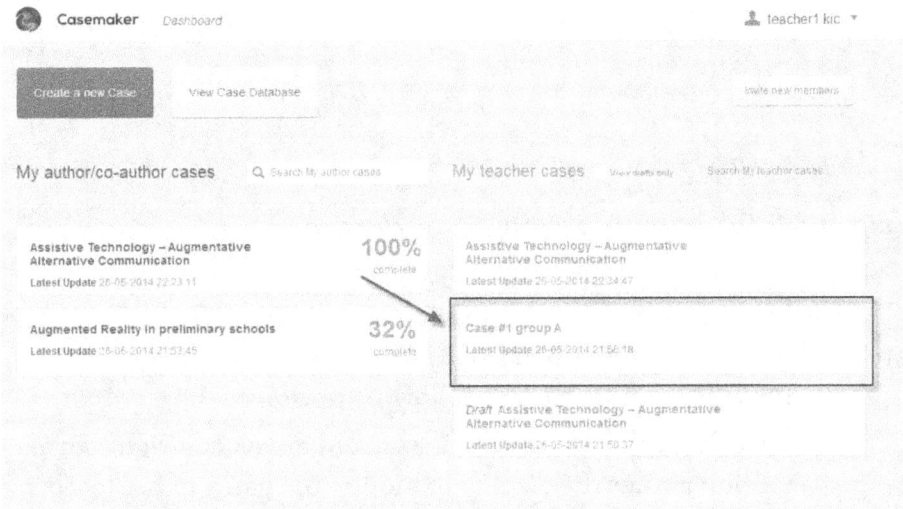

Figure 33: The Teacher Dashboard showing that a case has been assigned to the students.

The teacher's cases that are suffixed with the word *Draft* in red (see Figure 33) are cases that have been saved by the teacher but not yet released to students.

4.3. Surveying and annotating the teaching cases

4.3.1. Overview of a teaching case

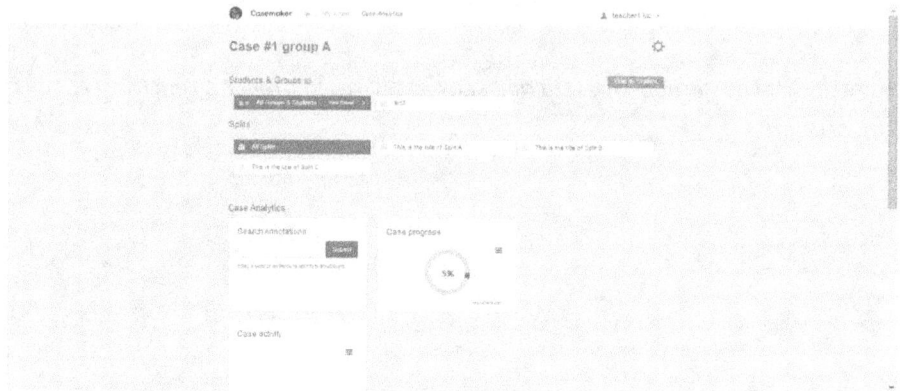

Figure 34: The overview panel of the teaching case

By selecting a case from the teacher's dashboard (Figure 33) the teacher goes to the **Case Analytics** page as shown in Figure 34.

The teacher now has the following options:

- Click on the **'gearwheel' symbol** at the top right corner. This enables the teacher to modify the name of the teaching case.

- Click on the **group name** (here 'kic3'). The teacher can now edit list of participating students.

- Click on **All Splits** or the **title of a Split** to review the case analytics.

- Click on the **View as Student.** The teacher can now view the reports and annotations of the students in group 'kic3'.

4.3.2. Viewing reports

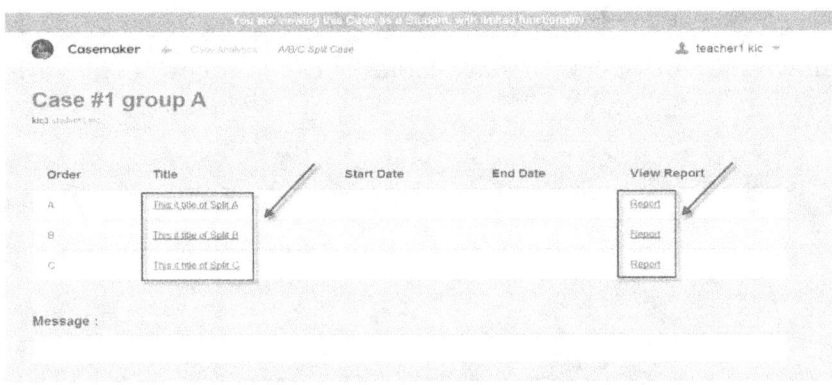

Figure 35: The teacher and the student can view the reports of that student's work on a case.

The teacher can survey the student's work performed on a case, or on each split of that case if applicable. The functionality available to the teacher is similar to the functionality given to the student – and this is described in detail in section 5 (Figures 36-44).

5. The Student's Dashboard

5.1. Operation flow

The flow chart of operations available to the student is shown in Figure 35.

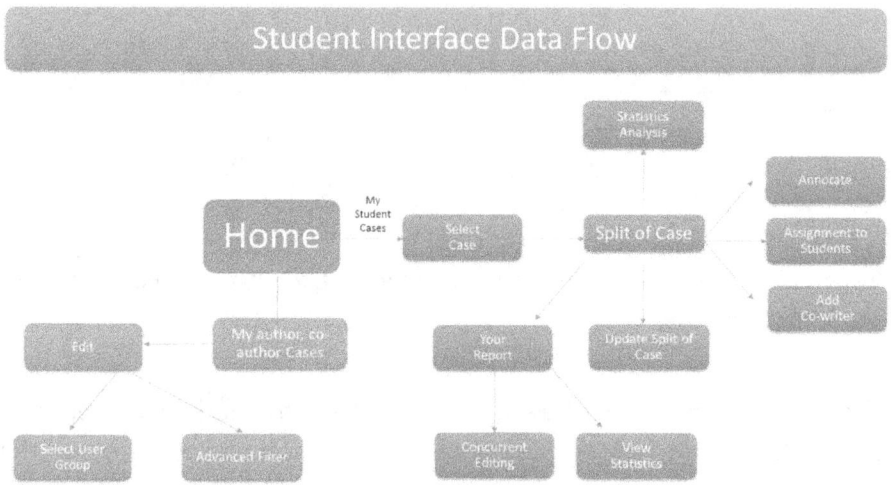

Figure 36: The student interface process flow.

The student's dashboard provides the student with the following options (Figure 36):
- select a teaching case,
- work on a split of a case,
- annotate information and multimedia files of a case,
- view the assignments and tasks for a case or part of a split case,
- add other students to participate in solving the teaching case,
- view statistics and analytics,
- participate in the preparation of a case if an author invites him to become a co-author. In such cases the authoring dashboard becomes available to the students.

5.2. My student cases

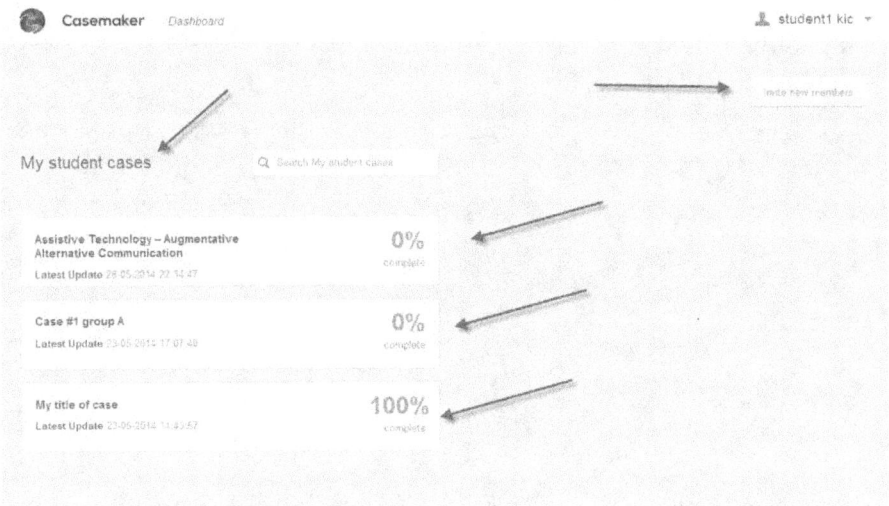

Figure 37: A student can view a list of the cases where s/he participates.

In Figure 37 the main dashboard of the student displays all the cases available to a student named 'student1 kic'. In this example the student has three assigned cases described by their title, date of the latest update and work progress percentage.

5.3. Search my student cases

Figure 38 depicts the front page of a split case named "Assistive Technology – Augmentative Alternative Communication". The student studying this case has the following options:

- To click on the titles of the splits
- To view and/or edit the report of each split
- To view the instructional message from the teacher (see Figure 31 in section 5.2.3).
- To view the start date and end date of the split parts of the case set by the teacher (see Figure 31 in section 5.2.3).

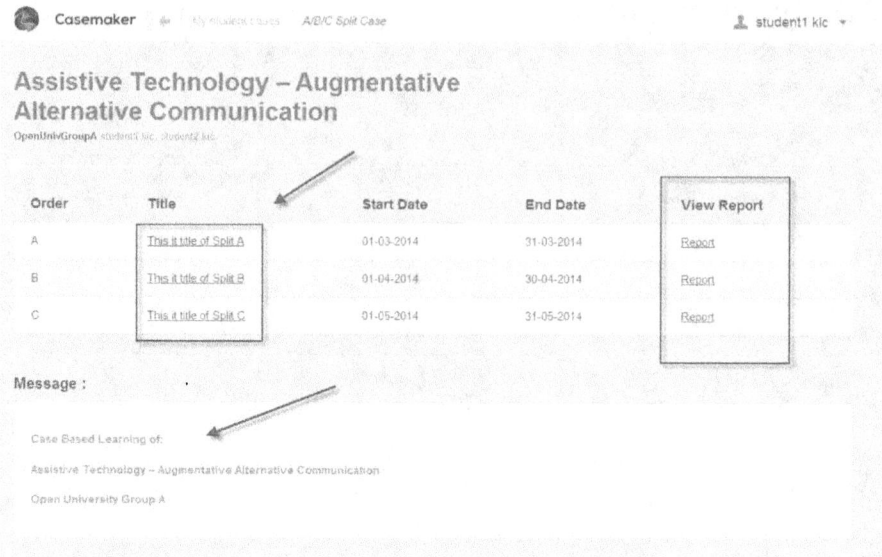

Figure 38: *The student can view the parts, reports, and message of an allocated case.*

5.3.1. Working on case splits

When the student clicks on the title of a split case (eg: as shown in Figure 38) a new page opens like that illustrated in Figure 39 below. The student can now start working on that part of the split case and can make separate annotations to each file (i.e. exhibit) provided with the case.

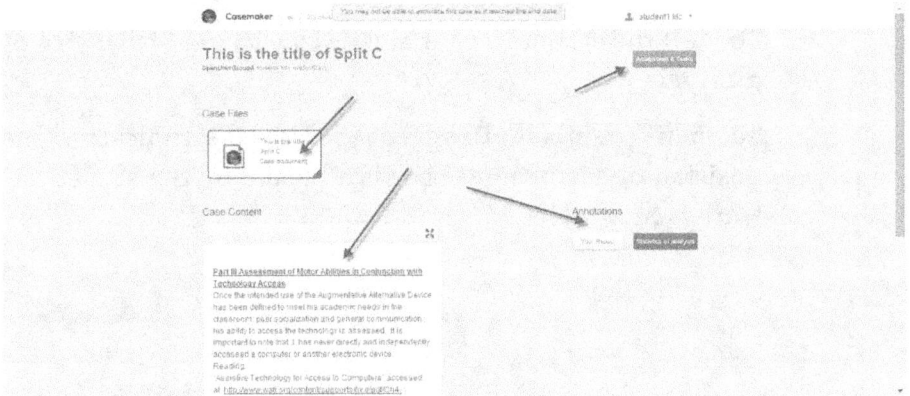

Figure 39: The student view of content, annotations, and files of the case.

In this example the student named 'student1 kic' can annotate the case document that was set by the teacher in section 4.2.2. In addition, if s/he then selects the pdf file named "A chapter to read" the student will be able to place a fresh annotation related to this file, as depicted in Figure 40 below.

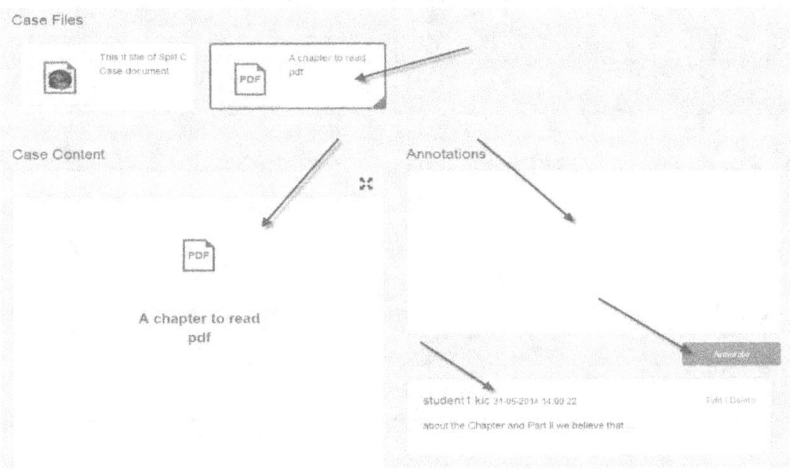

Figure 40: The student can place annotations concerning an attached file

The lower section of the page for the part of the case being worked on offers three main options, as indicated in Figure 41:

- To view or edit the report by clicking **Your Report**
- To view the statistics of analytics by clicking **Statistics of analysis**
- To view the **Case Progress** percentage indicator. The position of the progress bar is adjusted by the student as work is progressed.

Figure 41: *The student can view a report of progress on that part of the case being worked on.*

When the student clicks on the **Assignment & Tasks** button (as indicated in Figure 39) the instruction from the teacher will appear in a pop up message in the fashion shown in Figure 42.

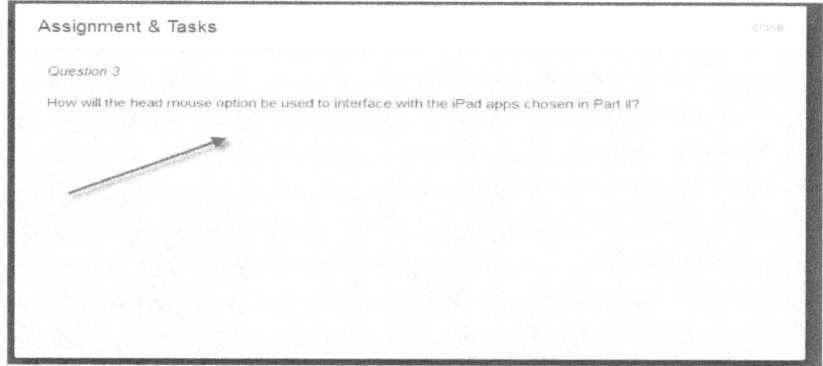

Figure 42: *The student has to answer to each assignment and task of the case.*

The **Co-Writers** button that is indicated in Figure 39 allows the student to open a pop up window, as illustrated in Figure 43, to add people who will collaborate in solving the teaching case.

Figure 43: *The student can add a co-writer to the case.*

5.3.2. Annotating and reporting

When the time allowed for working on a case has reached the end date set by the teacher (see Figure 31 in section 5.2.3) a pop up message is displayed to the student and system disables the annotations feature. These steps are depicted in Figure 44 below.

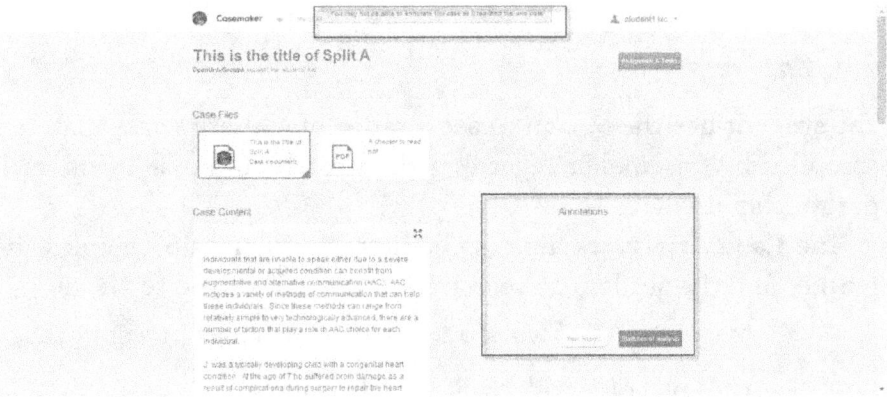

Figure 44: *What the student sees when the end date set for a case has been reached.*

The reporting tool (see Figure 45) is based on an enriched editing box with ordinary text formatting and work tracing. The report editor offers:

- Import and Export to/from alternative file formats.
- A Time slider in order to see recorded text changes.
- A Revision saver which will also appear in the time slider with a special character.
- Real-time Chat tool between the online students that work on this report.

Figure 45: The reporting editor that offers real time editing by multiple students.

5.4. Case analytics

The student has the option to see a range of statistics and analytics compiled by Casemaker regarding their work on a case or on each part of a split case.

The **Case Analytics** area (as depicted in Figure 45) enables the teacher and the student to search for annotations and to view:

- the progress of work on a case or each part of a split case
- the level of work activity on the case
- the number of clicks resulting from work on the case.

- the number of annotations - displayed as a pie chart - for each file of the case
- the number of annotations - presented as a pie chart - made by each student within a group of students.

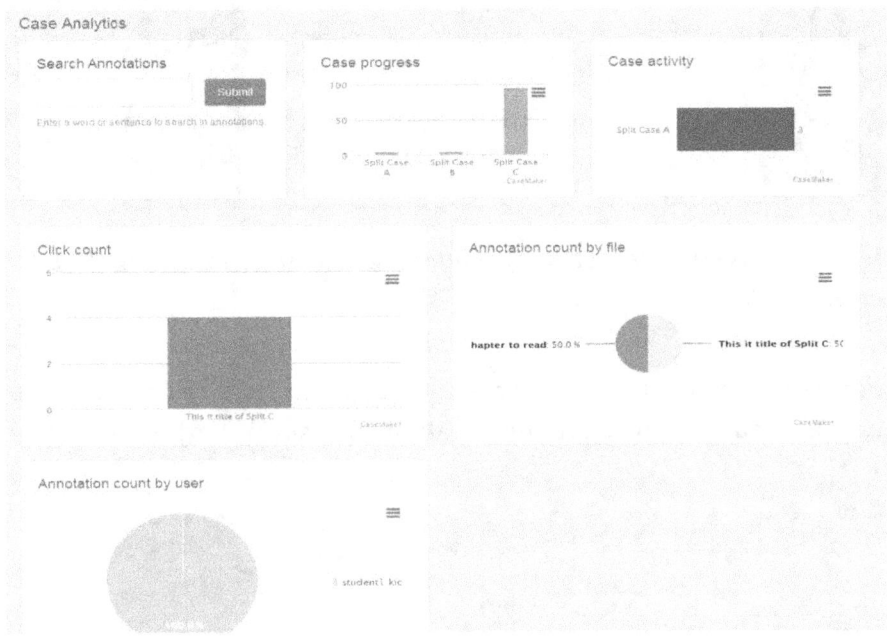

Figure 46: A typical representation of the statistics for a student's work on a case or part of a split case.

5.5. Student as co-author (in the CaseDeveloper area)

In Casemaker it is possible for a student to invite other students to work as co-authors. This case creation process takes place within the CaseDeveloper software and in this situation its functionality is exactly the same as described in section 3: The Author's dashboard.

To enable this feature, the teacher must invite registered students by adding their email addresses (as indicated in Figure 47).

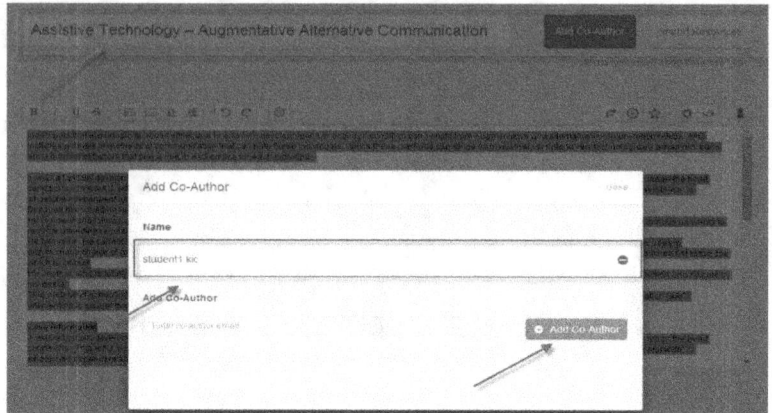

Figure 47: A student invites a co- author to a case by providing the email of the student.

Figure 48 depicts the home screen of a student who is co-author of a case as well as being a student dealing with several other cases.

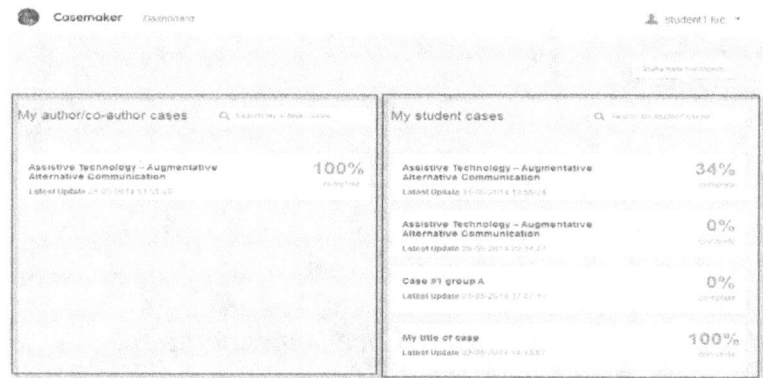

Figure 48: The Student's Dashboard of the student named 'student1 kic'.

www.ingramcontent.com/pod-product-compliance
Lightning Source LLC
Chambersburg PA
CBHW071215080526
44587CB00013BA/1387